NEWS IN THE R

NEWS IN THE REGIONS

Plymouth Sound
to Moray Firth

Alastair Hetherington

For Michael Ryle,
in hope that he may have
time some day to read
a little of it
Alastair Hetherington

29 June 1989

MACMILLAN

First published 1989

Published by
THE MACMILLAN PRESS LTD
Houndmills, Basingstoke, Hampshire RG21 2XS
and London
Companies and representatives
throughout the world

Printed in Great Britain by
Billing & Sons Ltd, Worcester

British Library Cataloguing in Publication Data
Hetherington, Alastair, *1919–*
News in the regions: Plymouth Sound to
Moray Firth
1. Great Britain. Journalism
I. Title
072
ISBN 0–333–48231–X (hardcover)
ISBN 0–333–48232–8 (paperback)

Contents

List of Plates

Acknowledgements

The author and publishers wish to acknowledge with thanks permission from The Broadcasters' Audience Research Board Ltd for the figures in Tables A1–A8 of Appendix B, and to Central Television for the seasonal data on audience patterns in Table A9 of Appendix B. We are grateful also to the Audit Bureau of Circulation and other journals for the figures in Appendix A; and to the Newspaper Society for further information on daily and weekly newspapers. The maps on pp. xiv and xv were drawn by Stirling Surveys.

Preface

The subtitle 'Plymouth Sound to Moray Firth' has a double meaning. In Plymouth you can find the most southerly BBC and ITV television studies, and at Inverness, on the Moray Firth, the most northerly. 'Plymouth Sound' is also the name of the most southerly ILR radio station, and 'Moray Firth' the most northerly. As to newspapers, the *Western Morning News* is based in Plymouth but Inverness has no daily newspaper, the nearest being the *Press and Journal* in Aberdeen.

This is a study of regional news as presented on television, on radio and in newspapers. It grew out of an Edinburgh conference on national and regional identity, out of talks with journalists and political people in Scotland and the south, and out of discussion in the Media Studies Department of the University of Stirling.

The study has been funded by the BBC, the Television Fund, and Stirling University. My warmest thanks therefore go to all three, in particular to Geraint Stanley Jones and David Barlow at the BBC, to Lord Thomson of Monifieth at the IBA, and to colleagues at Stirling University.

Thanks are also due to the 24 newspapers or broadcasting units who let me observe them at work, to others such as Granada Television and the *Manchester Evening News* who were helpful, also to Moray Firth Radio and BBC Highland; to my wife for constant advice and support, to Kay Weaver as research assistant, and to Keith Povey for his sharp spotting of errors and omissions.

ALASTAIR HETHERINGTON

Glossary

ABC	Audit Bureau of Circulations (newspapers)
AIRC	Association of Independent Radio Contractors
AM	Amplitude modulation – better known as Medium Wave (MW) transmission
BARB	Broadcasters' Audience Research Board (tv., BBC and ITV)
BBC	British Broadcasting Corporation
C3	Channel Three, to replace ITV in 1993
C4	Channel Four
C5	New fifth tv. channel, due 1991 or soon after
FM	Frequency modulation – or VHF or short-wave radio transmission
IBA	Independent Broadcasting Authority
ILR	Independent Local Radio (commercial)
IRN	Independent Radio News (part of London Broadcasting Company)
ITC	Independent Television Commission (to replace IBA, 1992–3)
ITV	Independent Television (companies)
JICRAR	Joint Industry Committee for Radio Audience Research (ILR)
LBC	London Broadcasting Co.
Network	Broadcasting to the whole of the UK; or to all Scotland, Wales or Northern Ireland
NUJ	National Union of Journalists
PA	Press Association (UK news agency)
PSC	Portable Single Camera unit
R.	Radio (in titles of radio stations)
S4C	Welsh Fourth Channel
Sc. Tv.	Scottish Television (company)
TSW	Television South-West (company)
TVS	Television South (company)

VDU	Visual display unit
VHF	Very high frequency: see also FM
VT	Video tape
YTV	Yorkshire Television (company)

News Content by Categories: a Guide

A & S	Arts, science, culture, incl. theatres, scientific research (other than medicine), music (incl. pop and rock), history, books
Ag.	agriculture
Crash	accidents, disasters, fires, floods, wreck (in the measurements, this is split with *Human*)
Crime	courts, crime (other than *Terror* below)
Crime C	civil cases in court
Crime W	if specially a women's interest case
Env.	countryside, environment, preservation, RSPB, National Trust, etc. Also mountaineering (unless *Crash*)
Health	NHS, hospitals, doctors, medical (also quite often split with *Human*)
Health A	local or regional
Human	stories about people *not* covered by preceding categories or by *S & S* or *Stars* below. Also strong human stories mainly or partly in another category, such as families affected by a court case
H/Women	if specifically about women's interests
Int.	international
L & L	leaders and letters (though these are generally omitted from the news measurements)
Money	City, finance, business, etc.
Pets	dogs, cats, etc.
Pol.	political, economic, social, industrial, unemployment (UK)
Pol. A	local, regional or Scottish
Pol. W	as above, but primarily women's affairs
Pol. Ed.	education (but this was merged into *Pol.* or *Pol. A* in some of the measurements)

Terror	= IRA, Provos, Loyalists, bombings, RUC, etc. (but Anglo–Irish meetings count as *Pol.*)
Sport	sport, incl. horse racing
Stars	personalities, celebrities, stars, tv. people, Royals
S & S	sex and scandal (or either)
War	war, peace, arms and disarmament, nuclear, CND
Weather	weather

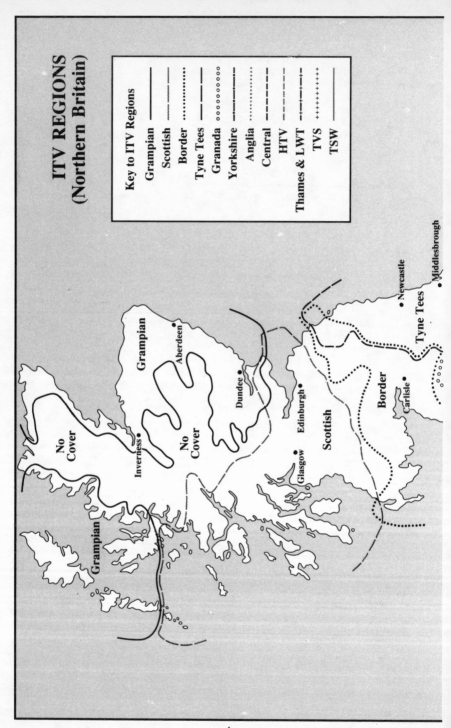

ITV REGIONS
(Northern Britain)

Key to ITV Regions

Grampian	————
Scottish	- - - - -
Border	··········
Tyne Tees	— — —
Granada	ooooooooo
Yorkshire	··········
Anglia	·············
Central	– – – –
HTV	—·—·—
Thames & LWT	+++++++++
TVS	————
TSW	————

Grampian

No Cover

Inverness

Grampian

Aberdeen

No Cover

Dundee

Grampian

Edinburgh

Glasgow

Scottish

Border

Carlisle

Newcastle

Tyne Tees

Middlesbrough

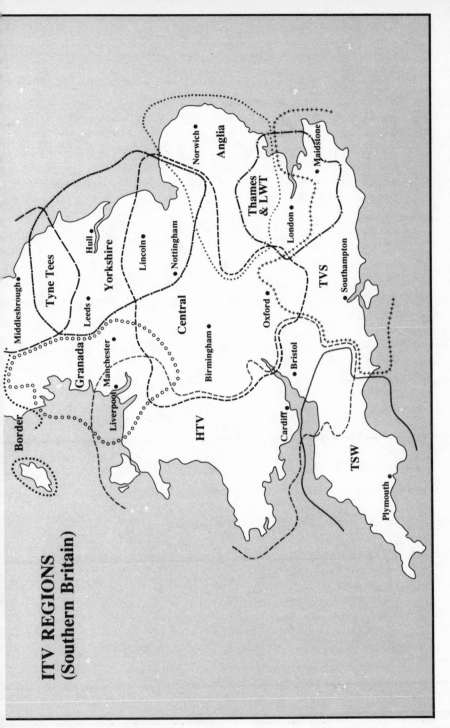

ITV REGIONS
(Southern Britain)

Border

Tyne Tees

Middlesbrough

Granada

Manchester
Liverpool

Leeds

Hull

Yorkshire

Lincoln

Nottingham

Central

Birmingham

HTV

Cardiff

Bristol

Oxford

Norwich

Anglia

Thames
& LWT

London

Maidstone

TVS

Southampton

TSW

Plymouth

1 News Where You Live – and Who Controls It

People in Britain buy more newspapers than people anywhere else in the world – about 15 million national newspapers each morning and about 8½ million regional morning or evening papers. That means on average more than 1 newspaper each day in every household. We also spend many hours watching television or listening to radio at home, in cars, and sometimes at work. The audience figures for regional television news are about level with viewing of national network news, and numbers listening to local or regional radio news are not far short of those for national radio news. Much of our daily information, therefore, comes from regional or local sources.

What is the character of this news? Who decides on regional news priorities? How well is it presented? And who owns or controls the newspapers and the broadcasting media?

This study looks in detail at four regions – Yorkshire, the Midlands, the South-West of England, and Central Scotland, using these as a cross-section of the country. Within each of these it looks at two or three newspapers, two television stations (one BBC, one ITV), and two radio stations (one BBC, one ILR). There is also a brief look at other regions towards the end of the book.

Yorkshire was chosen because it is distant from London and has a strong character of its own. It lived up to its self-confident reputation. The Midlands provided a contrast, being closer to London and lacking a common identity – factors which make regional news harder to prepare and present. Devon and Cornwall in the South-West have many common interests – though they sometimes deny it – and there is rivalry between the two counties. Their broadcasters and their one morning newspaper help to hold them together. Central Scotland differs from the English regions, because of the Scottish identity and the complexities of Scottish politics. Its morning newspapers have higher sales than any others based outside London, and solid content. It is well served in radio, having both Radio Clyde – in many ways the

1

best of all the ILR stations – and a highly competent BBC Radio
Scotland. The two evening television programmes, *Scotland Today*
and *Reporting Scotland*, are both of a high standard. These are the
basis of the study.

WHO DOES WHAT

Overall, BBC television provides network news on BBC 1 and BBC 2
from London, complemented by early evening regional news programmes from 12 centres – Belfast, Birmingham, Bristol, Cardiff,
Glasgow, Leeds, London, Manchester, Newcastle, Norwich, Plymouth and Southampton. These centres also broadcast brief news
bulletins throughout the day.

The ITV structure provides for network news mainly from ITN in
London (owned collectively by the ITV companies), plus TV-am at
breakfast. In addition, each of the ITV companies broadcasts its own
early evening news and its daytime bulletins. The companies are based
in the same cities as the BBC centres, plus Aberdeen, Carlisle and
Guernsey. But Central Television in Birmingham also provides separate services for the East Midlands (from Nottingham) and the
Thames Valley (from Abingdon). Similarly TVS has separate programmes from Southampton and Maidstone, as does Yorkshire
Television from its major transmitters in the east and west of its
territory. Thus there are 18 ITV early evening programmes, against
the BBC's 12.

Channel Four's news comes from ITN, with no regional element.
S4C, the Welsh fourth channel, provides news in Welsh from the BBC
in Cardiff and Welsh current affairs from HTV Wales, also in Cardiff.

For radio (we shall come to newspapers later) the BBC has no
regional news as such. But no fewer than 49 BBC local radio stations
broadcast news in the morning, midday, and evening – as well as
hourly bulletins from most. They include not only the 39 local
stations in England (by the autumn of 1990) but also the 7 part-time
stations in Scotland, 2 in Wales (Gwent and Clwyd) and 1 in Northern
Ireland (Foyle). On a bigger scale, Scotland, Wales, and Northern
Ireland each have their own full-time network radio news and
substantial current affairs programmes.

For ILR (Independent Local Radio) a UK network news service is
available from LBC, the London Broadcasting Company. Each
station can choose how much or how little it will take. Altogether 47

stations are in operation in 1989, and others may follow. Pennine Radio, Mercia Radio and Plymouth Sound are among those described later. For most, the transmission areas are smaller than for BBC local radio. Thus, for example, Plymouth Sound broadcasts only to the immediate area of Plymouth, and DevonAir only to the south coast of the county, while BBC R. Cornwall and BBC R. Devon each cover almost the whole of its county and both can be heard in Plymouth.

Supervision of BBC output lies with the BBC's Governors, the Director General, and for the regions more specifically with the Managing Director Regional Broadcasting – since 1986 a Welshman, Geraint Stanley Jones. The BBC is a massive organisation, in its own terms 'a £1000 million company', with news and current affairs costing one fifth or one sixth of its total expenditure – a relatively low sum compared with the hours of broadcasting. As far as possible, authority is devolved from Broadcasting House in London to its regional production centres. The regional budgets are less generous than for network news and current affairs, and very much less than those of their ITV competitors. An extreme example is in the Midlands, where the BBC's television news in Birmingham and Nottingham has a total staff of 21 journalists (including sport), while for its output from Birmingham, Nottingham and the Thames Valley, Central Television has 84 journalists (again including sport).

For BBC staff, however, numbers are not the only worry. In recent years – from 1982 onwards, if not earlier – there has been anxiety and insecurity through much of the corporation. Pressure from Governments, Labour as much as Conservative, was not new. But Mrs Thatcher's Government has packed the BBC's Governors with Conservative supporters, breaking the tradition respected by all previous Governments that these appointments should be representative of the country as a whole. During the Falklands war Mrs Thatcher and others, including many Conservative backbenchers, had been highly critical of the BBC's 'unpatriotic' cover – though in reality the BBC had tried to provide reliable reports when news was scarce. Later the Government had shown its dislike for funding the BBC through the television licence fee, setting up the Peacock Committee to look at alternatives such as advertising on BBC 1 and BBC 2. Peacock, however, recommended against that move. Then there had been a series of public rows over reporting from Northern Ireland, over the *Secret Society* series, and over the SAS action in Gibraltar. In news and current affairs – before, during and after the 1987 General

Election – the conviction grew that the BBC's governors would not back anyone who dared to ask awkward questions or present critical reports. The 'play safe' disease filtered through to regional newsrooms.

The ITV companies had a different problem, one that will plague them until 1993. Following a Peacock Committee recommendation – reached by four votes to three – the Government decided that the next round of franchise renewals should be by competitive tendering. In theory, that could knock out every one of the existing companies. In practice, it is unlikely to do so. Some will probably be outbid by newcomers; some of the bigger companies may bid not only for renewal of their own franchise but also for the right to take over the territory of smaller companies. The predators want to reduce the English companies from 10 to 4, and in Scotland from 3 to 1. Meanwhile, however, you are unlikely to encounter in ITV newsrooms the anxieties evident within BBC. They are well staffed, well paid, well equipped and cheerful. Which is not to say that they always produce better programmes than the lean and harried BBC: the surprise is that, with exceptions, they do not. Read the later chapters for the evidence.

Two maps, on pages xii and xiii, set out the areas at present covered by the ITV companies. The BBC regions are almost identical, except that the Reading–Oxford area is covered from London instead of the Midlands, and the whole of Scotland is covered by BBC Scotland. One difference, though: the ITV companies compete with each other in the border areas, some of which involve extensive overlapping – for example in the county of Lincoln and in East Anglia, or in the Gloucester–Cheltenham area reached both by Central and by HTV. The BBC stations are complementary, working with each other and sharing news resources. BBC local radio is also an important source of news for BBC regional television.

The overlord of ITV and ILR at present is the IBA (Independent Broadcasting Authority). That, too, will change in 1993, or sooner. For the past 34 years (since 1954) the IBA has kept close control over the ITV companies. It has insisted on multiple ownership of each, with no dominant financial interest in any, and although company shares are bought and sold on the stock exchanges, the IBA can block purchases by anyone whom it thinks unsuitable. As a result each company is owned by a diversity of shareholders and their boards of directors are drawn from a variety of interests. One consequence is that the professional executives – programme people, heads of news and current affairs, advertising sales directors, chief engineers and others – have a great deal of freedom, always provided that the company is profitable and pays its dividends.

From 1993 a 'lighter' regime will apply, with the IBA replaced by the ITC (Independent Television Commission). The companies who win the new franchises – possibly as few as 6 or 7 or as many as 16 or 18 – will be regionally based but with fewer restrictions on shareholding. Newspapers, as before, will be limited to 20 per cent of holdings in any company.

The IBA has maintained close supervision of programme plans – too close and too nit-picking, some ITV people say. The IBA has also insisted on maintenance of education, religious and other programme categories, not least the half-hour early evening news magazines. Just how much of that is to be swept away in 1993 remains to be seen, for the Government still (summer 1989) has to get its legislation through Parliament. At present, however, the Government is insisting that the regional news services must be carried on. Deregulation is not to be as total as the free market advocates want. If the requirement for regional news survives, so much the better.

NEWSPAPERS, BIG AND SMALL

Newspapers are less institutional, having no high authority to watch over them, and are varied in character. The nationals – 6 'popular' and 5 'quality' – cover the whole UK. That is to say, they are distributed throughout the country, but they take much less interest in events outside London than in the affairs of South-East England. Altogether there are 16 non-metropolitan daily morning newspapers in the UK and 75 evening papers. The biggest morning sales are in Scotland – the *Glasgow Herald* at 126 000 a day, the *Dundee Courier* at 124 000, and the *Press and Journal* (Aberdeen) at 109 000. The highest in England – the *Yorkshire Post* and the *Eastern Daily Press*, both at about 91 000 – are level with Scotland's fourth morning, *The Scotsman*. The largest evening distribution is the *Manchester Evening News* at 292 000, followed by the *Express and Star* (Wolverhampton) at 245 000. The smallest, but still profitable, are the *Paisley Daily Express* at 12 000 and the *Scarborough Evening News* at 19 000.

Ownership is no less varied. Northcliffe Newspapers, part of the Associated Newspapers group (publishers of the *Daily Mail*), have 12 regionals in England and Wales. Thomson Regional Newspapers also have 12, stretching from Aberdeen to Cardiff and Reading. Their parent company also had *The Times* and *Sunday Times* in London before they were sold to Rupert Murdoch in 1981. The Westminster Press, linked with the *Financial Times* in London, has nine regionals; United, with the *Daily Express* and *Star*, also has six regional dailies. Other companies with regional interests are the East Midlands Allied Press, Eastern Counties Newspapers, and Reed – each with four dailies. Lonrho and Ingersoll each have three. There are 12 or 13 companies with a single daily. (More detail can be found in Appendix A.)

One clear distinction should be made between the regionals and the nationals. Even those dailies owned by Lord Steven's United Newspapers or those owned by Lord Rothermere's *Daily Mail* group are, broadly speaking, free of the political direction and prejudice that emerge in their related nationals, especially during general elections. Further, the vulgarity and triviality of some of the 'popular' nationals are to be found in no more than a small minority of the regional newspapers. That is partly because the regionals and locals are closer to their readers, who include supporters of all the political parties. Their editors, reporters and photographers encounter readers – often articulate and critical – more often than the men of Wapping or other ex-Fleet Street offices do. And, living in smaller communities, their neighbours are more likely to know who they are, and to identify them with what they write.

Much the same applies to the weekly or twice-weekly papers published by almost all of the regional daily companies or by others producing weeklies only. These range from a big and prosperous company such as Johnston Press (UK), with weeklies in England and Scotland, to the one-man single (editor, manager, reporter and photographer) and his wife operation of the *Arran Banner*, on the Island of Arran, with winter sales of about 2000 each week and summer sales of over 3000. Since Arran's winter population is barely 4000 people of all ages, its sales are a great achievement, but – as its editor-proprietor knows to his cost – angry readers are apt to invade his office, however accurate the report may have been. The more accurate, indeed, the bigger the risk, but he lives with that.

The regional and local newspapers are less subject to political pressure than the nationals, who in turn are much less troubled than the BBC or ITV. To begin with, the non-metropolitan newspapers individually are a much smaller target. They number just over 100 dailies owned by about 50 companies, whereas there are 16 ITV companies and 1 BBC – the last being by far the biggest target. Further, political people and senior civil servants regard television as now more influential than newspapers. Top politicians and civil servants, it is true, are sensitive to the reporting and comment in the 'quality' newspapers, and telephone calls to editors are quite frequent. On the whole, though, they are capable of looking after themselves.

In the regions and locally, Ministers and MPs will have occasional contacts with those in their areas. Very rarely, however, does that seem to amount to serious pressure. Nor does there appear to be much political direction from proprietors. At one time the Westminster Press – one of the most liberal and broad-minded companies – used to circulate leading articles which editors could use or not use as they wished. Northcliffe Newspapers did something similar. But for the most part individual newspapers are left to make their own decisions. They are sensitive – or should be – to the differing opinions among their readers.

WHY THE REGIONS MATTER

Londoners, as Brenda Maddox once said, 'don't give a damn about regional news'. It is no coincidence that the television early evening news for the London area is probably the most boring and least colourful of all of ITV's 6 o'clock and the BBC's 6.30 programmes. London itself is too diverse for people to identify easily with its news other than national news relating to the capital. To quote Brenda Maddox on London again, 'the region is simply too big to capture any flavour that can be labelled as local'. Unfortunately for the rest of the country, some able television people in London – BBC and ITV – have built their assessment of regional news on what they see in London. It gives them a false impression.

In the rest of the country the regional television news, the local radio news, and the variety of daily newspapers are generally appreciated, although often criticised. The audience figures and the newspaper sales are evidence of their popularity. True, the viewing of regional news is influenced by the network scheduling of what comes before or after it – but, as we shall see later, there is often an upward 'blip' in audiences when the regional news comes on. True also, people buy local newspapers for the advertisements, the sports sections and the listing of local events, as well as for political and social news. Yet the newspapers, television and radio are our primary sources of information, not least on political and other public affairs. They are the main channel by which the Government, the Opposition, and Whitehall departments and the local authorities can reach their constituents. Regional television and local radio are valuable to MPs of all parties. They are equally valuable to people at home, as a means of keeping up to date with public events and assessing the policy-makers. Without the flow of information, a democracy cannot work.

As to news priorities, in the regions I found them much the same as in nationals and the network television news studied three years earlier. The 'seismatic scale' projected in *News, Newspapers and Television* (Macmillan, 1985) still characterised the approach of most reporters, news editors and editors. It set out the primary influences in the choice of news. Its categories, in order of priority, were these:

1. *Significance* – social, economic, political, human
2. *Drama* – the excitement, action and entertainment in the event
3. *Surprise* – the freshness, newness, unpredictability
4. *Personalities* – royal, political, 'showbiz', others
5. *Sex, scandal, crime* – popular ingredients
6. *Numbers* – the scale of the event, numbers of people affected
7. *Proximity* – on our doorsteps, or 10 000 miles away
8. And – for television news – good pictures, visually attractive

Journalists must, of course, often work at high speed. Their judgements are instinctive rather than analytical. Nevertheless my questioning of them in 1984–5, repeated in preparing this study in 1988, confirmed that behind the instinctive judgements based on years of practice were instant assessments ruled by priorities such as these. In regional or local newspapers or radio or television the 'proximity' factor is automatic. News of what is happening close to home comes first.

Is there bias? Only the usual 'socio-centralism' – which is to say the tendency in the media to reinforce the established society, uphold law and order, and accept social reform only gradually. Newspapers and broadcasters usually reflect what they perceive as the attitudes of their readers and audiences; and since most people want peaceful, prosper-ous and orderly lives, events such as riots and strikes are unpopular.

2 What to Look For

The chapters which follow are case studies of individual newspapers, regional television news, and local radio. They deal with daily routine – how the news is gathered, how decisions are taken on what to publish or broadcast, and how the news is presented – but they also reveal the responsibility placed on young journalists. Men and women only 2 or 3 years out of school or university may find themselves in charge of early morning radio news bulletins. They are often alone, with nobody to whom to turn for advice, and they must make their own decisions. They must read the news, precisely on the hour or half hour, and push the right knobs to bring up pre-recorded items or interviews. And mostly they love it, in spite of the nervous strain.

You, the reader, will also find examples of the higher forms of journalism – where initiative uncovers important information, and persistence by the journalist secures its publication, often followed by action on the part of local authorities or Central Government or industry. Remember that these are random examples. As author I was able to spend only one or two days, or three at most, with each of the 24 offices or studios in the main study. Review and analysis of the newspaper or broadcasting content had to follow. I emphasise that these are random examples, not a systematic catalogue of achievements. They illustrate how much can be done by regional initiative and enterprise.

Let us look at some examples.

The Birmingham hospitals

The source is the BBC's *Midlands Today* (Chapter 13), a unit with 21 journalists to cover all the West Midlands and East Midlands. The two people chiefly involved were Clare Harrison, a general reporter and script writer with a brief also to watch NHS affairs in the region, and one of the regular producers, Peter Hiscocks. Together, they played a major part in making the hospital crisis into national news in the winter of 1987–8. For Clare Harrison it began as a single story at a

9

single hospital, the Queen Elizabeth in Birmingham, where a consultant told her that cancer patients were dying because beds had been closed and a waiting list had developed. That was followed in the autumn by a dramatic series of events at the Birmingham Children's Hospital, with delayed or cancelled heart operations on babies.

One of those cases (that of William Pound) was well covered by *Midlands Today*, thanks partly to an articulate father. But network news in London was not interested in the story. Clare Harrison then went back to the Queen Elizabeth Hospital, where she was told that 20 people a month were dying 'needlessly'. But at first neither *Midlands Today* nor network news wanted the story. 'I could not interest anyone in that', she said.

Peter Hiscocks, however, had a baby daughter with a serious heart problem, and she was on the Children's Hospital's waiting list. He produced a 40-minute programme on the background to the hospital crisis, bringing in a past president of the Royal College of Surgeons and a Conservative MP who was highly critical of the Government's 'folly' in not funding the hospitals adequately. That programme had an impact in the Midlands, but network news was still not interested. National newspapers, however, were beginning to pay attention.

Then followed further cases, in one of which parents took the hospital to court because their child's operation was delayed. More of that and its consequences can be found in Chapter 13. The newspaper coverage galvanised BBC network news into calling for reports; and at one point ITN, being unable to get into the hospital, filmed (without consent) Clare Harrison interviewing one of the consultants. She was nevertheless still disappointed that the problems of the Queen Elizabeth Hospital and others in the area received little attention from the media; but nationally, through the spring and summer of 1988 and beyond, the financing of the NHS continued as one of the top political issues.

The Passport Backlog

This, too, originated in Birmingham – with BBC R. WM. Its ethnic reporter-producer, Anita Bhalla, in early 1988 received a number of telephone calls from people whose passports had become stuck in the Home Office centre at Croydon, so they could not travel. She started making inquiries, and found that there was a big problem. Through talking to one of the Leicester MPs, she learned that there was a backlog of over 200 000 letters. She got him on to her radio programme and on to *Midlands Today* – from which it 'snowballed' into the national newspapers and network television, leading eventually to Home Office action.

The Royal Dockyard Redundancies

This is a case of well organised preparation, bringing strong results in news, reaction, and analysis. It was the work of TSW in Plymouth, on one of the days when I was there. The Devonport Royal Dockyard was and still is the biggest employer in the South-West. It had been privatised in 1987, and a year later, in June 1988, there were indications of a drastic reduction in jobs. When the news finally broke, on 11 June, the loss of jobs was put at 3300 over the next two years – one third of the workforce, and much worse than had been expected.

As will appear in Chapter 17, TSW had arranged to get the figures just before the start of the 11.30 am press conference at the dockyard. As a result it had the core of the news on its 11.25 am bulletin. More important than that, it had reporters lined up for interviews with unions, workers and three MPs; and live in its 6 pm programme it had a vigorous interview with the Defence Minister directly concerned. It gave 11 of the 27 minutes of its programme to the item. The BBC, because of other commitments, could not offer the same detail and analysis.

The Wednesday Walk-in

An initiative by Plymouth Sound, the ILR station there: unique, so far as I know. but almost certain to be copied. On Wednesdays from 2 to 3 pm it invites listeners to come to its studios and express their views live. When necessary, it extends the programme beyond 3 pm. It discourages political people, national or local, from taking part on Wednesday, but next day it gives them and others affected by the Wednesday comments the chance to come in and explain or reply.

Scottish Universities' 'Own Goal'

Really a goal as much as an 'own goal': a shrewd piece of interpretation by the *Glasgow Herald*'s economics editor, Alf Young. The bare bones of a report by the Fraser of Allander Institute on the finance of three Scottish Universities had been covered by radio news one morning, but Alf Young believed that there must be more to the story. At first glance, the report said that the reduction of Government support would mean, by 1990, the loss of a much larger figure to the Scottish economy through the loss of direct and indirect jobs.

But Alf Young, who prefers unravelling complex stories to accepting simple messages, looked at the figures more deeply. He found that while the losses had been severe – over 9 years probably £55 million and 1805 jobs – the three universities were offsetting their losses through fees from more overseas students, winning more commercial research grants and other such means. An 'own goal', he thought, in that it might encourage the Government to squeeze the universities further. But Young mentions the possible distortion of academic priorities and the failure in Britain to educate a greater proportion of its youth beyond basic school level. Industry and commerce, he says, are reporting serious shortages in skills.

These are just five examples drawn from the chapters which follow. Others will be found there. Good journalism depends on that kind of initiative and persistence. It is true that newsdesks are sometimes slow to react to what their own specialists tell them, and that they are sometimes more impressed by what appears elsewhere. Hence the 'snowball' effect in national and regional news. But it is also true that confident news editors will seize on original material supplied by their reporters and specialists, though they may also at times ask for further evidence.

A common criticism of regional and local news, whether in print or on air, is that it is 'trivial'. Again, the evidence presented later counters that – though individual readers must make their own judgements. It may apply to some, though not all, of the smaller newspapers; and it does apply to a few of the smaller ILR stations, with minimal staff. But the detailed content analysis in the individual chapters is relevant here.

Look in particular at the proportion of content devoted to the categories *Pol.* and *Pol. A* – the first being the general political group, which covers political and economic news, social and industrial affairs, jobs and unemployment, and the second being regional or local items belonging to the same group. Look also at the *A & S* category, covering Arts, science, culture, music, history and books; and at the *Health* and *Human* categories. Newspapers or broadcasts with a fair proportion of these are not likely to be trivial, at least to people concerned with the counties or cities within which they work or live. Publications heavily dependent on the *Crash* category (accidents, disasters, fires, floods, etc.), on *S & S* (sex and scandal) and on *Stars* (personalities, celebrities, Royals) are more likely be of little lasting significance. The *Human* category can be ambiguous, especially when it depends on the general character of a newspaper. A guide to the 25 categories used in this study can be found on pp. xi–xii.

Just as critics living in London or the South-East may be inclined to dismiss regional affairs as trivial, so journalists and others elsewhere criticise the parochial tendencies of national newspapers and network news. During my research in Yorkshire, the Midlands, the South-West and Central Scotland I encountered many complaints on this score. Specifically, in Yorkshire while I was there the 'Sgt Speed' murder trial took place – Sgt Speed having been a police officer who was murdered outside Leeds Parish Church, while another police officer was badly wounded. It was ignored on network television news, and of the national dailies only the *Daily Telegraph* gave it much space. It was an extraordinary case, linked with crime in other areas and the abduction of a member of the Guinness family in Dublin. The almost universal comment among Yorkshire journalists was that if it had happened on the steps of St Paul's it would have been the lead in every national newspaper and in every network bulletin. (In fairness, it may be noted that the BBC's *Crimewatch* gave it extensive cover before and after the trial.)

Then in the Midlands there was the hospital issue, with the reluctance of London to take anything until the national newspapers caught on, rather late, to the cancelled operations at the Birmingham Children's Hospital. In the South-West, with the start of the Single-handed Trans-Atlantic Race, there was astonishment at the BBC in Plymouth that the Television Centre in London (1) when advised beforehand of the event said it was not interested, (2) only hours before the start changed its mind and demanded cover, and (3) when supplied with good pictures and commentary did not use them, while French television – and BBC *Breakfast Time* next morning – did). And in Scotland, though there was no great surprise about the

English reaction, the controversy about separate or joint Catholic and Protestant schools received little or no attention south of the Border.

Style and presentation are important – the layout of pages in newspapers, the credibility and authority of television presenters, and the clarity of speech on radio. In newspapers an orderly layout is preferable to a fussy one, but the pages must not look too rigid. For television news the presenters must be chosen carefully and must not change too often if audiences are to identify with them. Probably the most effective is a combination of one man and one woman, with the woman often in the lead. To have two can speed up the programme and mark changes of topic more readily. They need to speak with apparent authority, interview with firm precision, and yet not be too formal. While seeing a live programme is the only way to assess performance, let me draw attention to those which seemed to me the most effective – the BBC's *Look North* from Leeds, TSW's *Today* from Plymouth, and the two programmes from Glasgow, Scottish Television's *Scotland Today* and the BBC's *Reporting Scotland.* It is, of course, a hazard for competent presenters that they are likely to be offered jobs in London. It may be relevant to the four programmes named above that most of their regular presenters have either chosen to stay where they are or have worked in London and preferred to come back.

So read on and form your own conclusions. For the benefit of readers who may be considering a career in newspapers or broadcasting – and perhaps for the interest of others – a few brief biographies of a cross-section of journalists have been included at the end of relevant chapters.

3 The News in Yorkshire

North Yorkshire is mainly moors, dales and the beauty of the Herriot country. East Yorkshire is the flatlands of the Vale and the gently rolling Wolds – all good farming country. West Yorkshire has the Pennines and the industrial centres of Bradford, Halifax and Huddersfield. South Yorkshire has the coalfields, the steaming power stations, and surviving remnants of the steel industry. For broadcasting purposes, Lincolnshire and much of Nottinghamshire must be added, for the huge transmitters at Emley Moor in the east Pennines and Belmont near Lincoln serve them as well.

Based in Leeds are the ITV company Yorkshire Television and BBC North-East. YTV's early evening *Calendar* is broadcast in two versions – one from Emley Moor for most of North, West and South Yorkshire, and the other from Belmont for East Yorkshire, Humberside, Lincoln, Notts and north-west Norfolk. Most items are common to both programmes, but Belmont breaks away for 8–10 minutes of its own. (Eventually Belmont is likely to have a completely separate programme.) The two versions come from neighbouring studios in Leeds. The BBC's *Look North* also comes from Leeds in the early evening, and within its 25 or 27 minutes 5 or 6 minutes are reserved for what it calls its 'slip edition' for the Belmont transmitter.

Within the region there are four BBC local radio stations – R. York, R. Humberside (in Hull), R. Sheffield and R. Leeds. Not far away are R. Lincolnshire and R. Nottingham to the south, R. Lancashire to the west (and easily picked up in much of West Yorkshire) and R. Cleveland to the north. ILR has four stations – R. Aire (Leeds), R. Hallam (Sheffield), Pennine Radio (Bradford) and Viking (Hull). In general, the ILR transmitters cover smaller territory than the BBC's for local radio, but that gives the ILR companies an advantage in calculating the percentage of listeners reached.

One daily morning newspaper covers the whole area – the *Yorkshire Post*, with average daily sales of about 92 000 and owned by United Newspapers. Ten evening papers also serve the region, based in Bradford (sales average 82 000), Grimsby (73 000), Halifax (37 000), Huddersfield (43 000), Hull (106 000), Leeds (143 000), Lincoln

(34 000), Scarborough (19 000), Sheffield (138 000) and York (54 000).
(More detail of ownership can be found in Appendix A.)

Although there are many 'Yorkshires', in character and occupa-
tions, all or nearly all of its people appear to have a common pride
and interest in the four counties. On my first visit to Leeds, an account
of its nature was given to me by a man who had lived in Yorkshire for
all his life, Derek Foster, then Acting Deputy Editor of the *Yorkshire
Post*.

> They say that in Bradford anybody who's got any money will invest
> it in stocks and shares, whereas anybody in Leeds who's got any
> money puts it straight in the building society. That's one example of
> different character in people ten or twelve miles apart. All brought
> about probably by the environment in which they grew up, in that
> Bradford was born on wool and wool was always a gamble but Leeds
> was born on tailoring and commerce, and that was always pretty
> straightforward – you knew where you were with it, you knew you'd
> got a steady income.

> Out in the farming areas, the rural areas, like any rural areas, they
> are more parochially-minded because their world is smaller: but even
> that world has grown big with television and with the onset of
> modern farming methods that have become standard, instead of
> everybody knowing his own bit of land and how it works and what's
> best for it . . .

> Then South Yorkshire – that really does have a character of its own.
> Still populated heavily by mining communities all of whom are
> fiercely loyal to each other and yet who buy our paper [the *Post*] in
> quite good quantities, which may be because we've got a good racing
> page . . . But the South Yorkshire character – you have to live there
> to understand it. The people are very friendly when they get to know
> you and very loyal to one another – easily led, gullible in the sense
> that it only takes any rumour to be spoken of as a fact and it goes
> round and they accept it. I come from South Yorkshire and I've lived
> there and I know what happens; but that apart they're an absolutely
> grand bunch of people.

> There are so many kinds of Yorkshiremen: the only thing that binds
> them together is that if there's any brass around then they are after it,
> and they know what everything is worth because in days gone by
> they've had to work hard for it – fight for it – and they mean to keep
> it.

The voice of Yorkshire. Here we are studying mainly the news, and for television the links between regional and national are relevant. YTV has the privileged position of being one of the five major ITV companies. For 20 years that has given it a guaranteed right to provide a substantial part of the network programmes for the main ITV channels – though that privilege is likely soon to be phased out. Its centre in Leeds has four big studios and an air of confident prosperity. Close to the newsroom where the daily news and *Calendar* are produced for the region, network programmes – *First Tuesday* among them – are being prepared, as well as single documentaries and other series. The interchange between them is of mutual benefit. The newsroom has also been the source for *Calendar Commentary*, a half-hour political programme on Mondays for 35 weeks a year.

The Leeds branch of BBC North-East – it has a brother in Newcastle – is also contributing to network, though on a smaller scale. With Newcastle, it produces a half-hour series *Up North* with BBC 2 documentaries in 1988 on topics such as the business companies that redundant Yorkshire miners have established for themselves, a Hull-based charity to combat child abuse, and the black economy in the vegetable fields of Lincoln. Bill Greaves, Head of Broadcasting for the North-East, regards 'an element of networking' as crucial to the development of his region. He has also secured commissions for a drama series and a daytime series.

As to resources, YTV's *Calendar* has 35 journalists and 8 news crews – 3 in Leeds and others in Lincoln, Sheffield, Hull, Grimsby and York. It has access to 12 freelance single-man camera units. YTV can also feed items directly from Scarborough and Northallerton to Leeds. The BBC's *Look North* has 17 journalists and four video crews (2 Leeds, 1 each Sheffield and Huddersfield). Although it has access to freelance single-man units it makes only limited use of them. It has no fixed facilities for feeding tape from Sheffield, York or other centres, relying instead on despatch riders.

The *Yorkshire Post* calls itself 'A three dimensional newspaper' – international, regional and local. Its policy is to put on the front page the strongest stories of the day, regardless of their location, but with a marginal preference for 'a good regional story, particularly if it is an exclusive'. On average, two thirds of the front page goes to national or international events, whereas in the paper as a whole more than two thirds of the content is regional or local. The distribution of reporters and specialists also gives an indication of priorities. In London there are two for parliamentary and political news, and two for the 'Money' and 'Business' pages. In Leeds there are between 20 and 25, including the political and industrial correspondents and others primarily covering the environment, agriculture and ethnic interests. A further 20 are in 'strategic centres' such as Sheffield, Hull, York and Bradford. Then there are the Sports and Business staffs in Leeds, and the sub-editors who handle the texts, headlines and page make-up. And the leader writers (3), the literary editor, the letters editor and the features people. In all this, the total is over 100.

The owning company used to be called 'The Yorkshire Conservative Newspaper Company' but it is now 'Yorkshire Post Newspapers Ltd', a subsidiary of United Newspapers which owns the *Daily Express* and a host of others. Its articles of association still require the *Yorkshire Post* to be a Conservative newspaper, though as its senior staff say 'not necessarily Thatcher Conservative'.

Most newsrooms are cramped, noisy and stuffy, though with the arrival of electronic equipment conditions are improving. The *Yorkshire Post*'s newsroom is much above the average, with its high domed ceiling, plenty of space and good air-conditioning. It is comparatively quiet, since nearly everyone works in front of his or her VDU terminal screen. Access through the screens means also that anyone with a terminal can call up to the current news list, can see much of what has been written in Leeds or York or Hull, and can tap the Reuter and Press Association (PA) files. Sheffield, equally, can tap in to what is happening in Leeds.

Returning to the broadcasters, at the BBC in Leeds there were few signs in the spring of 1988 of the tension, uncertainty and demoralisation then evident in parts of the BBC, particularly in London, with pressure from the Government, an unsympathetic Board of Governors, and many internal upheavals. Nor were there any such anxieties at YTV, apart from a slight uncertainty because the company was beginning to commission some programmes from small independents – in keeping with the Government's requirement that 25 per cent should come from independents within four years.

In BBC R. Leeds there was also some uncertainty because all local radio budgets were being cut by up to 10 per cent. It must be said, however, that to me the youth and enthusiasm of many of the journalists and supporting staff at Radio Leeds were impressive. They had devotion and self confidence.

Arthur Scargill, Sgt Speed, Militant Nurses and 'Militant' Bradford

During the 5 weekdays from Thursday 2I January to Wednesday 27 January 1988, YTV's *Calendar* and the BBC's *Look North* were mostly of one mind about news priorities. The single exception was the decision by the Labour Party's National Executive, meeting in London, to mount a further inquiry into the activities of 'Militant' in Bradford. *Look North* led with it that day, while *Calendar* relegated it to half a minute towards the end of its programme. (The reasons for their decisions are recorded later.)

They were at one when an RAF Red Arrows jet crashed in Lincolnshire – the third in 18 months – barely 2 hours before their programmes went on air. Both revised their running orders to lead with it: both followed up with pictures next day, and both gave prominence to the pilot's funeral 2 days later. They were equally at one on the day Arthur Scargill was re-elected as president of the NUM, each having substantial studio interviews with him: network news had no more than brief extracts from a press conference early in the day.

Unquestionably, though, the biggest event of the week for both – as for radio and the Yorkshire daily newspapers – was the Crown Court murder trial in Leeds. 3 years earlier Sgt Speed of the West Yorkshire police had been shot dead outside Leeds parish church, and another policeman had been badly wounded. The trial was dramatic in its revelations. On the day of the verdict, both *Calendar* and *Look North* devoted more than two thirds of their time to it – $17\frac{1}{2}$ and $18\frac{1}{2}$ minutes respectively. Yet network news and the national newspapers ignored it, to the surprise of Yorkshire journalists.

A full content analysis appears later. Meanwhile, let us look at the treatment of these four events and at one day's decision-making at YTV and at *Look North*.

Sgt Speed

It may be asked why a murder – any murder – should be regarded as significant news. Part of the answer must be that in the North of England such murders are rare. Even in London they are not often so calculated or cold blooded, nor can it often have happened that, when the whole story is revealed, the principal characters turn out to have been such successful thieves over a long period while appearing to have harmless characters.

Before the trial, both *Calendar* and *Look North* had prepared their background features. The trial was not of the man who fired the gun but of the accomplice, the gunman having accidentally shot himself during a police chase a year earlier. The BBC programme had one advantage through using a *Crimewatch* reconstruction, with a dramatic presentation of one policeman being shot outside the church but sending a radio call for help, with an exact description of the gunman, followed by the gunman's attack on Sgt Speed on his arrival at the churchyard and the pursuit of him by a third policeman. It also had a revealing interview with the gunman's former wife. These points apart, there was little to choose between the two versions. Both were factually cool but gripping; both traced the long search for the killer and his accomplice; both mentioned the 30 convictions of other armed robbers that were by-products of the search. Both also ended with moving interviews with Sgt Speed's widow – proud of her husband, protective of their children, and sad that 'you never get a second chance'.

The NUM Presidential Poll

In the run-up to the NUM voting, the campaign and background had been covered – more thoroughly by the BBC than by YTV, though adequately by each. As the Scargill v. Walsh campaign drew to a close, with Mr Scargill's policy of confrontation with the Coal Board a major issue, *Look North* went back to the family and home of a Cortonwood miner whose fortunes it had followed during the 1984–5 dispute. A thoughtful man, the miner concluded thus:

> I feel I owe a certain loyalty to Mr Scargill, but I can say quite categorically I won't be voting for Mr Scargill because we need a new leader, we need a different approach to things . . . He's had a shot at it and he's failed.
>
> You hear his rhetoric and you stand up at his spiel and he gets my blood going and I want to side with him. I chanted Arthur's name throughout the strike and I voted for him in the first election, and I do feel that I'm letting him down that tiny bit by not voting for him now.
>
> But I've sat down and thought about it in the quiet of my home and I firmly believe it's time for a change.

Cortonwood, of course, had closed and he had moved to another colliery which in turn was about to be closed. His wife hoped, nevertheless, that having struggled through and with household debts still to pay because of the 1984–5 strike they would get to prosperity in the end.

When a triumphant Arthur came to the two studios after the result was known, he was in a cheerful and confident mood. Each pro- gramme preceded its interview with statistics and graphs to show his reduced majority and the voting pattern, with Yorkshire crucial to his success. YTV's *Calendar* followed on with pre-recorded interviews with John Walsh, then the Yorkshire president Jack Taylor, the UDM's Roy Link, and the Energy Minister Cecil Parkinson – then to Mr Scargill. The BBC's *Look North* had a shorter but similar lead-in, including two minutes with a Newcastle professor who thought that it would now take longer to reach the essential agreement on flexible rostering which was the key to new investment and cheaper coal.

As to the interviews that followed – $4\frac{1}{2}$ minutes on YTV and just over four minutes on BBC – the former tended towards being mild and cosy while the latter was harder and more specific. Mr Scargill is, of course, one of the greatest masters when it comes to fending off awkward questions and saying what you meant to say all along. When asked by Richard Whiteley of YTV how he could claim a 'stunning victory' with only 54 per cent on his side and, taking account of the UDM members who had not voted in the ballot, how he could claim that a majority of miners were on his side, he sidestepped by saying that Mrs Thatcher had had the support of only 30 per cent in the general election. When asked persistently by Judith Stamper of *Look North* why he did not lift the overtime ban to permit negotiations, he replied as persistently that the Coal Board did not want to talk. When she put the point that the Board wanted investment leading to productivity, and that the alternative was a spiralling of pit closures, he replied that the Board wanted 6-day working, the closure of 32 more pits, the 'axing' of jobs – all to get ready for privatisation. The hard approach drew more information.

South Yorkshire remains Britain's biggest coalfield and all York- shire is concerned about its future. The attention given by the Yorkshire broadcasters to the NUM vote is readily justified. The nature of the two interviews was no doubt predictable: but they still seem preferable to the network choice of a brief summing up by industrial correspondents, competent though those correspondents are. If there is a criticism, it is that YTV at the end of its interview tried to be too cosy and gave the game away on its own expectations.

The final question was 'You'll be sweetness and light, then?' and the reply 'I'll be the same Arthur Scargill you've always known – the moderate Arthur Scargill'. At which both presenter and NUM president subsided into beaming laughter.

The Red Arrow's Crash

Again there was no hesitation in either newsroom. It was the third such crash in south Lincolnshire in 18 months, though this time there was no danger to civilians. It was a tragedy to an RAF unit whose displays are popular. Scampton is some 50 miles from Leeds, so there seemed little hope of getting pictures with less than 2 hours to transmission. (Since then, YTV has installed a direct link to Lincoln.) So each newsroom put together a package with library film and placed the item first. *Calendar* gave the report extra prominence by putting the whole of it before the news headlines: *Look North* kept to its normal format.

The Troubled Nurses

One topic came up in both programmes every day. The troubles of the National Health Service had been getting increased publicity since the previous autumn – troubles due to the success of the NHS with new but more costly treatments and to the shortfall of funds. Now, almost without precedent, nurses were contemplating a strike. On 21 January *Calendar* gave 10 minutes to a preview of the issues, including interviews with four individual nurses – one a student who talked about the mental pressures and physical demands of her work, one an experienced NHS nurse (male), one a private hospital sister who had left the NHS because she was unhappy about changes there, and one an NHS intensive care nurse with 3 years' experience in her post, mainly dealing with children. Their weekly pay rates respectively were £80, £120, £120 and £110. It then had some street interviews, all sympathetic to the nurses but divided about a possible strike. Finally there was a studio discussion with officials of COHSE (the Confederation of Health Service Employees) and the RCN (Royal College of Nursing) – one in support of a token strike and one against. The BBC's *Look North* had a similar item, much shorter at 3 minutes and not distinguishing between the COHSE and RCN positions.

On Friday 22 January both again carried short items about the votes expected next week, and on Monday 25 January they gave the result at the Leeds St James's Hospital. Since the result was declared at about 5.40 pm (earlier than expected) *Calendar* could carry only a voice report from its man at the hospital, but *Look North*, half an hour later, was able to show its reporter in vision at the hospital. On the next 2 days, both carried short reports from hospitals in Hull, Sheffield and York, including brief interviews with Health Service managers.

The Bradford Militants

On 27 January *Calendar* started the day with this as a possible lead, but by the evening had relegated it to 21 seconds near the end of the programme. *Look North* took an opposite view, having started by listing it low but in the end putting it at the top of the programme with 2½ minutes. *Calendar*'s view was that the Labour Party National Executive had done no more than 'order another inquiry', that the dispute in Bradford North had become a bore, and that nobody had anything new to say. *Look North*, however, thought the continuing Militant activity was politically significant. The *Yorkshire Post*, no great friend of the Labour Party, led with the story on its front page next day and with a reminder of its own inquiries. It quotes the MP, Pat Wall ('a founding father' of Militant from which he withdrew on becoming a Parliamentary candidate), as saying of the named party members 'All are able individuals whom this movement can ill afford to lose'. *Calendar* may have been right in judging that the dispute had become a bit of a bore, but there was still some political mileage in it.

Wednesday 27 January was a day which both *Calendar* and *Look North* thought 'poor' in news – as will emerge later.

Let us now look at the programme makers in detail.

Appendix: Content by Categories

Content by categories

The table below shows the nature of events reported in Yorkshire over five weekdays, using the categories outlined on pages xii and xiii. Similar tables appear for the Midlands on pp. 87 and 139, for the South-West on pp. 164–5, and for Scotland on pp. 201, 214 and 233. The 'crime' figures for Yorkshire are unusually high because of the Sgt. Speed murder case, a major interest in the North.

5 weekdays, Thursday 21 January to Wednesday 27 January 1988

Category*	Look North		Calendar		Yorkshire Post***	
	No. of Items	Total duration (min./sec.)	No. of Items	Total duration	No. of Items	Total space (sq. cm.)
A & S	3	7.35	6	10.29	18	5604
Ag						1505
Crash	7	7.02	7	6.15	14	1159
Crime	14	32.01	10	26.55	26	2956
Crime A					15	2851
Crime C					2	120
Crime W	**		**		2	228
Env.			1	0.25	7	473
Health	6	14.43	11	14.38	26	3022
Human	2	3.05	6	6.36	24	2556
Int.					69	5701
Money						21 434
Pets			2	1.47	1	48
Pol.					33	4923
Pol. A	15	34.25	11	33.36	57	5426
Pol. W					2	30
Terror					11	2586
Sport	4	8.27	3	8.15		18 521
Stars	1	2.33	3	9.58	12	1280
S & S					1	28
War	1	1.48	2	3.08	10	1578
Weather	1	2.20	2	3.32	2	182
Other			1	7.40****		

Notes:　*For explanation of categories, see pp. xi–xii.

　　　　**The conviction of Mrs Guest is treated as *Crime*, being linked with her husband's conviction.

　　　　***Note that the *Yorkshire Post* listing does not include features, leaders, letters, etc.

　　　　****Australian bicentenary, as seen from Yorkshire.

4 'The People Nearest to the Ground': BBC R. Leeds, Thursday 21 January 1988

Narrative, *Good Morning Yorkshire* **and** *Peter Levy Show*

4.40 am

Tim Dower (presenter *GMY*) arrives. Starts to go through material for programme, due on air 6 am. Pays particular attention to sports items prepared for him previous night – 'It can be a bit fiddly, you want to get the hang of it, reading it once or twice so you are sure of it'.

4.55 am

Nicola Hill (bulletin producer for GMY) arrives. Starts on 'hectic' hour of preparation. Reads overnight note. Takes messages off answerphone – one from reporter drawing attention to late night news item. Makes check call to W. Yorkshire police overnight control at Wakefield; also to fire control, Wakefield. Tears off texts from 'rip and read' channel from London. Begins to think about priorities for 6 am bulletin. Types or clips each item on to separate sheet so that running order can be revised instantly, if necessary.

5.50 am

Liz Haven (early reporter) arrives. Quick consultation with Nicola.

5.52 am

Tim goes to one of three linked studios downstairs, to self-drive start of programme at 6 am.

5.57 am

Nicola goes to neighbouring studio (glass panels between them) to read 6 am news. Normal 7–9 items: duration 5 minutes.

6 am

On air, with Tim and Nicola.

After 6.05 Liz makes further check calls to police main headquarters Leeds and Bradford and district headquarters Halifax and Wakefield; also fire and ambulance services. Also to BBC R. York, though it has already sent some material by printer. Decides which items worth further inquiry by telephone. Goes thoroughly through *Yorkshire Post*, again in search of anything not already covered – 'but we never lift something from the papers without checking with official sources or police'. Also scans other newspapers.

Behind the desks being used by Nicola and Liz, but within arm's reach, are 7 machines. They include 3 big (10 in) recorder/player/edit for output and for the London circuit; a 'cart' machine for instant play of short items, two telex printers, and a fax machine, much used for sending texts to BBC television in neighbouring building.

6.20 am

Jenny Billington arrives, as p.a. for Tim in studio. Also drives 'carts' on which news inserts (voice pieces, interviews) are pre-recorded for Nicola's 7 am and 8 am news bulletins and later news.

6.30 am

Nicola in studio, reading 2 minutes of headlines. Soon afterwards she prepares 1 minute of headlines for Tim to read at about 6.45 am. She will be back to read 10-minute bulletins at 7 and 8 am.

(Nicola Hill has been a news reporter at Radio Leeds for 2 years and is now an 'acting news producer'. Previously she had experience with local newspapers and as a freelance for nationals in Manchester, and in freelance work for local radios in Lancashire.)

The Programme Routine, *Good Morning Yorkshire*: 6 am to 9.30 am

GMY, five days a week, aims at about 75 per cent speech and 25 per cent music. Tim Dower conducts it at a fast pace, with vigorous commentary of his own and frequent trailers for coming items. When anything has to be repeated two or three times within the hour – road or rail travel or a weather summary – he varies the wording and throws in a joke or two ('if you're travelling on the 7.39 from Skipton to Leeds don't worry; it's just that it's going to be nice to cuddle up a little closer to your fellow commuters this morning because instead of the usual four coaches there will be only two.').

The news on the hour is followed by a pop or rock record – bright and cheerful – then 2 or 3 minutes on today's newspapers, adapted from the London text to give it a Yorkshire flavour. Then traffic news live from the AA in Leeds, followed by other travel. Then another record. At 20 minutes after the hour, for 5 or 6 minutes, the sports news with pre-recorded interviews or inserts. Next, a pre-recorded short feature (see below). Then, at the half hour, travel and the news headlines and another record; and about 35 or 36 minutes after the hour another feature, and then another record before brief headlines about 45 minutes after the hour.

For the features on Thursday 21 January, Tim Dower had five already prepared in the newsroom the previous day and one interview to be broadcast live. The five prepared items were each run twice between 6 and 9.30 am. The live item was to have been just before 8 am but because the guest arrived late, after a minor motor accident, it was run at 8.35 instead. That meant a swift change of plans about 7.45 but was handled smoothly by Tim and Jenny (who had been trying to find out what had happened to the guest).

The prepared features were these:

- 'Illustrator', an interview with an Allerton artist on her success in illustrating children's books.
- 'Gas lady', about a Bradford woman's 'tussle' with the Housing Department who wanted the Gas Board to undertake work in a flat where her 91-year-old mother lived ('I told them she would die').
- 'Miners' Election', a look forward to the Scargill–Walsh vote due at the end of the week, with commentary by the BBC's industrial reporter Nick Jones and inserts from the two candidates.
- 'Howarth Playwright', a jolly interview with a teacher whose first play (about a parents' evening) was to be broadcast on R. 4 at the weekend.
- 'Heart Support Group', with Dewsbury volunteers helping victims of heart attack.

The live item was about a 'jail break' being organised for charity by a group of prison officers at Armley in Leeds. The running order was recast at 7.45 when Jenny reported that Mel Mox, the prison officer due in, had left home but failed to arrive; it was recast again at 8.15 when he still had not come, but he turned up at 8.25 and went on air at 8.35, having been taken into the studio while one of the discs was on. Tim had about 1 minute to talk to him before going on air, with only an opening cue and a couple of possible questions ready; but, as Tim said afterwards, 'luckily he arrived with some extra information and some photographs which gave me an idea of how to approach it'. Mr Mox gives a moving account of the 11-month baby for whom money was to be raised – she had a rare growth for which treatment is available only in California – and he goes on to the 'fair and foul' means to be used by three prison officers to 'escape' and get as far as they could from the jail (with airport and bus stations being watched). A touching and unusual item.

Activity in the Newsroom

The main events up to 6.30 have already been outlined. Thereafter, though it was seen by the journalists as a fairly easy day, these followed.

6.35–6.45 am

Liz picks up from printer detail of House of Commons written reply to question by Leeds MP on money owed to local authorities for unpaid rent. Nearly £200 million owed in England overall, with substantial sums unpaid in Leeds, Bradford and West Yorkshire. Much heavier arrears, however, in London boroughs. 1-minute item written and recorded (voice) by Liz for 7 am bulletin.

6.58–7.12 am

With Nicola in studio reading news. Liz simultaneously keeps an eye on TV BBC *Breakfast Time* and an ear on 7 am news from rival ILR station in Leeds, R. Aire. Nothing so far that's not already covered by R. Leeds.

7.40 am

Circuit from London offers new, short comments from NUPE and

Royal College nurses in London who may decide to join 1-day strike in early February. One extract put on Cart for 8 am bulletin, together with existing comment from General Secretary of Royal College.

7.50 am

John McGill, 'day editor' today, arrives. Checks stories already in hand. Notes that Michael Meadowcroft, president-elect of Liberal party and formerly a Leeds MP, is holding 10.30 press conference in opposition to Lib–SDP merger. Is telephone interview possible before 10.30? John Mac starts chasing.

About 8 to 8.15 am

Arrival of Peter Levy (presenter of the *Peter Levy Show*, 9.30 am to 12.30 pm) and others. Producer, Alison; programme assistant, Nick. Discussion with John Mac and others: should they mount today a studio or telephone debate on David Alton's Bill to amend Abortion law, in Commons tomorrow? Peter says they did it 6 weeks ago; only worth doing if they can get two named participants. Liz and John Mac try, but eventually cannot. Idea dropped.

8.45 am

Nicola revising running order, to give variety at 9 am. Nurses story to go first, in altered form with Yorkshire aspect. Further revision, to provide three Yorkshire stories before going into national news. (BBC policy is that national news should be kept together, whether at the beginning or middle.)

8.50 am

John Mac, after talk with Alison Lister (Peter Levy's producer), pursues two possibilities. (1) Get someone from Bradford University School of Peace Studies on their report on over 200 nuclear accidents – published today, big story in *Yorkshire Post*; also in *Bradford Telegraph and Argus* last night. (2) On Alton Bill, try for Leeds MP John Battle who will vote for Alton but may be deselected by his (Labour) constituency party as a result.

Around 8.45 am or soon after

More arrivals, including:

- News editor, John Cundy, who is much preoccupied by murder trial which opens today before jury after 6 days of legal argument without jury. He is preparing a documentary.
- Angela Piears, producer working on documentary about NHS in Leeds and Bradford, due for transmission at end of next week. She has 3 days to work on it this week but returns tomorrow to Nicola's role, producing *GMY*. (She remarks on how much better it is having 3 clear days to work on the documentary – 'when you've got a clear head' – rather than old system of doing documentaries in spare time and then getting compensating time off.)
- Annabel McGoldrick, Day News Desk and news reader; briefed by Nicola when she returns from studio at 9.06 am.
- Two more reporters. (Still to come, one for late duty, 3 pm to 11 pm.)
- Three sports staff (one retired but back part time, one full time, one freelance on contract).

9.02 am

Liz, listening to R. Aire news, picks up story that Yorkshire soldiers on winter training in Highlands were in crash near Inverness during night. Phil rings Northern Constabulary, Inverness, who say one dead and four or five injured. Rings Raigmore Hospital, Inverness, who give detail of injured. Dead man from Leeds; others from RAMC unit, Sheffield. Rings BBC Radio Highland, Inverness, to ask for fax of their text; they'd be delighted to help but don't have a fax machine. Rings Army, York, who provide home addresses of injured (including two Territorial Army women). Vehicle left road at Bridge of Brown during night, midway between Balmoral and Inverness.

9.10 am

John Mac says John Battle MP refuses to discuss Alton Bill. He complains that R. Leeds never ask him about anything else. Some surprise on news desk, since they think they've given him quite a lot of cover in the past, though not often with his voice.

9.15 am

Nicola and Liz off to breakfast. They invite me to join them. I'd like to, but there's too much happening. They will be back soon – Nicola being on 10 hours' shift, until 3 pm, and Liz until 4 pm.

9.16 am

John Battle MP rings back to John Mac; he has changed his mind.
Yes, he will give phone interview about why he intends to support
Alton. But it will have to be soon. It is fixed for 10.05, immediately
after news. Slight panic for producer Alison, because she has just
fixed another interview for then. It's agreed to take Battle first and
then go straight on to the other interview.

9.20 am

Annabel on phone to *Look North* (next door) to tell them about
Inverness story and John Battle MP. *Look North* morning conference
is at 9.30 am.

9.30 am

Phil recording voice piece on soldiers' crash in Highlands, for use at
10 am. Has to record it again at 9.40, after further information from
Army headquarters in York. Annabel will lead bulletin with this.
Further rewrite and re-recording at 9.50 after further call to Inverness.

9.30 am in studios

Tim Dower winds up *Good Morning Yorkshire* after 3½ hours, and
hands over to the *Peter Levy Show* for the next 3 hours.

The Eight Programmes of the Leeds Day

As we have seen, from 6 am to 9.30 *GMY* carries news, sport, travel
and weather, six to eight background items or interviews, and some
cheerful music between the dominant items of talk. It is the most solid
and fast-moving programme of the day.

Then comes the *Peter Levy Show* from 9.30 am to 12.30 pm, with a
slightly higher ratio of music (average 30 per cent) but with more live
interviews and features. The eventual running order on 21 January,
after four changes while the programme was on air, included:

am
– *10.00* news (5 minutes)
– *10.05* John Battle, MP, on the Alton Bill (phone interview)

- *10.15* Librarian from Sheffield (live from Sheffield studio)
- *10.25* Radio car interview with airline chief (Capital Airlines), leading in to
- *10.40* Joint live discussion with Radio Jersey, to mark opening of direct flights to Jersey; Peter Levy works hard to persuade Jersey people to come to see the Yorkshire Dales, Bradford's Museum of Photography, etc.
- *10.50* NUPE man on Leeds nurses (phone interview)
- *11.00* News (5 minutes)
- *11.05* Interview from Bradford on jobs for graduates (live) (Merlyn Rees, MP, was then to have been on about coming debate on televising Parliament but could not be located)
- *11.25* Phone interview with men's tie designer in London, coupled with Radio car talk with three wives buying ties in Leeds city centre (lively and funny 10 minutes; example, tie designer, when asked to identify character of a man who wore plain dark brown ties instantly replied 'intellectual and reserved')
- *11.45* Phone interview (live in studio) with two women who help illiterate school leavers (again good, because of the results they seem to achieve)

pm
- *12* News (5 minutes)
- *12.10* Radio car interview on problems for pub landlords with under-age drinkers
- *12.20* Bradford Peace School man, from Bradford studio, on nuclear accidents; he said that they had not had access to any classified information but had gathered much material from scrutiny of American magazines
- *12.25* 'Truffles' – studio interview with biologist on hunting in Yorkshire for underground truffles, French style
- *12.30* Hand over to the lunchtime programme

Not a bad line-up, by any reasonable standard. A strong sequel to the news-based *GMY*; and clips from the interviews contribute to the later news bulletins. As producer Alison says; 'It does the big interviews in the area. Peter fits into two categories – he's a personality and well known in the area, and he'll do the interviews with famous people; and because of the time when the programme is on he'll do the more serious current affairs. Quite often, with a big story breaking, News will develop the story through an interview in our programme'.

From 12.30 pm to 3.30 pm, a period of lighter programming (until the spring of 1988) but there is now a more solid programme mixing speech and music, including an 'action line' to help people. Part of the afternoon is given to Arts and Education – in a broad sense for both. *Drive Time* between 3.30 and 6 pm is aimed at homeward-bound motorists. Finally there is an Ethnic (Asian) programme from 6 pm to 6.40 pm including Asian news; an *Access* programme from 6.40 to 7; and an evening music programme, a joint production by the four Yorkshire stations, from 7 to 9 pm. The Ethnic programme is in English from Monday to Friday, though using dialect phrases, but in Urdu and Punjabi on Saturdays.

The co-operation between radio and television can be seen from telephone calls from R. Leeds to the television newsroom in the neighbouring building, to provide briefings on the Territorial Army casualties in the road accident in Scotland and on other items. And the joint operation among BBC local radio stations was evident in the presence in the Crown Court at Leeds, for the murder trial, of a senior reporter from R. York (Graham Thomson); he was telephoning hourly from the court to York, and his copy was being immediately relayed to R. Leeds and R. Cleveland. Later in the day, when the Court adjourned, he came to R. Leeds to record a voice report for use in Leeds, York, Cleveland and (if wanted) in London.

Commentary

To anyone accustomed to a newspaper office or television newsroom. the isolation and individual responsibility of journalists and presenters on local radio in the early morning is striking. Yet that is the time when local stations are building up towards substantial audiences. As the narrative shows, the news producer was working alone – with the presenter as the only other person in the building – until going on air with her first bulletin at 6 am. Nicola Hill had substantial experience behind her, both in newspaper journalism and in radio; and if she wanted advice or a second opinion during that hour she could talk to Tim Dower as he thought through all the non-news content of the coming $3\frac{1}{2}$ hours. Neither Nicola nor others who are assigned to the early duty seem at all bothered by their isolation

News Content: a Sample

These were the items at 7 am on Thursday 21 January 1988:

Item	Duration (min./ sec.)
7 am	
Following weather, travel, pips and jingle	
Headlines: trial, nurses, blinded patient	0.19
Trial of York lorry driver starts today, murder of policeman outside Leeds Parish Church. (Graham Thomson of BBC York)	1.5
Voting for NUM presidency at weekend (Leeds reporter, with Scargill and Walsh inserts)	1.25
(These two opening items can be taken as both local and national; the next five are national or adapted from London circuit, and the remainder all Leeds/Yorkshire)	
More London nurses to consider striking (with Royal College insert)	1.5
Two children and stepfather killed in fire, Manchester	0.47
and mother and two sons in Redhill fire	0.13
Police in London interview three, over poisoned Iraqi	
Reagan on aid to Contras	0.23
Brighouse woman, blinded during routine medical test, seeking compensation (Insert from Bradford Health Council)	0.52
Teachers in Kirklees may strike over staff cuts	0.35
Local authorities in England owed large sums – W. Yorks, Leeds and Bradford among them (Parliamentary reply)	0.55
Leeds based epilepsy lobbying in London (spokesman insert)	0.50
W. Yorks police employ multi-lingual officer to deal with complaints against police	0.15
Main points again (reverse order)	0.22
Weather	0.18
Total	9.38

Content Analysis

Aggregrating the news at 7 am, 10 am and 5 pm as a sample, we find:

Category*	No. of Items	Total duration (min./sec.)
Pol.	11	
	of which, national 1.4, local 0.4	6.36
Crime	7	
	of which, national 1.41, local 3.0	5.11
Health	7	
	of which, national 2.19, local 2.07	4.26
Crash	6	
	of which, national 1.41, local 1.13	2.54
Int.	1	0.23
Human	1	0.57
		(local)

Note· *For explanation of categories, see pp. xi–xii.

and responsibility, though if they stopped to contemplate it could seem daunting. The pressure of work leaves no time for that.

With hourly bulletins through most of the day, and a summary at least on the half hour in peak periods, fast working is required. The general rule appears to be that after use in two of the hourly bulletins an item must be dropped or rewritten with a fresh aspect and after three bulletins it ought to be dropped anyway unless of prime importance. Thus it can be seen that on 21 January none of the 7 am items survived in the 10 am bulletin, apart from the national news item, almost wholly rewritten, on the NHS nurses.

What of the news values? They follow established conventions. As can be seen from the analysis above, *Political* news in its broad sense dominated the scene – 'politics' being taken here to include economic affairs, social issues and industry as well as parliamentary and local authority events. Crime came second, perhaps inflated here by interest in the 'Sgt Speed' trial in Leeds Crown Court, and the smouldering dispute over financing the National Health Service came next. Regional and local news are given more time than national events, taking on average about two-thirds of each bulletin, but since R.

Leeds is bound to be in competition with R. 4 for much of the day, it rightly includes the major UK and international items.

As to balance and impartiality, no reasonable complaint could be made against the bulletins that I heard over a 3-week period. One or two of the developing feature items could have upset or irritated individuals who are themselves partisan, but that is a risk that a lively and often impromptu programme must take in holding its audience. On issues such as the NUM presidential election the two contenders, their supporters and the wider public reaction were all taken into account. Inevitably, middle-of-the-road broadcasting such as the BBC's tends to be socio-centralist: in other words, its attitude is conservative rather than reforming and – intentionally or not – it is likely to reinforce the status quo. Governments, whether of the Right or of the Left, are likely to receive greater attention than the Opposition just because they are in power and making executive decisions. This socio-centralism is reflected in the output of R. Leeds as of other BBC stations – and of ILR and ITV.

But the justification of stations such as R. Leeds is in the local service that they provide and their identity with the communities whom they serve. R. Leeds calls itself 'The Voice of West Yorkshire' – a bold claim. Its territory is the whole of West Yorkshire and it can be heard in parts of North Yorkshire; if its weekly reach is put at 17–18 per cent, it is being heard on average by just under 400 000 people.

That puts it well ahead of ILR's R. Aire and Pennine Radio – though with a bigger area than either of them – and about level with R. 4 in West Yorkshire. Considering the diversity of interests in the county and the separate characters of its cities and districts, these appear to be good figures.

In terms of its journalism, it is reliable and conventional. It sets out to be accurate, though nobody can hope to be completely accurate when covering controversial events. It has good antennae of contacts and good relations with the neighbouring BBC local stations and it helps to serve the Leeds television newsroom. Its journalism lacks originality, being too heavily dependent on telephone interviews, but that is a factor of staff shortage.

People

John Cundy, news editor
From school in Liverpool to weekly newspapers, Warrington, 1965–9. Reporter then night news editor, *Liverpool Daily Post* and *Echo*, 1969–74. News producer, BBC R. Merseyside, 1974–8. Chief News Assistant, BBC R. Scotland, 1978–9. News editor, R. Leeds, from December 1979. (Also 6-month attachment to office of BBC Assistant DG, London, 1985–6.)

Tim Dower, presenter *GMY*
'Born in early 1960s within sound of London's Bow Bells' and 'started listening to radio right away'. 3 years in Hospital Radio. BBC R. York from 1986. To R. Leeds 1987, presenting breakfast show 6 days a week.

Siobhain Fitzgerald, Radio Car operator
Manchester University, graduated 1986 English & Media. 1 year public relations in Sheffield weekdays; Saturdays at BBC R. Sheffield. Then BBC basic training course. Freelance with R. Leeds from winter 1987–8.

John MacGill, acting producer
Dundee University (Hons Philosophy). While there started working for ILR R. Tay and hospital radio. 'On strength of this small experience and ability to talk himself out of trouble', gained a place on BBC local radio training. Trainee at a number of northern stations. Staff job as reporter, R. Leeds, from winter 1986.

Angela Piears, producer
London University, Westfield College (Hons History). Freelance in Yorkshire 'with about two days off in six months'. Reporter, BBC R. Sheffield. Producer's attachment, R. Leeds 1986, and producer since then. Comes from Coventry and 'never been north of Birmingham' until she began as freelance in Yorkshire.

5 From Miners to Majesty: BBC *Look North*, Leeds

Narrative, Monday 25 January 1988

The day begins with reporter Nick Farrow arriving about 4.30 am or soon after, followed by reporter-presenter Sue Wilkins at 5.45 or thereabouts. They prepare for the 2½ minute North-East bulletins, to be inserted into BBC 1's *Breakfast Time* at 7.15, 7.45 and 8.15, and then for a 3-minute bulletin just before 9 am. (As before, the term 'reporter' is used in its broad sense, not in the terms of BBC hierarchy.) The late reporter ought to have left enough to fill the bulletin, but Nick wants to get in as much new material as he can. 5 to 7 items will be the average. Sue will be reading the bulletins – putting herself on air, alone in the studio and on cue from London, pushing the buttons for the pictures. There is no teleprompt. It is just 6 months since she completed the BBC training course, but she had had 3 or 4 years' experience as a newspaper journalist (mainly at the *Wokingham Times*) before that; previously, London University, English degree.

Normally the early staff are released about 9.30, but today there is a shortage of reporters so both are kept on duty. Meanwhile another Nick – reporter Nick Wood – has been assigned to cover pithead reactions to the NUM vote and to find John Walsh. He is doing it both for network and for *Look North*, and before 9 am he is on his way to Castleford (mining town 12 miles away). Network wants as much as possible for midday; *Look North* wants an interview in studio or at Castleford or anywhere else. At present Walsh is 'missing'.

At 9.30 the morning conference is inevitably preoccupied with Mr Scargill's success. The result of the ballot had come at 10.20 last night and had led all news bulletins since then. What was to be done for this evening's *Look North*? John Lingham, presiding over the meeting as Head of News, thought reaction to the result must be the main story in the evening. Scargill was to hold a press conference in Sheffield soon and it would be covered by network's Martin Adeney, with the North-East's Sheffield crew; Walsh's plans were not known, but Nick Wood was on the way to Castleford. Peter Knowles, programme editor for the day, thought the network lunchtime news would 'go mad' with the story. What would be left for the early evening? John Lingham thought it would still be the strongest story.

Lingham hoped that they (Leeds) would not get to 'loggerheads' with network over the use of crews. Network demands take precedence over regional requirements in allocating crews; the BBC has only 2 in Leeds, 1 in Sheffield and 1 in Humberside. But there was also a network links vehicle in Sheffield to permit transmission direct to London. As will become clear later, in a television newsroom much more time has to be spent on the mechanics and logistics of news gathering and presentation than in a radio newsroom or a newspaper.

Next was discussion of how to handle Professor Ian Fells, of Newcastle University – the specialist on the mining industry, with whom arrangements had been made the previous week for a comment on the result. Should he go live into the programme at 6.35 or be pre-recorded? If live, how great was the risk of losing the Newcastle line at the last minute? (Engineering work was going on there.) Last week he had said that if Scargill won with a narrow majority it would be 'the worst possible result'. Would he hold to that? Was it worth trying to get him into a live discussion with Scargill – or, better still, Scargill and Walsh? Peter Knowles, programme editor, thought it would be prudent to record him at about 4.30 when they were sure of a Newcastle studio and a line from there.

Other items were discussed.

For one story there was a plea from Sport and others for a crew that day, though the story as such could wait a day or two if necessary. That afternoon Bradford Grammar School's rugby team, with an unbroken record after 49 matches. was to play the visiting 'Belgrano Day School' team from Argentina. 1t must be covered. That was agreed, though with a warning to be careful about the commentary: 'No "Gotchas" please'. (It was used two days later.)

Back in the newsroom, after the conference, two of the more senior journalists were marshalling information. Pat O'Hara has been reporting on the coal industry for 16 years, 6 with the *Yorkshire Post* and 10 for broadcasting. He was keeping in touch with the reporters in Sheffield, Mansfield, Castleford and at the Sharlston colliery near Wakefield. Throughout the day he was to 'pull together' the elements of the story, make sure that network news in London received what it wanted, and edit the item for *Look North*. It was supposed to be Pat's day off, but because of his big experience of the NUM he had come in. In parallel Russell Peasgood – a senior journalist – was in touch with the reporters at the Crown Court for the murder trial, at the inquest on the dead Red Arrow's pilot, and out in Sheffield on NHS matters. He was also keeping a check on the whereabouts and allocation of the mobile crews.

Tonight's 2 presenters are the regular pair: Judith Stamper and Harry Gration. Judith has some years of experience and is familiar with the industrial and political issues of the North-East. To interview Arthur Scargill and John Walsh – if both come in to the studio, as hoped – will be nothing new, but she will prepare for it thoroughly beforehand. Judith arrives at 11.15 and is immediately in discussion with John Lingham on the day's prospects. They are agreed that the programme must 'look ahead' to how the Coal Board and NUM will react. Will they start to talk again? Harry Gration, a sports specialist as well as an experienced presenter, is on his way back from a rugby league international in the South of France. Will he get back in time? There is a standby ready in case he doesn't.

By mid-day Nick Wood's pithead interviews are complete and back at base – some extracts are on their way to London for network lunchtime use – but John Walsh is still 'missing'. Mr Scargill, although extremely busy, has confirmed that he will come to the Leeds studio to be interviewed in the late afternoon. 'It shows confidence in us', Lingham says. 'He generally won't do anything unless it's live, to keep control'.

At 12.40 official confirmation of the Duchess of York's pregnancy comes (though it turned out to have been on ITN at 12.30). What to do for Yorkshire? Obviously, the York connection. News desk is mobilising interviews in York, statement from Lord Mayor (who is sending a telegram of congratulation) and request from York (Archbishop?) that the child should be christened at York Minster. John Lingham says it will be the final item in the programme, because the Duchess's baby is almost sure to lead the BBC 6 o'clock news; so it's more appropriate to put the Yorkshire element at the end – 'a nice little extra to the overall national story'. So 'Fergie' is planned to end the programme, at $2\frac{1}{2}$ minutes.

Much of the afternoon is taken up with technical planning – and with anxious inquiries about John Walsh. At 2.45 it is confirmed from Barnsley that he is there, at the Yorkshire miners' headquarters, and

that the Sheffield crew are standing by, just 5 minutes away. That is
relayed to London, since network still want him. Meanwhile a group
of six, including producer, director and presenter, is having a lengthy
(25-minute) discussion about studio layout and camera positions.
Producer Peter says it is essential to get the right grouping of the
NUM element, to provide a 'smooth, fast presentation'. but it means
breaking up the reactions to permit a quick change of camera
positions and studio layout before the Scargill–Walsh interview. After
20 minutes Judith says it's time to think about the content as well as
the physical structure, and departs to her dressing room to think in
peace about the sequence of questions. The technical debate continues
for another 5 minutes.

At 3 pm a call from London crew and links van now at Barnsley.
They want to get home, having been away over weekend. Too bad:
they will have to wait until Walsh appears. At 3.20 London on line
saying they need an interview with Mr Scargill for *Newsnight,* before
Leeds records for *Look North.* They want it by 4.30 if possible, but
there's no certainty on when he will arrive. The usual *Look North*
informal conference about 3 pm has been ditched because of the long
technical debate; but the running order is thought to be more or less
self-evident.

Content Summary

Before 3 pm also, producer Peter had set out what he hoped would be
his final running order, with estimated duration and his running time
(in reverse to show how many minutes are left):

Item			(min./ sec.)	(min./ sec.)
				23.40
Titles	VT		0.50	22.50
2.	NUM result	Judith PSC	2.45	20.05
3.	Prof. Fells	Judith VT	2.00	18.05
4.	Miners' reaction	Judith PSC + Parlt. + Notts	1.40	16.25
5.	Scargill		3.30	12.55
6.	Walsh	Judith live 1 + 1	2.30	10.25
7.	Consultant	Harry PSC St James + PSC	3.15	7.10
8.	News	Harry Red Arrows PSC		
		Judith Halifax fire PSC	2.55	4.15

Table *cont.*

9.	Rugby	Harry PSC	1.15	3.00
10.	Duchess	Judith PSC	2.00	1.00
11.	Payoff	Harry PSC	1.20	0.40
12.	Weather		0.40	

Note: the running order is important as a guide to presenters, the floor manager, gallery and studio staff, and engineers. The reverse timing in the last column is vital in making decisions to drop items, when necessary, and to make sure of ending the programme precisely on time.

The list in itself, however, hides a number of complexities. First, the 'Consultant' item covers two separate but related stories. The stronger in news terms is to be a vote by COHSE and NUPE nurses at St James's hospital in Leeds – one of the biggest in Britain – on whether or not to join the 1-day strike 10 days hence. But that vote is not expected until between 6 and 6.30 pm, by which time the programme will be going on air. The other item, the 'Consultant' of the catchline, had already been on air briefly but is worth more time. A children's specialist in Sheffield has launched a public appeal for funds for his NHS Hospital's baby care unit, which is suffering because of its own success in dealing with up to 450 serious cases a year. But the crew who are to interview him are still caught up with the NUM, and the '15.00' time for arrival of the tape in Leeds has already been passed. It has to be brought back by road. A further complexity, of course, is that nobody yet knows whether, when or where John Walsh will be found. And (item 9 on the list) Harry Gration is still not back from yesterday's rugby match at Avignon and he is bringing that tape with him. (He turns up, however, at 3.45 and says it will make a strong item of whatever length Peter wants.)

An event lost; Sue Wilkins. at work since 5.45, had gone to Dewsbury to cover unusual court case but no decision reached before the crew had to leave at 2.30 for York, for the more urgent 'Duchess baby' story.

Producer Peter is now (4.10 pm) worrying that the NUM in leading the programme may turn into 'a shooting gallery' with Arthur Scargill as the target. Their success in getting both Cecil Parkinson (Energy Minister) and the break-away Union of Democratic Miners, as well as Professor Fells, is loading the critics too heavily. He may have to drop one element.

The Last Two Hours

4.15 pm

Jake Fowler, Hull reporter, in edit room to put together Red Arrow's inquest and to record commentary. Using freelance cameraman's shots of wreckage, taken Saturday with RAF consent, but not yet seen. RAF Scampton won't make any comment because inquiry impending; so it's only a short item. Whole edit and sound recording takes about 50 minutes.

4.30 pm

Arthur Scargill arrives, just as Judith Stamper is going into studio to record Professor Fells from Newcastle. Mr Scargill in cheerful mood.

4.36 pm

Judith starts recording Fells, after 3 minute discussion of content ('steering him off politics', she says afterwards, but he wanted to talk about flexible rostering and competitive costs anyway). Interview completed at 4.40, but both Judith and Peter feel it was 'a bit ragged', so it is done again. Second recording shorter and sharper.

4.50 pm

Back in newsroom: still no word of Walsh, though he is known to be in Barnsley. No hope now of getting him in studio with Scargill; but Nick Wood (reporter) and crew are at Barnsley. So Scargill will be recorded solo – he is now in 'broom cupboard' waiting for *Newsnight*. They are late but he is still cheerful.

4.55 pm

John Lingham, Peter, and Russell Peasgood in discussion of legal problem over recording (not for tonight) of Leeds-based Opera North production of *West Side Story*, with participation of 'Graffiti Gang'. It was all cleared with the BR Transport Police, but the 'gang' have now been reported to the Crown Prosecutor. No charge laid, but BBC lawyer advised 'keep off'. Decision to 'keep off' at present – taken regretfully, because the gang were 'deadly serious' in their opera role.

5 pm

Call from Barnsley. Walsh left NUM offices by back door. His aide 'can't say' when or where he will be available. Peter now expects the worst. Consultation with John Lingham; decision to let Nick Wood include Walsh in his commentary and use clip from last night's pub recording – total 20 seconds. This eases pressure for Peter; he can now give Scargill an extra 30 seconds, let the Duchess stay at 2 minutes, and be sure of giving the Avignon rugby $1\frac{1}{4}$ to $1\frac{1}{2}$ minutes.

5.10 pm

Judith and Arthur about to record. While they wait, Arthur tells Judith jolly story about nurse giving him anaesthetic in hospital recently. Peter tells Judith 'four minutes, not three'. Arthur jokes – 'that's worth the world'. Recording starts; Mr Scargill instantly looks serious. Hard questioning from Judith on narrowed margin of his support, possible loss of members to UDM, need for serious negotiation with Coal Board, the obstacle of the overtime ban, threat to investment and productivity; Mr Scargill adamant that Coal Board does not want to talk to union, and he accuses Judith of not listening to his replies. Interview ends at just over 4 minutes. Arthur Scargill, Judith Stamper and Producer Peter are all satisfied with it. But there is a small sound fault at start, so first question and answer are re-recorded. Mr Scargill then leaves for Yorkshire Television, still in cheerful mood.

5.18 pm

Another technical problem: how to link from Cecil Parkinson interview to David Prendergast, general secretary of UDM? Decision; after Judith's interview with Professor Fells, go to Harry Gration who will do joint lead-in to both Prendergast and Parkinson, putting the UDM man first because he is less well known than the Energy Secretary. The Prendergast interview is coming from BBC Nottingham but has not yet arrived, probably because they are tied up with their own Midlands programme, Peter says.

5.20 pm

'Not a single script in the rack yet', Peter notes. That is because of NUM changes and late arrival of other tapes – but all will be well. Does he know what will be in 6 pm network news, preceding his programme? 'No; but they will probably lead with the Duchess of York's baby, and we must have the courage of our convictions'. The miners' leadership was more important to Yorkshire, he believed.

5.30 pm

Nottingham interview with Prendergast now coming in.

5.40 pm

Peter back and forward to edit suites where NUM and other items are being put together.

5.44 pm

St James's Hospital nurses vote just in, big vote in favour of 1-day strike.

5.46 pm

West Yorkshire police on phone to Peter: statement by Chief Constable Colin Sampson on N. Ireland prosecutions available, but Sampson will give no interviews. Peter diverts call to 'copy', to take Sampson text, but it's very unlikely to warrant a place in the regional programme. It is relayed to London, since the Attorney General's statement that there would be no prosecutions of RUC Officers over 'shoot to kill' in 1982 had caused an uproar in the Commons 2 hours earlier, and mentioned in network news later.

6.0 pm

Watch network news headlines. They are leading with 'Fergie' pregnant.

6.05 pm

To studio to start rehearsals. Some changes of lighting, and moving of monitor. Checking of graphics and captions, including statistics of NUM vote, names for interviews, etc. Also check on 'Dogs' – pictures inserted above presenters' shoulders.

6.18 pm

Scripts still arriving.

6.19 pm

Producer and director checking possible cuts and changes. Walsh interview now deleted: news item on Halifax five likely to be dropped; Harry offers optional cut on rugby.

6.25 pm

Run-through on routine for opening and closing.

6.33 pm

Warning from newsroom of new text on nurses, with fresh detail. It will come in time for planned transmission at 6.47 or 6.48. (It does.)

6.35 pm

On air.

Commentary

The decision to lead with the NUM vote is almost indisputable, at least in terms of conventional journalism. The event filled standard criteria: it was politically important, affecting the future of a major industry; it was happening on home territory, with the biggest British coalfield in Yorkshire and the NUM's headquarters there; and it involved a colourful 'star' personality, in Mr Arthur Scargill. His leadership had been controversial, not least during the 1984–5 coal dispute which was disastrous for his members and had led to the breakaway of the Nottingham men. In addition, Mr. Scargill is an accomplished performer on the screen.

Look North was also well justified in looking ahead – in particular to the likelihood of a further period of conflict between the Union and the Coal Board. That was the underlying theme of the interviews. Mr Scargill was rightly given the opportunity to state his case against the Board.

His warning that the Board wanted to 'axe' jobs and prepare for privatisation, while not new, had to be heard. Inevitably there was some overlap with network news, but not much since only brief clips from the morning press conference were carried by the BBC and ITN main news. Both relegated it to a low place in running order because of the Duchess of York's pregnancy and the uproar in the Commons over the Attorney General's statement on the RUC. ITN dropped the NUM story completely from *News at Ten*, because of extended cover from Australia of the bicentenary celebrations (very colourful).

As to the style of interviews, Judith Stamper conducted hers with a cool severity which gave it authority. It also served Mr Scargill better than the amiable, chatty style of YTV's parallel exchange, since Mr Scargill thrives on hard argument. It was a fast and effective exchange, leaving viewers to form their own judgements. The questions were crisp and in the end comprehensive, quite evidently the result of careful preparation and quick thinking during the recording.

At the other end of the programme, was the *Look North* item on the Duchess worth doing? YTV's *Calendar* decided against carrying anything. *Look North* at least achieved some agreeable street interviews from young mothers in York, with such cheerful advice as 'get out plenty, don't stay at home' and 'get a babysitter'. The statement from the Lord Mayor was somewhat wooden; and last minute cutting clipped off the call for a christening at York Minster, trailed before the programme. Still, it made a pleasant ending to that day's news.

Just before the Duchess, there was the Avignon rugby league match, GB v. France. With a 28–14 win for the British team and some spectacular tries (5 or 6 fast clips with an equally fast commentary) it too made satisfactory viewing – the better for Yorkshire with three players from Leeds, two from Castleford and one from Halifax.

The news priorities of the *Yorkshire Post* next morning differed in detail from those of *Look North*, though echoing its approach. 'Yorkshire nurses back strike call' was its lead, with 'Mother-to-be Duchess flies high' at the top of page 1. The main headline on page 3 was ' "Yes" to confrontation', on Mr Scargill's plans for the NUM. The paper also had an exclusive on page 1 on plans by transport chiefs in five cities, including Leeds and Bradford, to sue British Rail over the failures of the Sprinter trains.

One evident disadvantage of the BBC output, by comparison with YTV's, was the more frequent use of still photographs rather than moving pictures on secondary news items. That follows from having fewer camera crews and a less extensive regional library.

The studio set is designed to give a changed character towards the end of the programme. Most of the time the two presenters sit at a desk – rarely seen since they are generally shown in medium close-up shots – with a plain light blue background. For the last part they move to a comfortable pale blue sofa, with plants behind, giving a relaxed look. Here wide shots of the pair are more frequent. The changed scene effectively indicates the softer context of the closing items.

Ultra close-up shots are rare, even during interviews, but since interviews hardly ever go beyond 4 or 5 minutes the intensity of the ultra close-up is perhaps not called for. The lighting is generally neutral, which can give too bland an effect in a long exchange. One exception in this programme was the lighting of the nurses' meeting at the St James's hospital, which with backlighting and side-lighting had a more dramatic effect.

Camera angles were normally at eye level, as news conventions require. Mr Cecil Parkinson, however, was shot from a low angle with enhanced light on his face and with Big Ben in the background, which critics may say gave him the advantage of looking forceful and authoritative.

As to clothes, the presenters were as usual in sober semi-formal dress. Judith Stamper wore a dark grey-blue suit and a thinly striped polo-necked shirt. This was offset by Harry Gration's pale grey-blue suit, plain grey shirt and a grey tie with slanted white stripes. As presenters, their differing characters – as they appear on screen – are matched. Judith is the more serious and commanding, while Harry has a slightly younger and lighter form. They regularly work together, presenting *Look North*, and give the impression of a confident and reliable source of information.

People

Harry Gration
Teacher for 5 years before joining BBC R. Leeds, 1978. Sports editor, 1980. R. Leeds tv. 1983.

Peter Knowles
St Catherine's College, Oxford, to 1983. Unpaid researcher, Newcastle, then with freelance agency, Carlisle, 1983–4. BBC training course, with various attachments, 1984–6. BBC Manchester as 'regional journalist' for 16 months. To BBC Leeds, Autumn 1987. On rota as producer *Look North* from January 1988.

John Lingham
Reporter and subeditor in weekly papers, then to BBC tv., Birmingham (producer *Midlands Today*). Acting news editor BBC tv., Newcastle; then to BBC tv. Leeds, head of news from 1984. (Coal dispute and Bradford City football club fire among items handled since then.)

Judith Stamper
Cockermouth Grammar School, Cumbria; University of Wales (BA

Hons English, and postgraduate diploma in journalism, distinction). BBC local radio, Carlisle and Liverpool. Researcher for David Frost at BBC Lime Grove. Assistant producer on *Money Programme* and *Newsnight*. To BBC Leeds 1980. Presenter *Look North* with Harry Gration from 1985.

6 Improvising on a 'Rather Quiet Day': YTV *Calendar*

Narrative, 27 January 1988

The trial of the accomplice in the Sgt Speed murder case was over, and only the case against his wife remained. The nurses of Yorkshire and the distress of the National Health Service continued to make headlines here as in other regions. The coal industry was still having trouble in some of its Yorkshire pits. But Wednesday 27 January 1988 was seen as a 'poor news day' in the newsroom of *Calendar*, as at the BBC.

From 7.15 am or so onwards the staff are arriving, most being in by 8.30. The morning conference is at 10 am, chaired by producer Andrew Darling. About 20 people are present. The conference is fast moving, with frequent quips (unlike the more solemn meeting at the BBC). Among the items taken up:

– *'Agony aunts' for the Army*
  An announcement in the Commons last night that WRVS people will be recruited as counsellors for young soldiers. It's part of the measures to reduce bullying of recruits. Can *Calendar* get a reporter into Catterick or Strensall to talk to WRVS and soldiers? Glynn believes they won't be very co-operative. They don't like the publicity over bullying.
– *Bradford North, the Labour NEC today*
  Could be a strong story if they take action, but not a lead. 'They may fudge it again', Darling says.
– *Mozart's anniversary*
  What anniversary? The 262nd, according to the *Independent*. Anyway, there is a 3½-minute piece about the new York String Quartet that's ready and ought to be used tonight.

50

– *The second day of sentencing in the Speed trial*
Mrs Guest, wife of the accomplice, has pleaded guilty to withholding information. Suspended sentence expected. Andrew says she should be 'doorstepped' – ask her about 'the spell of Gricewith' (the murderer, now dead after accidentally shooting himself when being chased by police cars). This leads to a discussion later in the conference on whether also to take up the alleged 'cock up' by the police in not allowing Guest's lawyer to be present during early questioning after arrest. Someone explains that the case law quoted by the judge came from a recent Appeal Court ruling, made months after Guest was arrested. Andrew sees 'no mileage' in reviving the legal argument, so concentrates on Alison Guest.
– *Catterick to be 'front-line' base for fighting Russians, with troops ready to fly to Germany*
Announcement late last night in Commons. News editor Glynn Brailsford says it had come as a surprise to Catterick when he phoned this morning. 'Ah, hold on, we'll have to check that out'.
– *Red Arrow's funeral*
Dead pilot's 3-week-old baby expected to be there. Lincoln reporter and crew will cover. Will try for pictures of baby.
– *And a dozen others are briskly discussed.*

Assessing the prospects at 11.20 am, Andrew Darling now thinks the Speed trial is likely to be his lead. The Army 'initiation rites' could be an alternative but he does not know how it will develop. If Jack Ashley, the MP who raised the matter, can come up with names in Yorkshire it's a possible. But the Army was being unhelpful both at Catterick and at Strensall. On the trial, he says that Mrs Guest has 'gone down' for 15 months instead of getting a suspended sentence, so she cannot be interviewed. But 'the woman who wouldn't tell the police what she knew' is still a good story, of much interest in Yorkshire. He does not think much of the Catterick 'front line' story because it means no extra troops there and no extra jobs, and anyway, the Army there won't talk.

Throughout the day the Belmont editor, Steve Cohen, works close to the news editor. He has 9 or 10 minutes to fill, when the Emley Moor (west) and Belmont (east) programmes separate. Steve cannot make final decisions until he knows what Andrew Darling will take as the early items, but he says he has plenty in prospect. Also in consultation from time to time are Richard Gregory (Editor, *Calendar*) and Andrew Darling.

Events in the afternoon of what Andrew Darling ultimately called 'a rather quiet day' follow.

2.45 pm

Glynn says there is still no news from Walworth Road (Labour headquarters in London). They are still discussing the NHS. Bradford will come later. But he has been trying to find someone to comment. Peter Kellner of the *Independent* is not available: James Naughtie of the *Guardian* cannot be found. Asked whether they should not be looking for someone at Walworth Road, Glynn says Kellner and Naughtie are both very reliable and they can pick up the news from their newsrooms.

On other news, Glynn says there have been two murders in South Yorkshire but both were 'false starts' in that they turned out to be domestic and with no police operation there was nothing to film. In the afternoon, he says, the main concern is not choosing the news but getting it in and editing. The Red Arrow's funeral is likely to be last in, with the flypast due about now or around 3 pm. The crew should be on the way back by 3.15 and here soon after 5 pm.

2.50 pm

Steve, dealing with the Belmont output, has 2 new stories. A 2-hour-old baby has been found in the River Trent – stillborn probably, and the mother is being sought. And a vicar has hanged himself in his vicarage, but it is 'down in deepest Lincolnshire', too far away now to be reached by a crew. Apart from those, he will certainly run Byron's 200th anniversary and the Cleethorpes banning of dogs on the beaches 'which always gets the viewers phoning'.

3 pm

Andrew has issued a handwritten running order. A printed one will come later. They will lead with four short news items, starting with Alison Guest going to jail. The Army will follow with 'what sounds a promising film with the WRVS' which is a 'nice sort of silly angle' but more fresh than the bullying which had been on ITN's *News at Ten* last night. The Red Arrow's funeral and flypast would come next.

He is not entirely happy, however, and is still looking at alternatives. Labour has suspended the party in Bermondsey and if they were to 'expel all those people in Bradford North' he might bring that forward again. Otherwise the story 'doesn't really go any further'. He had booked a studio for 4 minutes at Westminster just in case.

3.15 pm

Andrew scripting introduction for Army story.

3.23 pm

Penny Bustin, reporter and tonight's co-presenter, brings Bradford North decision to Andrew. It amounts to continued suspension for the constituency's General Committee until there has been a membership check, and further investigation of charges of 'Militant' membership against nine Bradford North members. There are other details as well. Andrew sums up: 'It's pretty mundane'. Nevertheless they discuss with Glynn whom to try to get from the lobby. Still no word of Naughtie, so try *Sunday Times* man. Who else to try, for possible studio interview? Andrew, emphatically, not Pat Wall who will only say what he's said before. Penny says she will see if she can raise anybody else – 'back in five minutes'.

3.30 pm

Andrew and Glynn discussing alternatives. There is a minute and a half gap, Andrew says, and they must have something to balance against Belmont. What about the 'splash' story in tonight's *Telegraph and Argus* (Bradford) about the people of Silsden (village north of River Aire) voting to be moved from West Yorkshire to North Yorkshire? Andrew says that if he had been voting it would have been for North Yorkshire because the rates are lower and the schools much better. Glynn will send crew and reporter out.

4.05 pm

To studio and gallery (control) with Nick Salmon, director. Floor manager, technical co-ordinator, and lighting director are there, plus eight other men and three in sound control and one in lighting. The next 20 minutes or thereabouts will be spent on lighting, and setting of studio cameras and furnishing will follow. Are not 15 people rather a lot for this? Question referred to management. Reply: look at the day's schedule. The studio crew were in at 8.30 am to set up for *Lunchtime Live*. They worked on the set and lighting until 9, when they had to bring in a complete car for an item on safety seats and chairs for children. From 9.30 to 12, recording inserts and rehearsal with car. On air 12 to 12.30. Dismantle (partly) 12.30 to 1 pm, then lunch break till 2 pm. Complete dismantling after lunch, then on call for inserts or rehearsals for *Calendar*. An easy programme tonight, with no studio interviews: hence lack of activity until 4 pm. Crew will not finish until 7 pm – a 10-hour day.

4.30 pm

Andrew bobbing in and out of video edit suites to see items. Also picking clips ('teasers') for use at start of programme.

4.50 pm

Glynn in edit suite revising the Sheffield–Everton football item for second time. Still not satisfied. 'No problems, really', he says. 'We just decided to incorporate a bit more of the match action from the other night. And we had to get the reporter – he was still on the road but I spoke to him on a Vodaphone – to come in to the Sheffield studio to send a new voiceover to key us in to the football. Quite simple, really'. (It's a replay tonight, which will bring both clubs a lot of money.)

4.55 pm

Just over an hour to transmission. Robert Hall, co-presenter tonight with Penny Bustin, says 'it's a presentation job tonight'. No interviews, so he's getting on with other work.

5 pm

Andrew finally cancels the Westminster studio. The only change of plan since 3 pm was in sending the crew to Silsden. All the studio scripts are now ready – earlier than usual. Yesterday they had not known until just after 4 pm that the Crown Court case was ending, so they had had two running orders ready. Rewriting the top half of the programme is a common experience, Andrew says.

5.10 pm

Glynn, in his words, 'strolling up and down that corridor (the edit suites) seeing that everything is edited on time'. The football voice-piece from Sheffield has still to come; the Arrows and Silsden stories have still to come.

5.18 pm

Small crisis. The Silsden story is stuck in heavy traffic: radio call from reporter who had completed interview and shots of village but is now held up on the road back. Glynn: 'We could be editing it during the programme, but it's in the second half'.

5.23 pm

A policy issue. Richard Gregory talking to Andrew and Glynn. The press officer at RAF Scampton has been on about the funeral. They say the filming was an intrusion. Apparently it is because shots were taken of the racing driver Nigel Mansell, who was a friend of the dead pilot. Glynn confirms that there are shots of Mansell. Andrew: 'Is it really a private service if they've got an RAF flypast? I think if Nigel Mansell was there it's a good news story'. Richard suggests that RAF 'think we were going to sensationalise the funeral'. Andrew says he had been surprised to see Mansell's name on the shot list. (The reporter on location phones back a 'link' text, suggested cutting instructions, and a shot list.) Glynn says he will look at the edit. All agree that they should go ahead with the item.

5.35 pm

Robert in studio recording 'promo' for transmission at 5.44, before the ITV news. It headlines three items thus:

- A North Yorkshire woman who kept silent about the identity of a murderer started a jail sentence today after admitting taking a payment of a thousand pounds
- The funeral's taken place of the Red Arrow's pilot who died when his plane crashed in Lincolnshire last week
- And as Sheffield Wednesday prepare for tonight's cup replay against Everton, the club officials are laughing all the way to the bank
- Full details on all those stories on *Calendar at Six*

5.45 pm

Andrew in studio gallery with director Nick. (Steve is at the same time in another studio to look after the Belmont second half.) Andrew reckons they are 1 minute 45 over. If they knock out Silsden and drop a 'ceramics' item near the end, they will be about right. Nick instructs everyone – gallery, studio, sound, lighting, ENG and film – to cut items 5 and 10 in part two (Silsden and ceramics). All have detailed lists, item by item, with texts, insert pictures, sound directions (e.g., 'low ENG sound and studio voiceover') and other directions.

5.47 pm

Call from newsroom. Rewrite coming on Doncaster item. Andrew standing behind director, with wall telephone beside him.

5.52 pm

Rehearsal of opening. Robert in studio, replying to double-edged question from gallery, says 'yes' his adrenalin is flowing. (He has a reputation for small, impish deviations from text when on air.)

6 pm

On air.

There are no hitches during transmission. The timing is exact. 3 seconds are cut on transmission from the last small news item in part two, to leave a clear run from the York String Quartet. The Belmont part two, however, has to cut nearly half its colourful railway museum.

Content Summary

Item	Duration (min./sec.)	Category*
Titles	0.24	—
Headlines	0.16	—
Extra trailer	0.15	—
News (Penny Bustin):		
– Sgt Speed trial – woman jailed for withholding information	2.19	*Crime*
– Red Arrow's funeral and flypast	1.52	*Crash/Human*
– Strike at Wistow colliery (Selby) and walkout at Barnsley Main	0.36	*Pol A*

– York District Hospital
  nurses vote for 1-day
  strike		

– concerned about roster changes	0.35	*Pol A/Health*
Bullying in army, 'Agency Aunts' for soldiers	2.43	*Human/War*
FA Cup Replay, Sheffield – the money	2.34	*Sport*
Aerobics for pensioners, Ilkley	2.23	*Human*
Link to break	0.17	
Break (ads)	1.06	

Note: *For explanation of categories, see p. xiv.

For part two, the Leeds and Belmont programmes are separate. Leeds (Emley Moor) opens with a colourful Viking Festival at York, with longboats on the Ouse. It runs for just over 2 minutes. Then there are 7 short items, the shortest 17 seconds and the longest 32 seconds (the Bradford Militants), with a longer item between the third and fourth. One of the short items is the Catterick anti-tank unit, two are crime cases, and the shortest item is about a Derbyshire guest house winning an award. The longer item is Doncaster's video to attract new business; and the programme ends with Mozart's birthday celebrated by the York Quartet (just over 4 minutes) and the weather forecast.

Belmont leads with the baby's body in the River Trent and the Baptist minister found dead in his house. It packs in 13 items, nearly all short. The longest is celebration of Byron's 200th birthday at Newstead Abbey (2.24), and the next in length is record trading figures at Immingham port (1.24).

	Part one		Part two Leeds		Part two Belmont	
	Duration (min./sec.)	No. of items	Duration (min./sec.)	No. of items	Duration (min./sec.)	No. of items
Pol	0.54	(2)	2.11	(2)	2.13	(3)
War	1.22	(1)	0.25	(1)	—	
Crash	0.41	(1)	—		0.28	(1)
Crime	2.19	(1)	0.51	(2)	—	
Human	4.26	(3)	0.37	(2)	1.00	(3)
A & S	—		6.32	(3)	2.45	(2)
Pets	—		—		1.54	(2)
Sport	2.34	(1)	—		0.36	
Weather	—		1.09	(1)	1.06	(1)

Commentary

Walking back from the studio, Andrew Darling summed it up as 'a
rather quiet day'. There had been some last-minute scrambles, he said,
but all had been handled smoothly. That was, of course, no more than
a modest assessment of a professionally competent performance by a
bright and experienced team. As an outside observer, I felt that the
Calendar newsroom must be a congenial and gratifying place to work,
with better pay and better resources than can be expected at the BBC.
Broadly speaking, *Calendar*'s objectives are to provide a reliable and
comprehensive news service for its area, but to leaven it with some fun
and entertainment. The second part of the programme looks for
variety and pleasure. All that, however, does not exempt *Calendar*
from some criticism.

Take, to begin with, the decisions on the 'new' role for Catterick
within NATO, on the Militants of Bradford North, and on the end of
the Sgt Speed sentencing. Catterick as a 'front-line' base had been
treated with sceptism or distaste from the start, because there was
little information and the Catterick Garrison itself was not prepared
to talk. Yet a more careful look at the newspapers – in particular the
Telegraph and the *Guardian* – would have provided a starting brief. It
was the top story on the *Guardian*'s page 6 and was well covered on
the *Telegraph*'s page 8, with precise information about the coming
conversion of the 24th Infantry Brigade into an air-mobile anti-tank
unit, with 16 Lynx helicopters carrying missiles capable of hitting a
tank $2\frac{1}{2}$ miles away. Andrew had two objections to the story – that it
meant no extra troops at Catterick and that there would be no
pictures. The Lynx helicopters, however, were expected to bring with
them a new regiment of the Army Air Corps; and as to pictures, the
BBC's *Look North* dug out some relevant ones from the 1987 NATO
exercises in Germany which had led to the Catterick decision. Its 2-
minute item, sixth in its running order, carried much more information than *Calendar*'s 25 seconds in its part 2.

There seemed also, at least to an observer, to be too simple a
response to the front page 'splash' in the *Daily Mirror* – 'Agony Aunts
for the Army'. It was a brilliant headline leading in to a populist
version of the annual Commons debate on the Army, and *Calendar*
was not alone in picking up the 'Agony Aunt' theme. But their pursuit
misfired, because the nearest WRVS were the tea ladies at St James's
Hospital. Their role is rather different and when interviewed for
Calendar they did not have much to say about counselling young

soldiers. As emerged clearly in a later programme on another channel, the WRVS to be deployed for this work are of a different background and training.

Then there were the infiltrating Militants in Bradford. While there was ground for saying that Militant had become a bore – and that it had been extensively covered when the constituency executive in Bradford North was suspended a month earlier – the Labour National Executive decision was perhaps less negative than it seemed at first. One can sympathise with producer Andrew's frustration on being unable to raise a political specialist to interpret the National Executive decision: but YTV could profitably employ its own political correspondent instead of having to hunt for the Naughties and Kellners of the newspaper world.

A third decision worth examining was the elimination from the final episode of the Speed trial of any discussion of the alleged police 'cock-up' over its evidence. At *Calendar*'s morning conference one of the journalists had correctly explained the true position. Because of the pressures the previous night, there had been no broadcast explanation of the judge's direction to the jury not to find Guest guilty of murder but only of lesser charges, nor had it been fully covered in the newspapers. The point was that the Appeal Court ruling on access for solicitors had come months after the West Yorkshire questioning of Guest, and the judge in the Crown Court had not suggested that the police had acted improperly at the time. But after the 5 days of legal argument at the start of the trial, with reporters and public excluded, he had had to rule out much of the police evidence. That was behind his direction to the jury against finding Guest guilty of murder. Was it not, one may ask, something that the public had an interest in knowing about?

YTV can properly say that *Calendar* is a news magazine, with less than half an hour in which to cover diverse interests. With that in mind, it must be acknowledged that much skilful reporting, camerawork and editing went into the 27 January programme. The Red Arrow's funeral had been beautifully shot and edited, with none of the intrusion or sensation that RAF Scampton may have feared. The widow and her tiny baby were seen at the grave only for a few seconds, in a sideways medium longshot, not in close-up. Nigel Mansell similarly was seen only at a distance, among a group of RAF officers. A piper playing a lament was in close-up and then the Lightning fighter thundered overhead. The general impression was sad and respectful.

Among the other items, the pictorial pleasure of the Viking Festival was great and the bearded oarsmen manning the longboats looked the part. ('We're all mad', one said, and his companions heartily agreed.) Equally attractive were the two closing, or near closing, items – the Mistry Quartet at York University celebrating Mozart, for West and South Yorkshire, and the 200th anniversary of Byron at Newstead Abbey for the Belmont audiences. It may be argued that these were too highbrow for a programme aiming to hold a mass audience, but that is doubtful and some others of its tail-end items (of which more is said below) must be repulsive to a fastidious audience.

Presenters are important. On 27 January both the regulars were away, and the substitutes were youthful – Robert Hall, neatly got up in a dark jacket with pale shirt and tie, serious and straightforward most of the time but with the imp coming out off and on with his one-liners; and Penny Bustin in a slightly more relaxed open necked dark jacket with white lapels, also serious but with a friendly touch. (Penny Bustin on other days varied from a stylish high collared military dress in bright leaf green to a severely tailored white blouse and navy blue cardigan, which suggests that women presenters are either allowed more freedom than men or expected to provide scenic variety.)

As to the tail-end items, some are excellent without being highbrow, middlebrow or any brow. On Thursday 21 January there was 'Disco Mix', with the winner of a Bradford 'DJ mixer' competition. He turned out to be a mixture of acrobat, juggler, studio manager and composer – and a brilliant performer. At the other end of the scale – and this is a personal view, though confirmed by others – was the windup the following Tuesday, running to almost 8 minutes. It was supposed to celebrate the Australian bicentenary. It began with Captain Cook's origins in Whitby, and that was tolerable. It then tried to get people in the streets of Whitby to talk with Australian accents. Next came three rugby professionals from Australia now playing for Leeds and a pensioner from Tasmania living in Bridlington: they were drawn into banal talk (not their fault), and were finally required to put on 'funny' (Australian) hats adorned with swinging corks and to sing *Waltzing Matilda*. It was torture.

There is a dilemma about how to pitch the later stages of an early evening news magazine. We shall encounter it again in the Midlands. Richard Gregory sets out ambitious targets for his *Calendar* – the core to provide 'the best and hardest news of the day and a balanced content with some humour'. He does not want 14 or 15 items that 'do not mean a lot'. Yet the Belmont second half, to take that as an example, contained 13 items of which 8 were less than half a minute long; and, again expressing a personal reaction, I found its opening with the dead baby in the Trent and the Baptist minister hanging himself singularly unattractive. There are days when *Calendar* seems to depend too much on short news items, with a bias towards crime, misfortune and catastrophe. The first half of the programme is generally well put together, attractive and containing relevant information. And in both part one and part two the longer items, in the 2- to 4-minute group, are frequently first class, whatever your political or artistic preferences. *Calendar* has the resources to maintain a permanently high standard.

People

Glynn Brailsford
School in South Yorkshire. *Nottingham Evening Post*, reporter, 1973–7. *Evening Gazette*, Middlesbrough, 1977–8. *The Star*, Sheffield, deputy chief sub-editor, 1978–81. BBC R. Nottingham, producer, 1981–4. YTV from 1984; news editor 1985–8; producer, YTV promotions, and network *Pick of the Week* from 1988.

Andrew Darling
Penzance Grammar School; Cornwall Technical College. Trainee reporter, *East Kent Gazette*, 1967–71. Reporter, *Kent Evening Post*, 1971–3. Local government and political correspondent, *Sheffield Morning Telegraph*, 1973–8. District Editor, *Sheffield Star*, 1979–82. Newsdesk sub., YTV 1982–3; news editor 1983–5; producer, *Calendar*, since 1985.

Robert Hall
Radley College, then Leeds University (BA, Hons, English). Channel Television, 1977–80. YTV, Grimsby district office, 1980–2; Leeds 1982–8. Then to ITN, London.

7 A Conservative Newspaper's News: The *Yorkshire Post*, 28–29 January 1988

The front page of Thursday 28 January was overwhelmingly Yorkshire. All five of the main items were about Yorkshire or about *Yorkshire Post* investigations, and of the 11 brief digests in the end column five were Yorkshire stories. The lead was 'New inquiry on Militants in Yorkshire' – about the Labour Party's investigation of Bradford North, on which the divergent views of Yorkshire Television's *Calendar* and the BBC's *Look North* have already been recorded. The *Yorkshire Post* report was factual, with much more detail than the broadcasts gave. It was the combined work of a *Yorkshire Post* political staff member at Westminster and one in Bradford.

The other main items were an 'exclusive' by a staff reporter on an EEC grant of £100 million to Bradford for industrial development, to be matched by another £100 million from the UK Government and Bradford City Council. It was likely to bring 5 000 new jobs, and it was more than four times the regional grant to be given to the West Midlands as a whole. The third and fourth items both related to long-standing *Yorkshire Post* campaigns – a Commons committee's view on ways to restrict drinking by young people in pubs, and a Government decision to extend its coming ban on polyurethane foam in furniture. The fifth item was about a trial in Belgium over child sex in which a man recently convicted in Leeds was implicated.

Given this exceptionally high Yorkshire content on the front page, I asked Derek Foster (Associate Editor and Head of Newsroom) to explain the editorial decisions. His account:

– Militant

This is a story we've been working on very hard for a long time, to get to the bottom of the Militant Tendency activity in the Bradford North party. At the election before last [1983] the sitting member was a moderate Labour man. He was deselected and Pat Wall was nominated. When the election came both of them stood – one as an Independent Labour and one as Labour. The outcome was that the Conservative got in.

Then at the last election [1987] it was a straight run between Pat Wall and the Tory, and Pat Wall won so the status quo returned to what is normally a Labour seat. But there has been an aura hanging over the Bradford Labour selection process for a long time. It was one of those places where Militant had got their hooks in and decided they didn't want the moderate. Now Pat Wall, although he was a founder of Militant as a movement, declared before he was adopted this time that he no longer had any links with it ...

But there is still a big question over Bradford North – that Militant Tendency really were the people who were running the executive there, although it was denied, denied and denied. And we kept producing evidence suggesting that they had taken control of Bradford North. And this was the final outcome – that the National Executive was to have a proper investigation. That's why we made that the splash'.

– The EEC cash for Bradford

That had the double virtue of being exclusive and being important to a significant part of our constituency. It came late, long after our 5 o'clock conference'. (The extraordinary story of how the *Yorkshire Post* got the news comes later.)

– The Commons all-party committee's view on legislation to restrict young drinkers in pubs

On this, Derek Foster said it mattered to the *Yorkshire Post* because the paper's long inquiry into the problem had been a key part of the MPs' discussions.

– The extended ban on polyurethane foam in furniture

This again was a direct consequence of the work led by the *Yorkshire Post* reporter Brian Kay. It had been 'a long running campaign' which had succeeded, and deserved its place on the front page. (Kay was later 'Campaigning Journalist of the Year' in the British Press Awards.)

Asked what alternatives he saw to the events on that front page, Derek Foster said that the strongest in his view was the one on the extension of AIDS through prostitutes. It had led one of the inside pages. 'Maybe not a splash', he said, 'because you don't know how alarmist these people [the AIDS counselling service] are. It may be gloomy, but everyone is interested and they have a right to know'.

Narrative: Evening of 28 January 1988

2 pm

The Conference has a short print-out of primary items, extracted from the longer lists prepared by the Leeds newsdesk and by the Sheffield, Bradford, York, Hull and other offices. (The full lists are all available through the computer.) The top item is the North-East Transport Commissioner hearing evidence today on how a small bus company was 'elbowed off' a route by the aggressive tactics of a big South Yorkshire bus company. The evidence appears to be quite lurid.

The Editor, John Edwards, commends that morning's reports on Militant and on the £200 million cash bonanza for Bradford. As for today, it sounds 'pretty dull' in Yorkshire, apart from the bus company. But the verdict on the appeal by the Birmingham pub bombers could come tonight.

3.15 pm

Reporter Robert Schofield (also environment correspondent) is working on an exclusive for tonight, but he breaks off to tell me about last night's exclusive on the cash for Bradford. It was not really his work, but he had put the story together. The *Yorkshire Post*'s chief reporter in Bradford went to the theatre last night, to review a new production, but at the first interval he took a phone call from the deputy leader of the Conservatives on Bradford Council, who told him there was 'an agreement in principle' with the EEC to the grant under the 'integrated status' operation. Mike Clarke in Bradford had phoned the information to Robert Schofield and returned to his reviewing in the theatre, while Robert in turn talked to the Conservative deputy leader, to get the details. He felt it necessary, however, to check with the Labour group, and a little after 9 pm had tracked one of them down, who confirmed the information. So he 'carried it on from there', writing about 500 words with direct quotations from Labour's deputy leader and the Conservative deputy leader. He thought that the way the story had come to the *Post* was a tribute to the Bradford chief reporter's contacts.

3.45 pm

Derek Foster is running through the news lists on the computer. The bus company 'dirty tricks' is still at the top of the Yorkshire list, followed by court cases, a Scarborough inquest on two girls who disappeared from the beach in 1985 but no bodies have ever been found (but their mother believes they are alive), the Hull assault 'exclusive', and schoolboys building a bridge with spaghetti in a structural engineering competition.

The parliamentary list begins with Labour 'fury' because the Home Secretary is said to have made an announcement on revision of the Official Secrets Act during a BBC radio broadcast instead of to the Commons. Altogether there are 17 staff items on the Yorkshire general list, 6 on the parliamentary staff list, 11 on the staff features, arts, and 'people' lists, and 2 foreign. The Hull district list has 16 items, Sheffield has 17, Wakefield has 10, York 20 (and a substantial picture list), Bradford and Pennine 16, Huddersfield 5 and Harrogate 8.

Looking at the lists, Derek Foster notes that the Official Secrets row in the Commons could be interesting, and he is curious about an item on one of the Leeds MPs pressing for deregulation of airports – because the MP represents the area of the Leeds–Bradford airport, but the last thing most of his constituents want is night flying from there.

4.40 pm

Press Association says the Birmingham pub bombers have lost their appeal. The Lord Chief Justice and two other judges have upheld the convictions.

James Greenfield, tonight's Night Editor, says that it will almost certainly make the front page lead. But extensive background features have been prepared for an inside page, and they were based on the assumption that the men will be freed. All that will now have to be scrapped.

On picture prospects, he says that the Old Bailey is unlikely to produce anything, because of the tighter police restrictions in the vicinity of the court. But he is hopeful of something for the front page from the Portland navy base, where the Duke and Duchess of York ('our Royals') will be photographed together tonight for the first time since announcement of the Duchess's pregnancy.

5 pm

The main conference, chaired by John Edwards. James Greenfield goes through his priorities, with occasional comments from the editor. The list starts with the pub bombers, then NHS questions in the Commons and Mrs Thatcher saying there will be no 'bed and breakfast' charges in hospitals ('a U turn on a U turn', someone says), and then Hurd's broadcast tonight.

There is discussion on three or four items. On the Birmingham six, John Edwards asks whether there is space for the features: Jim Greenfield says it 'must be made' on page 8 or page 9. When the airport deregulation story comes up – the one that had intrigued Derek Foster an hour earlier – there is some hilarity because John Edwards at first fails to recognise that it's his MP and the night flights may go over his house. Others present also live close to the flight path. The possible exclusive from Robert Schofield is mentioned, but it is not confirmed yet. On the bus war, the Traffic Commissioner is said to have 'come down hard though he hasn't fined them as we hoped he would'. He has said that the war must stop. (It turns out later that the small company has more than doubled the number of its buses on the road.)

The back page leads for each of the five editions are also discussed. For Sheffield there is an unusual story which may be wanted for general news: the South Yorkshire fire chiefs are upset because the Home Office has refused them an extra grant on the grounds that they have had the money already, but they can find no trace of having received the money. Anyway, they are going ahead with recruiting more firemen.

5.25 pm

Leader writers' conference, again with John Edwards. Five issues are discussed. The choice goes to the Birmingham bombing, the Official

Secrets Act, and reform of the NHS. Debate on the lines to be taken is not extensive for there is common ground among those present. The Appeal ruling has come as a surprise, but the line will be that after the longest and most costly hearing in British legal history the outside observer cannot expect to pass judgement on this judgement. More immediate is the question whether the rift between London and Dublin will widen, for if it does terrorism will be the only beneficiary. On 'Goodbye to Section Two', the Home Secretary's apparent move towards a more liberal law is to be welcomed – and what is wrong, the leader will ask, with Mr Hurd 'tossing a few ideas around on BBC Radio'? (There is some concern to make clear to me as a visitor that the *Yorkshire Post* had supported the recent private member's bill on reform of the Official Secrets Act and in its leaders had disapproved of Mrs Thatcher's opposition to that Bill.) On the NHS, the line is to be cautious about radical change: while the NHS is recognised as being in deep financial trouble, some of the ideas coming from within the Conservative ranks are seen as being less than helpful.

5.50 pm

While the leader writers have been talking, the Night Editor and his newsroom colleagues have agreed on which items will be held for the front page, which will go on inside general news pages, and which will go to the five local back pages. Martin Robinson, in charge of the back pages, is beginning to assemble 'electronic baskets' with items for each of the five editions. Next he will embark on layouts.

For the front page, James Greenfield says there is no competitor with the Birmingham story. There is 'nothing moving' on the regional front that would displace it. The bombers' appeal has been a 'cause célèbre' for so long that it is 'overwhelmingly' the contender for the splash: the dimensions of the killing, the uncertainty about the conduct of the police, and the possible repercussions on relations with the Republic were all factors. On top of that, he says, there are the implications of what would have happened in Northern Ireland if the men had been released, and the fact that if it had not been for the 1965 Act they would definitely have been hanged, as one of the background articles made clear. Whichever way the verdict went, it was bound to be a strong story.

Of the Yorkshire alternatives, he says that they are all 'lightweight', though interesting enough in themselves. And as to pictures, if the Duke and Duchess of York did not turn up, for the front page he would use Prince Charles playing the cello in Australia – a novel and pleasing picture that would certainly find a place in the paper. (A little later, the Yorks' picture came.)

6.45 pm

Robert Schofield has got his exclusive after much telephoning and quiet talking to 'very twitchy' sources. The Forestry Commission have been holding today a regional meeting to consider a grant for planting 668 acres of conifers on Cam Fell, a sensitive area of North Yorkshire close to the Pennine Way. The Countryside Commission, the Nature Conservancy Council and the Dales National Park are all opposed to it, but the Forestry Commission's advisory committee favours it. The conservation bodies are seething.

7.30 pm

James Greenfield is sketching out his front page. The Birmingham six will go across 5 columns at the top, with a library picture of the Lord Chief Justice. Underneath will be 2 stories which were not listed at 5 pm. One is about an athletic policewoman (Welsh women's athletics team captain) who pursued a dangerous escaped prisoner whom she spotted near the Severn Bridge; after running 400 yards he collapsed and was recaptured by PC Alyson. It is seen as a small drama. The other is about a huge IRA arms dump being found on a beach in County Donegal. These will be flanked by a two-column picture of the York 'Royals'. That leaves no room for the forestry exclusive, which must go inside. The 10 short items in the end column will include cross-references to the NHS and Mrs Thatcher's supposed 'U-turn', the bus war and the firemen's missing funds.

From that point onwards the routine proceeds without complications. Greenfield says that late changes are easier now, with the computerised direct input. Although the journalists are generally slower in setting their texts on screen than the NGA (National Graphical Association) men were, the end result is very much quicker. A page can be changed in 10 or 12 minutes instead of the old 25.

Calm and quiet prevail in the *Yorkshire Post* newsroom, as men and women concentrate on their screens, but I am told that it is not always so peaceful as this.

Content Summary:

Front page, Friday 29 January 1988 (final edition)

Item	Total extent (sq. cm.)	Category*
'Bombers lose plea'	352	*Pol.*
'PC was too fast for killer on run'	167	*Crime*
'Huge IRA arms dump found on quiet beach'	179	*Terror*
'Royal couple reunited at naval base'	155	*Stars*
'Spy who made a superpower'	85 (and 172 p. 3)	*War/human.*
'Trade gap hits tax hopes'	175	*Money*
'Ford on verge of a strike'	46	*Pol.*
Short items, total	146	

Note:
*For explanation of categories, see pp. xi–xii.

(None of the main items were about Yorkshire, though three of the short items were 'Yorkshire political'. By contrast, on the previous day all five of the major items were Yorkshire stories.)

The back page lead and second stories, by editions:

Sheffield and South Yorkshire
'Essential fire cash may be "missing"': about the Government grants to South Yorkshire fire authority which had not been traced; and 'Last minute plea over disco scheme', about Rotherham residents' opposition to a discotheque and wine bar.

Hull and East Yorkshire
'Drinking game ended in death', about the inquest on a girl who died during a 'whisky race'; and '£2.3m pool design "like a cattle store"', about the design of a Northallerton leisure pool.

York and North Yorkshire
'"Problem pupils" centre approved', about plans for a centre for disruptive pupils; and '"Boring" Roman museum seeks more rates cash', about the Roman relics museum in Malton which wanted to make itself less boring.

Bradford and Pennine
'Minister deals blow to buses', about cuts being enforced on West
Yorkshire bus services: and 'Father wins £2000 for foster "error"', on
a civil court case over a mistake by social workers.

Final edition
'Minister deals blow to buses', as above; and 'Grim catalogue of
school havoc', on hooliganism at a Heckmondwike school.

Aggregating those *front pages* over the 5 days, we find these priority
news categories (figures in sq. cm.):

- *Pol.* 1127, plus *Pol. A.* 1384
- *Crime* 737
- *Health* 673
- *Stars* 524
- *Crash* 364
- *Int.* 178
- *Terror* 82
- *Sport* 29
- *Human* 24
- *War* 8

In assessing these figures, it is worth bearing in mind that *Stars* was
inflated by the Duchess of York's pregnancy, *Crime* by the Birmingham Six appeal (here treated as *Crime* rather than *Terror*) and by
the Sgt Speed murder trial, and *Crash* by the King's Cross fire inquiry.
It is clear, nevertheless, that political events – in the wide sense of
covering politics, the economy, social issues and industry – have a
long lead in *Yorkshire Post* primary news priorities. National and
regional political affairs account for almost 50 per cent of front page
news, taking these 5 days together; and if *Health* is added, at a time
when NHS policies were a major topic, then the total is just above 60
per cent.

Commentary

One can understand the 'frustration' of Editor John Edwards in not
being able to provide a completely comprehensive newspaper, such

that his north-eastern readers would not want to buy any other. Nevertheless, in terms of what is happening in Yorkshire and in neighbouring areas the *Yorkshire Post* offers an extensive service – far more than any of the nationals, and covering a greater territory each morning than any of the evening papers attempt to report. I had expected to find a number of trivial stories each day, but on looking for examples could find few. Vandals destroying the headstones of some war graves might be one example, and the inquest on a dead farmer another, but even these five-liners could not truly be called trivial.

As the summary of contents has shown, the primary news priority is in the political, social and industrial category, with a preference for Yorkshire or North-Eastern events. That must be the proper priority for a serious newspaper. Sex, scandal and gossip are absent from the *Yorkshire Post*'s pages. The coverage of national news is necessarily more limited than in the 'quality' nationals, and only the most pressing of international news is carried. The business and financial pages provide a competent service, again with a leaning towards Yorkshire news but altogether on a smaller scale than the major nationals.

But what about bias, and the required 'Conservative' outlook? In the day-to-day reporting it is not obtrusive, though I did hear some complaints about the paper's reluctance to carry news of Labour or Alliance activities during the 1987 General Election. In the fortnight of our fieldwork in Yorkshire there was no perceptible evidence of bias. The nearest to being questionable was, indeed, the decision on the night of 27 January to lead with the further Labour national executive inquiry into Militant penetration of the Bradford North constituency. The reasons for that choice have already been stated – with the Acting Deputy Editor's view that this was not only an issue that the *Yorkshire Post* had been watching for a long time but also one where there was a 'big question' about who was running the constituency party. The BBC in Leeds, with no axe to grind, also led with that topic; YTV relegated it as 'boring', but that was largely because *Calendar* had no political reporter to whom to turn. The *Yorkshire Post*'s report was factual and contained detail not available in any other newspaper or in any broadcast. There may have been an underlying readiness to stir up trouble for Labour, but on a quiet night it was a legitimate lead.

More open to question, in my view, is the quality of writing in some *Yorkshire Post* reports. Whereas the item on the Bradford Militants was clear and straightforward, with economy of phrasing, the front page story on the morning after the Sgt Speed verdict was contorted and confusing. The legal aspects of the judge's direction to the jury were important, but readers were left with no clear comprehension. That was a front-page failure.

The 'letters to the editor' are (or were) another area of deficiency. They are few and less than stimulating; but that, I was told, was going to change. More space for letters would probably bring more variety, for *Yorkshire Post* readers cannot be inarticulate.

On the ethnic minorities in Leeds and Bradford – in particular in the deprived inner city area of Chapeltown in Leeds – the *Yorkshire Post* claims to have done as much as it reasonably could. It has no ethnic journalists on its staff, though it has tried to recruit them; like other newspapers, it finds that the few who are trained tend to be snapped up by television or radio. To have reporters with Moslem or Hindu backgrounds could make access easier and might possibly reduce suspicion and hostility. It has nevertheless carried, among occasional series, studies of how the younger people in those communities see their own future. Those born and brought up here are said to have a different approach to life, particularly over arranged marriages. That series was the work of a young reporter, Susan Mitchell, and there have been useful contributions also from the *Yorkshire Post*'s Bradford staff.

The *Yorkshire Post*'s news values are orthodox, which means that it is socio-centralist or a little to the right of centre. It is cautious and not much concerned with women's issues. But as someone who spent much of his life working for a Lancastrian liberal newspaper, I nevertheless have respect for the Yorkshire conservative.

People

Derek Foster

From school to *Wakefield Express* series. To *Yorkshire Post* 1952, as Wakefield district reporter. Then 2 years with Beaverbrook's *Farming Express*, as northern correspondent. Back to *Yorkshire Post* 1962 – agricultural correspondent. To news desk 1968: latterly as Associate Editor and Head of Newsroom.

James Greenfield

Boston Grammar School to 1961. *Lincolnshire Echo* as reporter to

1967, sub-editor to 1970. *Daily Express*, as northern correspondent. Back to *Yorkshire Post* 1962 – agricultural correspondent. To news desk 1968: latterly as Associate Editor and Head of Newsroom.

Susan Mitchell

Economics degree (2:1). Postgraduate journalism course, City University 1985–6. To *Yorkshire Post* as graduate trainee 1986. Joint Campaign Journalist of the Year, British Press Awards, 1987.

Robert Schofield

BA (Hons) Geography. To *Yorkshire Post* as graduate trainee 1978. Now reporter and environment correspondent. Commended, British Press Awards Young Journalist of the Year 1979. Commended, Top Informative Journalist, Argos Awards 1987.

8 A 'Solid' Community Newspaper: The *Huddersfield Daily Examiner*

Until bypassed by the M62, Huddersfield was the first bastion of West Yorkshire that a traveller from mid-Lancashire met after crossing the Pennines. It is still the focal point of Kirklees district. It sits in a hollow, with hills rising to 600 or 800 feet on nearly all sides, and with a tall chimney or two as reminders of its industrial heritage. It still prospers with high-quality textiles, engineering and chemicals. Though no more than 20 slow miles from Leeds and 8 from Halifax, it is a separate community with strong pride in itself.

The *Huddersfield Examiner* is in keeping with its community. It sees itself as 'solid', unlike the more frivolous and 'pop' *Telegraph* and *Argus* in nearby Bradford. It has a long Liberal tradition in politics, which today leaves it free to take an independent line. It aims to report every significant event within 5 to 8 miles of Huddersfield city centre, and it restricts its distribution to that area alone. Its audited daily sales average 43 000 Monday to Friday and 37 000 on Saturdays – good figures in an area with some 350 000 people.

Ivan Lee, editor of the *Examiner* and chairman of the small company which owns it, describes it as 'a 24-hour newspaper'. But normally it has no more than 1 edition a day, going to press about 1 pm, but with page changes up to 3 pm, if called for. It prints only 45 000 copies, which implies that there are few unsold copies by early evening. Its standard size on weekdays is 16 to 36 broadsheet pages. On Saturdays it comes out in tabloid size. It has full colour printing facilities.

Its front page averages about two thirds Huddersfield and Kirklees stories and one third national news: the 'splash' story is nearly always local, unless major national or international news breaks between 8 am and midday. Some typical front page headlines: 'Surgeons sew

74

back man's severed hand', about how quick thinking by his fellow workers helped to save a Brighouse worker's arm; 'Hundreds evacuated after chemical blast', after an explosion at a factory in the upper Colne Valley sent toxic fumes into nearby houses; 'Legal threat to railway over Pacer train snags', over possible action by local authorities against British Rail because of defects in trains which were locally funded.

The *Examiner*'s claim to be 'solid' is confirmed by these content figures, based on measurements over 3 days in late January 1988 (figures in sq. cm.).

Page 1
- Local political (*Pol. A*), 1235
- *Pol.* (no local), 735
- *Human*, 377
- *Env.*, 300
- *Health*, 263
- *Crime*, 185
- *Crash*, 175
- *Int.*, 93
- *War*, 32
- *Pets*, 24
- *Ag.*, 14

The *S&S* category does not appear, nor does the *Stars* group. Overall, local events total 2396 and non-local 1185.

All pages on the 3 days, gave these fiures for space (sq. cm.) and number of items (excluding features)
- *Pol. A*, 4383 (44 items)
- *Pol.*, 2738 (29)
- *Pol W*, 171 (1)
- *Human*, 3617 (41, of which 30 local)
- *Crime*, 2398 (27, 18 local)
- *A & S*, 2360 (11, 8 local
- *Health*, 1472 (20, 11 local)
- *Int.*, with no local link 1003 (16), and with local link 379 (8)
- *Env,*, 992 (7)
- *Money*, 846 (5, 1 local)
- *Stars*, 522 (5, 4 local)
- *War*, 372 (5)
- *Teror*, 366 (3)
- *Pets*, 252 (4, 2 local)

– *Weather*, 248
– *Ag.*, 14 (1).

S & S again score nil.

From these figures, the *Examiner*'s strong interest in political and related news is plain, with local events taking nearly two thirds of the space in that category. Crime and courts feature little on the front page but receive substantial space on inside news pages. Sex and scandal do not appear (unlike the popular dailies). 'Star' personalities receive comparatively little attention. Human stories, the arts and science, and environmental issues all receive substantial space. One marked difference from the *Yorkshire Post* is the apparent lack of interest in farming, admittedly on 3 mid-winter days. Sports cover is extensive: the weather is given only brief notice on an inside page.

The office – a rabbit warren in an old building in the centre of Huddersfield – has an agreeable and friendly atmosphere. There are 42 journalists: 16 or 17 in the newsroom, 7 sub-editors, 7 in sport, 7 photographers and 4 feature people. The deputy editor is also the chief leader writer. The turnover of journalists is said to be less than in most newspaper offices, though not all are of Colne Valley or Yorkshire origin. Every member of the staff receives in January each year a copy of the managing director's report, covering progress in the past year and prospects for the coming one. The sales figures, advertising results, position of the related 'free' weekly and the 3 district weeklies, the 'no smoking' policy, and the pension fund are covered. A separate sheet deals with the journalists' pay scales.

The editor, Ivan Lee, regards the close identity and sense of community of Huddersfield as 'an enormous advantage'. He also puts emphasis not only on a thorough news service for the area but on special projects such as the 'Bodyscanner Appeal' through which in eight months in 1987 the Examiner raised £500 000 for a scanner for Huddersfield Royal Infirmary. That was followed in 1988 by a 'Pride in Huddersfield' campaign aimed at creating new jobs in the area.

Relations with Kirklees Council are said to be 'amiable on the whole' but there are occasional differences – 'they don't like criticism', Ivan Lee says, 'but none of us does'. One leading councillor thought they (the *Examiner*) were 'running a vendetta' against him, but that was because he had 'done some silly things' and was getting a bad press. On the whole, Lee said, the Council were open 'because they have to be – but we are partly responsible for that, we are the only paper which makes a serious effort to cover Kirklees'. Councillors knew that the newspaper was the only way the public could learn what they were doing. That also meant that the *Examiner* knew it must give the Council more space than it might otherwise wish.

My impression is that the radio stations give only sparse coverage to the Huddersfield area, and the *Telegraph* and *Argus* in Bradford treats it only as a fringe interest. The *Yorkshire Evening Post* could give it greater cover, but does not do so. The *Examiner* holds the ring.

The small independent company which owns the paper also owns the 3 local weeklies and the free newspaper (delivered to 75 000 households). It has a stationery shop and an office supplies division as well. It is a private limited company, with the editor as chairman: he and the managing director (Christopher Dicks) between them own 24 per cent of the shares. There is one other director, the accountant, and none of the company's £2.3 m investment in new plant in 1988 was borrowed. A compact board for a compact business.

9 Seven Journalists for Seven Days: Pennine Radio

Pennine Radio is the ILR station based in Bradford and covering also the areas of Halifax and Huddersfield, with a population of just over 1 million. East of Bradford there is also good reception of R. Aire, based in Leeds. Pennine Radio is owned by the company Yorkshire Radio Network with its head office in Sheffield, operating R. Hallam in South Yorkshire, Viking Radio in Hull and Pennine in Bradford.

Like many other ILR stations, between 70 and 80 per cent of Pennine's output is music – mainly pop. It provides news bulletins on the hour from 6 am to 6 pm, taking 3 minutes from IRN (Independent Radio News) in London and adding between 2 and 5 minutes from Bradford. Also there are evening bulletins shared with Hallam and Viking. The main bulletins are 7 and 8 am, with 4 minutes of local news, then at 1 o'clock and at 5 pm, when there is a 10-minute bulletin partly from IRN but predominantly with Pennine news. There is no mixing of music with news. After each bulletin the presenter takes over again with discs and chat.

To provide the Pennine bulletins there are 7 journalists – the News Editor (Dee Marshall in the spring of 1988), the sports producer and 5 others. On weekdays 1 reporter is on duty from 5.30 am to 1.30 pm, 1 from 1.30 pm to 9.30 pm, and 1, 2 or 3 (depending on availability) from 9.30 am to 5.30 pm or 10.30 am to 6.30 pm. One senior reporter is on duty alone each Saturday and Sunday but then has 2 weekdays off. Consequently, allowing for holidays and sickness, for the middle of the day there will be at best 5 journalists available to prepare and present the news, and at worst only 2.

Pennine does, however, draw on 3 local agencies for court material – covering magistrates, county and crown courts. It also makes occasional use of freelance journalists. The main burden, however, is on the 7 – making telephone calls to gather news, receiving calls, going out to record interviews, doing items in studio, keeping a check on IRN output in case there is anything relevant, occasionally listening to R. Aire (Leeds) or BBC R. Leeds in case they have anything new, and writing and reading the bulletins. There is said to be no shortage of news: with the wool textile industry and other manufacturing, the politics of Bradford and its neighbours, the employment problems and other issues, there are 'cracking stories', according to Dee Marshall.

As an example of their ability to move fast, she cites the Bradford football stadium fire in which 56 people were killed in May 1985. Pennine were lucky in that two of their staff were there – the sports reporter, on duty, and another reporter who had gone to the match for his own pleasure. As a result, unlike other radio and television stations, Pennine were on air reporting 12 to 18 dead when others were saying only that they could not bring their match report because of technical problems. All Pennine staff are required to live within 10 miles of the studio, and all were called in that afternoon. Pennine soon found itself supplying IRN in London and feeding continuously to Ireland, Europe and Australia. They had to send some of the staff home in the evening, in order to maintain a 24-hour service for the next 4 days.

As with other ILR stations, they have a dilemma over the routine supply of news to IRN. If they send a good item to IRN, it is then used in the hourly bulletins from London and that prevents Pennine from carrying the story or developing it in their own bulletins that immediately follow IRN. They tend, therefore, to hold back for an hour or two before sending items to London. Their own policy – as with many other stations – is never to use any item in more than three consecutive Pennine bulletins unless there is fresh information which permits a rewriting of the item. But they nevertheless like to feed IRN, after an hour or two's delay, because of the prestige of getting their items on national news and because it brings the reporter extra money. They regard IRN as 'very London orientated' and they like to see or hear news from the north.

A comparison of the main stories at 8 am one morning, with priorities indicated by their running orders, gives us the following result:

Content Summary: *Monday 26 January 1988*

Pennine	*BBC R. Leeds*
'A leading West Yorkshire Liberal vows to fight the proposed merger with the SDP'	'Arthur Scargill is back in charge of the NUM driving seat'
'Production at the Halifax Wirework Company has been brought to a standstill after a blaze caused damage estimated at over £1 million'	'Michael Meadowcroft is poised to leave the Liberal Party'
'Health Union chiefs in West Yorkshire warn that strikes could break out among the region's nurses'	Health authorities in West Yorkshire are set to discuss controversial plans'
(Those were the headlines, followed by IRN national news with 4 items in 3 minutes: – Mr Scargill re-elected by NUM – Prince Charles insulted on arrival in Australia – Ann Diamond's former nanny dies in mysterious circumstances – Potholers rescued in South Wales) (Pennine then returns with 4 items each taking about 1 minute, including voice pieces in 3 of the 4)	(These headlines were followed by over 3 minutes on the NUM vote and its implications, including 4 voice interviews, John Walsh among them. Then came 11 items, taking about 7 minutes; 7 of these items are from Yorkshire and 4 are national On the NHS and the nurses, detail is given of the meetings of Yorkshire health authorities due that day)

Commentary

Three points stand out. First, the flexibility available to BBC R. Leeds in drawing together the local and national news is evident, but with only one journalist on duty Pennine could not achieve what two were able to do in Leeds. The BBC journalists also benefitted from the detail and interviews supplied from Sheffield, Castleford and Barnsley through their London newsroom. Second, IRN's treatment of the NUM was more partisan and prejudicial than that of R. Leeds as the opening words of each will illustrate.

IRN: 'Arthur Scargill is declaring war on Mrs Thatcher and British Coal after clinging on to power as boss of the National Union of Mineworkers. He has been re-elected President with a massively reduced majority'.

R. Leeds: 'Arthur Scargill is back in charge of the National Union of Mineworkers. In a closely fought contest he successfully beat off the challenge of John Walsh from Castleford'.

Third, with only one journalist on duty the Pennine news could give little detail of the local aspects of the NHS controversies, whereas the BBC covered three specific problems within 1 minute. Pennine was too obviously dependent on a single NUPE source. In fairness, however, it must be admitted that Pennine's closing item about a huge pink sculpture being put up in Bradford Art Galley and covered with plasticine was more amusing than anything in the serious Leeds output. Leeds made up for it a little later by playing the 'Marseillaise' before embarking on a discussion of the NUM vote.

Pennine's policy is to provide primarily for a 'popular' audience who do not want much talk. That nevertheless leaves room for a 10-minute news programme at 5 pm, when audiences 'shoot up', according to Dee Marshall, as people get into their cars to go home. That 5 pm programme is the only one when Pennine mixes the IRN output from London with its own.

One other service provided by Pennine deserves mention. From 6 pm to 7 pm on Mondays, Wednesdays and Fridays it broadcasts *Eastern Ear*. On Mondays and Fridays it is in Urdu, and is aimed at the older generations; on Wednesdays it is mainly in English, for younger Asians who do not speak much Urdu. The presenters and some contributors are paid on a freelance basis. The newsroom prepares both a local 3-minute bulletin and, for use after 7 pm, a longer international bulletin with news primarily of India and Pakistan; these are translated into Urdu. Pennine's advisory council also includes some Asian members.

Pennine is, of course, a commercial station. Its survival depends on revenue from advertisements: listeners consequently must accept the advertisements which come before and after programmes and in the middle of them. In its evidence to the Peacock Committee in 1985, the AIRC (Association of Independent Radio Contractors) placed Pennine among the three lowest in 'turnover per potential listener', but that was based on a population of 1 250 000 people in its broadcasting area, which seemed to me unduly high. It was shown as having made a small loss in the year 1983–4, as against a small profit in the previous year. (Hallam, on the other hand, was tenth out of the 39 listed stations in terms of profit: Viking was one of the seven who were not listed.)

The Peacock Committee itself – the majority within it, at any rate – seemed to show almost total unconcern with the consequences of more extensive advertising on radio through the possible privatisation of BBC R. and 2, even though it was pointed out to them that such a move would probably cripple the smaller enterprises such as Pennine.

People

Dee Marshal
Trained at London College of Printing (broadcasting course) 1979. Then with local news agency in Bradford; started to freelance for radio, including BBC Leeds and Sheffield. R. Aire, Leeds, for short time; then travel abroad. On return, freelancing at York, Leeds, and Derby. Was offered post as senior reporter at Pennine 1985; became News Editor in 1987.

10 The Midlands: 'From Wales to the Wash'

Yorkshire is big but has a clear identity. The Midlands are bigger, but are without any such cohesion. For broadcasters – both BBC and ITV – their task is to cover the whole of eight counties and substantial parts of six others. The total population is well over 10 million. But for broadcasters the Midlands is the only region with competitors on every side. As Bob Southgate of Central Television put it 'every border is threatened' – with YTV and Granada to the north and other strong challengers to the south. Anglia Television to the east and HTV Wales to the west might take a different view, seeing the powerful transmitters of the Midlands reaching well into territory that by rights is theirs. Even Thames Television and London Weekend must look enviously at Central's Oxford transmitter, reaching wealthy parts of the Thames Valley and providing better pictures to Reading than they can offer.

But covering such a vast and varied 'region' has its problems. While West Yorkshire differs in character from South, East or North Yorkshire, all four counties and their people have common interests. The Midlands lacks that unity. Even within the West Midlands, the cities of Coventry, Birmingham and Wolverhampton are not greatly interested in events among their neighbours, and to the East there is no close common interest between Nottingham and Leicester. Newspapers and local radio, of course, can carve out specific territories for themselves – as papers such as the *Coventry Evening Telegraph* and the *Express and Star* in Wolverhampton do, while ILR's Radio Trent or the BBC's R. Leicester or R. Stoke also provide for coherent communities.

For their early evening regional news, both Central and BBC Pebble Mill divide their programmes. Central prepares and transmits separate versions of *Central News* in Birmingham for the West Midlands, in Nottingham for the East, and at Abingdon for the Thames Valley.

The BBC, with more limited resources, splits its *Midlands Today* for about 6 minutes each day in order to report the lesser events of East and West separately. There is, though, a snag both for Pebble Mill and for Central: the West Midlands transmitter near Birmingham is more powerful and on higher ground than the East Midlands transmitter at Waltham, and as a result quite of lot of people in the East have their sets tuned to the Western output. The benefits and losses through splitting the programmes will be discussed later. But over the development in Oxford Central Television is in no doubt: 'people in Oxford don't believe they are Midlands and don't think of going to Birmingham for their shopping'. Also there is much revenue from advertisements to be raised from Reading, Oxford and the Thames Valley.

Among local newspapers there is subdivision, too. The *Coventry Evening Telegraph* is highly developed in that way. Unlike the *Huddersfield Examiner* with its one daily edition for the whole of its compact Colne Valley, the *Telegraph* runs up to 11 editions, 7 of them to provide for particular districts. 4 editions are for Coventry itself and the immediate neighbourhood. The first is on the streets about 11.15 am, the biggest at 2.45 or 3 pm (the 'City Final'), and the 'Night Final' at 5 pm. In addition, the *Telegraph* also runs special district editions with distinctive mastheads for Nuneaton, Leamington, Rugby, Stratford and Bedworth. These go to press at 15-minute intervals around midday – a considerable achievement, made possible by electronic typesetting and page makeup.

The *Coventry Evening Telegraph* belongs to the same owners as the *Post* and the *Evening Mail* in Birmingham, but there are marked differences in staffing and management. Until the spring of 1988 all three were owned (along with the Cambridge evening newspaper) by the Iliffe group, but since then Ingersoll Publications of Princeton, New Jersey, have bought all the Iliffe shares in the two Birmingham papers and 75 per cent of Coventry (with Lord Iliffe retaining 25 per cent). Ingersolls own more than 125 titles in the United States, and this is their first venture into Europe. They have established a subsidiary (Midlands Newspapers) for Birmingham and Coventry. In recent years, before the Ingersoll takeover, the *Post* as a morning paper had been losing money while the evening papers were profitable – Coventry especially. For a time between 1982 and 1986 Iliffes tried to run the two Birmingham papers as one, with editions covering 24 hours, but that was a failure from which the *Post* has not yet recovered. It did, though, rise from sales of 37 000 to 38 000 in the autumn of 1988, without extra resources. Today it still shares much of its news service with the *Evening Mail*, and it has only 60 journalists assigned to the morning paper. The *Coventry Evening Telegraph* has 100 and an atmosphere of confidence and certainty which is lacking at the *Post*.

There are contrasts, too, between the resources and wealth of Central Television and of BBC Pebble Mill – though Pebble Mill in 1988 was mercifully free of the anxiety and demoralisation then afflicting the upper ranks of BBC news and current affairs in London. because of Government pressure and the attitudes of the BBC's own Governors. With limited resources, indeed, the Birmingham BBC appeared to be providing a good service to its region. The main *Midlands Today* programme has (winter 1988–9) only 21 journalists, including its editor, producer, and presenters, though it also makes use of some non-contract freelance people. *Central News*, by contrast, has 43 journalists for the West Midlands, including sports, another 29 in the East Midlands, and 12 in the Thames Valley. The BBC has 3 'road crews' in Birmingham (cameraman, recordist and lighting man if needed) and 1 crew in the East. Central had 4 crews in the West, 5 more in Nottingham, and 4 in the Thames Valley (at Oxford, Abingdon, Aylesbury, and Gloucester) and 6 1-man units.

Even with 84 journalists and 4 senior executives working for Central Television, or 21 at Pebble Mill plus 2 or 3 freelance casuals and 2 senior executives, both have to keep an eye on the output of local newspapers. The newspapers, after all, can concentrate on particular areas, and are closer to their readers. Local radio is also a significant source of news within the BBC, with increasingly close co-ordination (as we have already seen in Yorkshire) between the BBC's local radio stations and the regional television news. Both also benefit from the two-way feed between the BBC's newsrooms in London and the numerous outstations.

Within the territory of *Central News* and *Midlands Today*, there are 12 BBC local radio stations, 13 ILR, and 16 daily morning or evening newspapers.

In the Midlands my study looks at the two main television centres (Central and Pebble Mill), at one radio station and one morning newspaper in the regional 'capital' (BBC R. WM and the *Post*) and two away from the 'capital' (Mercia Sound and the *Coventry Evening Telegraph*).

In that group, compared with the 100 journalists at the Coventry newspaper, the 84 at Central Television including both Birmingham and Nottingham, the 60 assigned to the *Post* within Ingersoll's

Midland Newspaper subsidiary, the 21 plus casuals at Pebble Mill's *Midlands Today*, there are 14 to 16 at BBC R. WM (though the number is difficult to define since there are mixed duties in its staff, who have to cover 16 hours of output). And – the least well staffed – there are only 10 at Mercia Sound including the Head of News; and one of the 10 has to be detached each day to provide the news at Coventry Cable.

The journalists at R. WM provide and present 10-minute bulletins at 7 am, 8 am, 1 pm and 5 pm, and 5-minute bulletins on the hour every hour from 6 am to 7 pm. Also $1\frac{1}{2}$-minute headlines on the half-hour in peak periods. At Mercia Sound, similarly, there are bulletins on the hour, every hour from 6 am to 7 pm, with a minimum of 5 minutes (3 from IRN in London and 2 of local news) and a maximum of 10 (4 from London and 6 local). There are headlines on the half-hour also at peak times.

Both Mercia Sound and BBC R. WM face tough targets. Proportionately to the population in its area, Mercia is one of the more successful ILR stations financially. It had in 1987 a profit of above 20 per cent of its turnover – more than double, proportionately, the profit of Birmingham's bigger ILR station BRMB. But the two companies were being merged in the spring of 1988, with Mercia expected to maintain its performance. At the same time, it had to prepare for the opening of BBC R. Warwickshire in the autumn of 1989. While the BBC station was bound to have a less popular and more middle class content, with speech predominant, Mercia nevertheless expected to lose some of its audience to the new station.

For BBC R. WM, the Governors in London had set a still harder target. It must treble its audience in the next 3 years – by the end of 1990, that is. The Governors recognised that the three biggest of their local radio stations were also the ones with relatively the lowest audiences. On the JICRAR surveys of audience reach, conducted twice a year, R. Manchester's weekly 'reach' was 16 per cent of people in its area, R. London's 11 per cent, and R. WM only 6 per cent. (By the autumn of 1988, R. WM was already up from 6 per cent to 9 per cent.) That compared with 47 per cent for R. Cornwall, 37 per cent for R. Derby and 32 per cent for R. Leicester. (Mercia has a 53 per cent 'reach', one of the highest for any ILR station in England, but the figure is based on a more compact area.) Tony Inchley had been brought in to R. WM as a new station manager (winter 1987), after experience in running Leicester and then Manchester, and had been set the task of trebling the audience. With pressure from Conservatives (and to an extent Labour) for the BBC to cut its local radio stations, and with a majority of the Peacock Committee in favour of privatising them, it must be a hard task. It is with R. WM that our Midlands study begins.

Content by Categories: *5 weekdays, 17–23 February 1988*

Category*	Midlands Today		Central News		Birmingham Post	
	No. of items	Total duration (min./sec.)	No. of items	Total duration (min./sec.)	No. of items	Total space (sq. cm.)
A & S	4	2.34	4	9.41	9	1354
Ag.					3	595
Crash	5	3.06	4	3.05	15	2370
Crime	12	7.19	11	9.28	30	2201
Env.	3	3.14	1	1.20	7	617
Health A	11	12.47	10	12.07	14	1672**
Human	12	20.45	9	12.28		
Int.			1	1.29	25	2574
Money					189	28 444
Pets			1	2.14		
Pol.					30	3970
Pol. A	26	34.02	24	35.39	37	5479
Terror	1	3.22	1	4.16	10	1840
Sport		11.46		18.18	122	21 836
Stars	1	0.15	6	13.08	10	967
S & S					1	25
War	1	0.20			8	1139
Weather	5	3.51	5	6.28	5	790
Other						

Notes: On categories *Crime A*, *Crime C*, and *Crime W*, *H/Women* and *Pol. W*, there were no items.
   *For explanation of categories, see p. xiv.
   **Made up of *Health*, 3232 and *Health A*, 1395 sq cm.

11 Big City, Big News: BBC R. WM

Narrative and Content, Wednesday 17 February 1988

5.15 am

Just arriving or recently arrived, 4 broadcasters (2 more than at R. Leeds, at this hour). They will put out the breakfast programme, starting at 6 am. It is mostly information – news, weather, travel, topical interviews – but leavened with a little bright and brisk music. The four are producer Bridget Sneyd, presenter John Taynton, news bulletin editor and reader Mark Whittacker, and reporter David Biddle. They are followed later by 3 more – another reporter, a production assistant, and a trainee. This is the most important programme of the day, with the peak audience around 8 am; but big efforts are being made to stiffen the lunchtime programme between 12 and 2 pm, including controversial interviews and phone-in discussion.

Soon after coming in reporter David Biddle departs in a news car to the Land-Rover plant in Solihull, in pursuit of what could be the biggest story of the day – an all-out strike by the 6000 workers at Land-Rover, due to start next Monday. 2 days ago the workers had voted by 2 to 1 for that strike, over what they saw as an inadequate pay offer. Yesterday letters had been sent by the management to all manual workers warning them that a strike could bring redundancies. Biddle wanted to get reactions at the factory gate.

The second reporter, Chris Nelson, leaves a little later with the radio car for King's Heath in the south of Birmingham for a live broadcast about road changes intended to reduce traffic jams at the peak periods. Both reporters will be working alone.

6 am

On air, with the first news, weather and travel. Disc immediately afterwards, then into background report on Land-Rover dispute (prepared last night) and promise of report on new developments after 7 am news. Another disc, more travel news, third disc and then travel.

John Taynton, the presenter, has a deep, clear voice and a friendly manner. In interviews he is firm and to the point, but cool in challenging the speaker. He gives the programme an air of certainty and authority.

Later items include a report and discussion of the Winter Olympics in Calgary and a summary of this morning's newspapers.

7 am

The news is now extended to just short of 10 minutes. The main items:

– Commons last night voted to renew Prevention of Terrorism Act. Home Secretary Douglas Hurd says the Act is to be made permanent. Labour objections led by Birmingham MP Roy Hattersley. (Voice extracts from Commons with Hurd and Hattersley speaking.)
– Union leaders at Land-Rover in Solihull (S.E. Birmingham) accuse management of 'dirty tricks' because of its decision to use Mori polling agency to gauge feeling about coming strike. The company says the workers were misled. Mori has been phoning workers at home. (Voice piece with T & G official, who indicates possible 'stoppage' today.)
– Ford unions say new pay deal, negotiated last night, represents a real victory. (London reporter with voice piece.)
– Parents of Matthew Collier, boy who died last Sunday after much delayed heart operation in Birmingham, have decided against asking for inquest. Funeral on Friday.
– Other items include two more on NHS controversy; voting in New Hampshire (US) presidential primary; eight died in California shooting; 270 technicians dismissed by TV-am; new funding system for universities announced by Education Minister; test cricket in New Zealand ends in draw.

Mark afterwards said his decision to lead with the Commons on anti-terrorism was because the 'actuality' of the two Ministers 'slagging' each other was stronger than the telephone 'clip' on Land-Rover. He had been swayed also by one being a Birmingham MP.

After the news, John Taynton runs again last night's tape on the background to the Land-Rover troubles. Travel then comes live from the West Midlands police control room, followed by rail and air from studio. Then into a 4-minute item on fund-raising for a QED (quick early diagnosis) scanner for Queen Elizabeth Hospital in Birmingham. At 7.20 am David Biddle comes in live with the first vox pops from outside the Land-Rover plant – reaction to the management and the Mori poll is bad.

Next disc comes after 7.30 am news summary. That is followed by vigorous interview on the 'barbaric blood sport' of hare coursing, with John Taynton questioning woman leader of a protest march which is passing through Birmingham. She likens hare coursing to 'two crocodiles with a human being in the middle', and she says the dogs can wrestle with the hare for 2 or 3 minutes while it is still alive. Taynton says the supporters of hare coursing would say the hare is very rarely caught; she replies that the hare is caught nearly every time, though some escape. So it goes on – he persists in putting the other side (though I learn afterwards that he disapproves of hare coursing); she maintains that it is totally immoral. A lively 5 minutes.

Immediately afterwards, at 7.43 am, producer Bridget takes a phone call from Ed Doolan, presenter and mastermind of the midday show *Tell Ed*. He wants the tape on hare coursing to be preserved – he will use an extract, to follow it up and get reactions from listeners. If possible, he will get one of the top people from the Waterloo Cup, the prime coursing event, to come on his programme. At the same time the production assistant and the trainee are both taking calls from listeners; some are asked to take part in the lunchtime phone-in.

7.46 am

More telephone activity. Wife of a Land-Rover worker complains that Mori had rung their number, which is ex-directory. How did Mori get it? Again, she is asked whether she will come on midday phone-in; her husband has gone to work, so she is reluctant. But there must be a story here. Bridget will take it up with newsman Mark as soon as he is free.

8 am

Today's third main bulletin, prepared and presented by Mark. He has changed the order slightly, still leading with the Home Secretary on the Anti-Terrorism Act but (to my surprise) dropping Land-Rover to third place and moving Ford up to second. He also has three new stories later in his bulletin, one a Coventry MP (Labour) with a blistering comment on a Conservative back bencher's proposal to help finance the NHS through a state lottery.

Asked afterwards why he had placed Land-Rover third, Mark said that he had hoped to put it first, before the Home Secretary or Ford. But the reporter Dave Biddle had come back from Solihull after his 7.20 vox pops from outside the plant, because he wanted to re-edit the vox pop interviews in a shorter form, which he could not do in the news car. He also wanted to provide a better script. He had arrived back about 12 minutes before the 8 o'clock bulletin. Mark had therefore thought it best to hold on for the new material. He'd been ready to put it in first or second, but it was not ready at 8 am. He slotted in the 'actuality' cart on Ford, which he had not meant to use, thus gaining another 25 seconds or so. Then as the vox pop cart was arriving he 'ad libbed' the opening of the third item (Land-Rover), saying that a majority of those who had clocked in that morning were in favour of the strike. The vox pops followed – one man angry at the company's challenge to the union ballot, one who had not voted but believing many of those who voted for the strike were doing it out of loyalty to the union, and a third 'fed up with the management's paltry offer'.

At 8.11 am, as the bulletin is ending, Bridget takes a call from Land-Rover with a statement on the Mori poll. She thinks it is only a repeat of what they said late last night, but she types it quickly for Mark. She also tells him about the ex-directory call. (That the news studio is a floor above the main studio means a 30-second sprint up or down the stairs, but the reporters have their own little cubicle studio within the newsroom. It saves them from having to sprint.)

Meanwhile, after the news and travel, the live report from the busy roadside in King's Heath comes up. Chris is there with Councillor Eve Brook, and the traffic is rumbling noisily past but still moving. She says that in another half hour it will be just about stopped, nose to tail, and she outlines the Council's plans to make life easier – together with some criticism of the plans. Then it is back to the studio for more weather and the travel, with the West Midlands police inspector adding his own comment on traffic jams at King's Heath.

9 am

There is another cliffhanger just before the 9 am news. About 7 minutes before 9, one of the Union officials at Solihull phones to say that there has been a walk-out. David Biddle has just revised his script for Mark; he leaves immediately for Land-Rover, to check how extensive the walk-out has been. Mark, in the last minutes before going on air, writes a new opening for Land-Rover, now his top item.

After the news, Bridget rings the Land-Rover press office. They say there has been a walk-out but 'production is not affected'. Questioned about the Mori poll and the ex-directory call, their man says that they gave Mori only the names and addresses of workers. Bridget says that since it was a selective poll they must have known which names they were giving, and asks how Mori could have got an ex-directory number if not from the company? She says the press office was 'very fudgy'.

David Biddle calls in about 9.30 am. About 2500 have walked out in protest over the Mori poll – nearly all the day shift, that is – and there is about to be a small meeting. He will provide a fresh report for 10 am. The management are now not saying anything. At R. WM's morning conference at 9.45 am the station manager, Tony Inchley, says that the reporting this morning has been 'very good'. At the small news conference afterwards the news editor, David Robey, says that they must find out more about the poll and ask Mori for their view. Land-Rover should be asked to put a senior management man to explain the poll, its motives and the selection process, because nothing else could now be convincing. Later in the day the Land-Rover company issues a formal apology, admitting that it gave an ex-directory number. It does not offer a senior spokesman.

With the Wednesday walk-out, the strike itself had effectively begun. It lasted about a month.

Bridget, with overall responsibility for the 6 am–9 am programme, is reasonably content. At first, before 6 am, she had been worried that they seemed light on hard news, but that had developed with Land-Rover. They had had to make a quick change of running order after the 7 o'clock news because the first vox pops were not yet available, but that had been no bother. She was 'happy' with the features arranged the previous night – the QED scanner and the nurses' balloons for fund raising, which they had run twice; the roadside interview about traffic at King's Heath, and the anti-hare coursing marchers who were going through the West Midlands today. On the hares she had been pleased also with the following item on greyhound racing, which she had put immediately after the hares to show the alternative to chasing live animals. On the extended anti-terrorist law, she had thought of trying for Roy Hattersley, but they had previewed that yesterday and Hattersley was 'appallingly bad' about doing anything for local radio so it would have been 'very hard work'. She was satisfied also with the detailed information that had been given on welfare rights in another item, for it was a difficult subject to condense, but important. The changes in supplementary benefit had been discussed in a live studio interview near the end of the programme. It had been allowed to run for $4\frac{1}{2}$ minutes instead of the planned 3, but she believed that that had been the right decision.

Asked whether she had any worries about political balance or bias in the programme, she said she was aware that it was something the producer must look out for. Most people had a one-sided opinion on party politics, as individuals, but she was convinced that this did not affect the broadcasting staff. That was mainly because of the training, but also because people did not want 'to leave themselves open as easy targets'.

John Taynton also was content with the programme. His main job, he said, was 'to keep on my toes'. They had had to switch the running order, but that was not hard. It was the only time he had had to ask the producer 'what next?' The interviews had all gone well. For each he was given an opening script and some suggested questions, but how he did it was left to him. He had been glad of the brief for the roadside interview, since he knew nothing about it. On the hare coursing, he was familiar with both sides of the controversy, so that was easy (though it can never be quite as easy as he implied). On possible political bias, he said that the breakfast programme had to be more sensitive than the lunchtime one, where it was possible to be a little opinionated. In general, he said:

> I think sometimes people criticise radio and television because you are commenting, maybe, on the activities of the Government of the day, and they see that as political bias – forgetting, of course, that it's just one party that will be in power, and you can't criticise the Opposition because it's not doing anything. When the Government changes, if it ever changes, the bias will be deemed to be the other way.

On his own role, John Taynton said that he enjoyed the more vigorous requirements of the morning programme, much as he had also enjoyed his 2 years as the lunchtime reporter.

The Rest of the Day

From 9 to 12 noon there is a lighter programme, simply named after
its presenter, *Gordon Astley*. From 12 to 2 pm *Tell Ed* – with Ed
Doolan seeking comment and reaction in telephone calls from the
audience – again takes up serious issues, though mixed with entertainment. From 2 to 4 pm *Gyn on the Wireless* again mixes music and talk.
Coming Home from 4 to 7 pm builds up the information element
again, especially between 5 and 6 pm. Later, with diminished
audiences, there are various music programmes. Important, however,
are the ethnic programmes running for half an hour on Tuesdays and
up to 2 hours on Wednesday and Thursday evenings.

On Wednesday 17 February, Gordon Astley's 9-12 midday show
was devoted almost wholly to the Chinese New Year. Astley regards
himself as a 'court jester' of radio rather than a journalist. He
describes his programme as 'cheap and cheerful'. For most of that day
he went out with the radio car to Birmingham's Chinatown.

Tell Ed, coming afterwards, stood out for two reasons. One was a
live discussion, taking telephone calls from people with problems,
about personal insurance problems. His guest was from the Association of British Insurers. He had been invited to come in because of
questions posed the previous day about insuring mobile homes, which
he now answered in discussion with the telephone callers. He then
took questions on car insurance and other problems, giving advice
and in some cases offering to supply, not on air, the names of people
who might be able to help with particular cases. Then there was the
follow-up to John Taynton's talk 4 hours earlier about the 'barbaric
blood sport' of hare coursing. Ed Doolan had succeeded in getting Sir
Mark Prescott, a Newmarket racehorse trainer and a committee
member of the Waterloo Cup. He put up an insistent defence of hare
coursing, saying that in a year with 1870 courses only 287 hares had
been killed and that the interest was in the skill of the dogs. Ed
Doolan continued to batter him with such questions as 'What's the
pleasure in seeing an animal put under such extreme stress', and
'what's the kick in it, seeing an animal chased to exhaustion?'. When
the calls came in, as they did, all were against Sir Mark – so much so
that Ed told the producer to put up 'at once' anyone on Sir Mark's
side.

Very different are the ethnic programmes in the evening. *East and
West* on Wednesdays and Thursdays is produced by Anita Bhalla,
herself born in Nairobi but brought up in Birmingham. She says that

hers have to be like other programmes, with the music for which the Asian communities are 'hungry', but it also contains 'a little probing into the more serious issues'. One such (mentioned in Chapter 2), began in *East and West* but was taken up by national newspapers and network television. It was the huge backlog of nationality and passport cases piling up at the Home Office centre in Croydon. It began with calls from listeners saying 'my passport is stuck, can you advise me?' She thought it strange, so rang two local advice centres who confirmed that it was true. 'The more I dug', she says, 'the more I found'. Finally she rang Keith Vaz, MP for Leicester, who said there was a backlog of over 200 000 letters. He was going to see the Home Office the following Monday. She therefore arranged an interview on the Monday morning between John Taynton and Keith Vaz, and spoke to the editor of *Midlands Today*, who took it on for television news. 'Then it snowballed', she says, as indeed it did in the spring of 1988 and after.

Commentary

The detail of one morning's early activity at R. WM shows once again that news does not arrive in neatly prepared packages. The effort put in by reporters and producers at R. WM that morning, particularly over the Land-Rover event, was routine to them. But it called for alert and fast thinking or action by those on duty, and they took this in their stride. The first reports anywhere of the walk-out at Solihull and the first explanation of why it had happened came through local radio; and the first disclosure of the ex-directory call, which became a factor in the dispute, came because a listener chose to ring R. WM to tell them.

It may be argued that no public benefit was gained by early reporting of the workers' reaction to the Mori poll and of the reasons for the walk-out. But in an open democracy such information cannot be hidden and it is the duty of press and broadcasters to find out what they can and to report it impartially. The Land-Rover company would have preferred to have the minimum publicity, as the inadequacy of their press statements showed. It was surely correct for R. WM to report the event as it did, stating the management's view that the workers had been misled about the pay offer, reporting the union reply that the ballot papers had been explicit, and following up with the latest news – that a walk-out was taking place – and with the vox pops of workers' opinions. It was surely correct also for R. WM to point out to Land-Rover's press office that what they were saying could not carry any conviction, as was done by Bridget Sneyd's call just after 9 am and by another longer call from the newsroom a little later. Strikes are never good news and rarely simple in their background, but the company's use of the Mori poll to try to reverse the union ballot was a new development, and the consequences had to be reported.

The narrative further illustrates, though journalists themselves are often unaware of it, that there are risks in the high-speed decision-making that radio news especially requires. If Mark Whittaker had played safe at 8 am, using the material he already had and not taking the risk of holding back the Land-Rover item until the vox pops had been re-edited, then probably nobody would have complained. If, however, he had held back and David Biddle, just back from the plant, had been unable to re-edit his tapes in time, then Mark might well have been given a black mark later in the day. Again, it must be remembered that a reporter on location at a factory gate in the cold dawn has to record a number of brief interviews, only a few of which will be fit for use. To pick the right 'clips' quickly from what may be a 15-minute reel is not easy. The station manager's 'Very good' at the morning conference was well earned.

As to possible political bias, it cannot be said that any was evident. The Commons exchanges on the Prevention of Terrorism Act, the lead story at 6, 7 and 8 am, gave equal attention to the conflicting sides and left listeners to draw their own conclusions – which could well be on either side. As John Taynton rightly said in his comment quoted earlier, Government action tends to get more publicity than an Opposition response just because one is executive action and the other is not. That can be – and often is – taken by Opposition supporters as bias in favour of the Government because it receives more attention. But the counterpart is that, because the Government is the executive authority, its actions are bound to be examined critically; and Government supporters then become angry with the broadcasters. Journalists have to learn to live with that. The comment on bias from Bridget Sneyd also seemed to me sound – that individuals have their own opinions but BBC training brings home the need for political balance: the training does drive home the need to set aside one's own opinions. It was understandable, though, at a time of tension within the BBC that she said that people did not want 'to leave themselves open as easy targets'.

The ethnic *East and West* programme must also deserve commendation for its disclosures of the chaos at the Home Office nationality and immigration department. An important public service was achieved there, rightly leading to network and national publicity. That resulted from telephone calls by listeners; and in my brief time with R. WM, mainly with the early morning and midday programmes, I was surprised by the number of calls being received. For a station supposed to have the lowest audience percentages of any BBC local station, R. WM was nevertheless generating much response.

The task set to the station manager, Tony Inchley, was and is a formidable one. To push audience 'reach' up by more than three times within 3 years must be extremely hard to achieve. It means moving the audience figures in the Birmingham area up from around 200 000 to above 600 000, allowing for the loss of potential listeners to the new stations at Worcester and Warwick. The BBC's Governors have set that target because of the corporations's restricted finance. Let us hope that it can be achieved.

People

David Biddle
LSE, graduated Economics and Economic History. Then to Australia via S.E. Asia. 2 years in advertising, Brisbane. London College of Printing, journalism course 1986–7. Freelance for R. WM from March 1987.

Anita Bhalla
Born in Nairobi; in Birmingham area since age of 8. Trained as teacher, College of Education. Community Relations Officer (Birmingham); then Community worker, Leicester. Lecturer, regional office of 'industrial language training unit' (one of six in West Midlands); also began presenting *East and West* in 1982. Full time at BM since autumn 1987.

Tony Inchley, station manager
Born in Wiltshire. Provincial newspaper and news agencies. News Editor, BBC R. Stoke early 1970s. Manager R. Leicester 1982–5. R. Manchester 1985–7, R. WM since winter 1987.

Bridget Sneyd
English and Anthropology degree, Oxford Polytechnic 1982. Then in

publishing. Radio course at Portsmouth 1985–6. Freelance, BRMB 1986. At R. WM as reporter from late 1986; producer since early 1988. Says social anthropology *does* have relevance. (Moved to BBC daytime tv., London, summer 1988.)

John Taynton, presenter *John Taynton at Breakfast* (freelance)
Various newspapers in Midlands, then into broadcasting from 1975. Presenter R. WM midday show 1985–7; breakfast programme since then. 'Enjoys radio immensely'.

Mark Whittaker
Durham University, BA Modern History 1979. Journalism training, Thomson Regional Newspapers, Newcastle, 1979. *Lancashire Evening Telegraph*, Blackburn. With BM as producer since early 1986. (Moved to R. 1 *Newsbeat*, July 1988.)

12 Bombers, Beds and a Birthday: Central News West, 18 February 1988

Content comparison

First, a listing of what Central News carried in its 6 pm programme, together with the content of Pebble Mill's *Midlands Today* on the same day. Then let us look at the day's activity in the newsroom at Central Television, to see how decisions were reached.

Central News duration (min./sec.)	Central News running order, 6 pm	BBC's place in running order and length (min./sec.)
4.16	(1) Birmingham pub 'bombers' given leave to appeal to Lords committee, plus interviews with family and solicitor	(2) 3.22
2.19	(2) NUPE demands investigation into private heart operation in Birmingham hospital for 4-month old child Queue jumping?	(3) 0.37
0.22	(3) Heart operation for child after three cancellations	—
0.25	(4) Inquest on soldier killed during training in Belize	—
0.21	(5) West Midlands unemployment up to 10%	(10) 0.16
2.6	(6) List of potentially lethal furniture on sale in Birmingham to be prepared	—

3.00	(7)	Report on inquiry into methane gas explosion which destroyed houses in Derbyshire; locals claim it's a cover-up	(1) 3.45
5.26	(8)	Mansfield man who has become TV personality in Finland (part 1, with part 2 tomorrow)	–
1.14	(9)	Weather	(15) 0.48

The BBC's *Midlands Today* carried six more items than Central News, but with a total length of 24 minutes, as against the 21 minutes of Central News (followed by 6 minutes of *Police Five*). Among the items not carried by Central News West were negotiations at Land-Rover to try to avoid the coming strike and scientists from Loughborough University testing a hovercraft to carry vaccine up the Yantse River. Central News East carried 15 items in 29 minutes (since it did not carry *Police Five*). It led with a death sentence in Greece on a Derbyshire man, whom it interviewed by telephone – an item also covered by *Midlands Today*, but without the interview. It finished with a colourful report on some Midlands firemen on holiday whose boat had capsized in bad weather, but they had rescued a windsurfer; that was carried the following evening both by Central News West and by *Midlands Today*.

Narrative, Thursday 18 February

The newsroom has been manned since before 8 am. The first news bulletin goes out at 9.25 am, with a single camera inside the newsroom. Some newsreaders like this, because it is convenient and atmospheric; others dislike it because of the background noise and the distracting movement of people behind the reader. The main 6 pm programme also goes out from a small area at one end of the newsroom – again convenient but also cramped, as is plain to perceptive viewers. At 9.35 am, the morning conference. Programme editor Owen Smith presides; acting news editor Peter Brookes goes through the day's prospects. The pub 'bombers' – lawyers at Appeal Court in Strand this morning, seeking leave to go to Lords; reporter there, with Birmingham crew, and lines booked from ITN at noon and 4.15 pm. Owen says they must get one of the lawyers for comment afterwards, and the family here because they are talking of going to the European Court. Liz Pike (reporter-presenter) is assigned to look after Birmingham end. Owen says 'it's the only good story today'.

Other possibilities: the Chief Constable of Staffordshire, appointed yesterday to conduct another inquiry into RUC 'shoot to kill' following Stalker, has refused all interviews. The newsdesk will persist in trying for him, and a profile is being prepared anyway. Owen is not enthusiastic: it's not a Midlands story. The hovercraft being displayed on lake at Exhibition Centre before going to Yangtse River will be covered; it is described at the conference as a military expedition, though it is actually medical relief. Kathy Alexander (reporter-presenter) is already there with crew. Furniture with fire danger: a 'hit list' is being prepared and will be launched today at 10.30 am, with demonstration burning which should give good pictures. (Owen: 'It's about the fourth time they've done it', but there's a 'new angle' in the phone hot-line being set up – it may make a lead for the 11.25 am bulletin.) More possibles are listed. Already there are seven news assignments for staff crew and four for sport today. Three events are being covered by the Stoke 'stringer' (man with video camera but low-quality sound) and commentary may be dubbed on afterwards.

Also discussed is a feature from Finland about a Mansfield man who has become a television star there. It was shot by a Central News crew in Finland for a sports assignment, to help cover the cost of going there. It could be used tonight, but if so the second half of it must be used tomorrow. Owen says that there looks like being room tonight, and tomorrow sport will be making heavy demands on facilities so the 'part two' could probably go then.

After the conference, news editor Peter says it is now his job to 'see it happens'. All the reporters and crews have bleepers or radio telephones for quick contact with any of them when away from the office.

At 10.55 am the result of the pub 'bombers'' appeal comes in, much earlier than expected. It is a complex ruling by which application may be made to the Law Lords for permission to make an appeal on a point of law. The Central News line in the 11.25 am bulletin will be that the lawyers have won 'a minor victory' in getting a preliminary hearing. For later in the day the reporter is now recording with his crew outside the Royal Courts in the Strand, and the tape will be sent up the line from ITN at 12 noon. Now the immediate problem is to locate the wife of one of the 'bombers' since she is the most likely person to be willing to talk. But her daughter is having a baby and she has gone to the hospital, so they may have to send the crew there. Liz Pike is working on that and looking for others who might comment.

At 11.15 am, the crew who were covering the hovercraft are back. Can they go with Liz to the Birmingham Six family and still get to their sports story by 12.30? Liz is still on the phone, so far unable to get confirmation that the wife is at the maternity hospital. She is reluctant to go without a crew because if she arrives by herself the family may say 'yes' and then back out when the camera arrives, so she sets off for the hospital with the crew.

Meanwhile Carol Proudlove, programme organiser, is talking to Central News East in Nottingham. They are covering the Derbyshire inquiry into the methane gas explosion from a rubbish tip which destroyed a house – something that was not on the Birmingham list, but it sounds a good story, looking at how this extraordinary explosion came about and who was to blame. Derby is common territory for East and West, so Nottingham will supply the West. Carol has already prepared a provisional running order and will provide a final one, with timings, at 3 pm. She has 'debriefed' the reporter who was at the hovercraft and has arranged the editing; enthusiasm for the story has grown since they discovered that the hovercraft is to carry vaccine for children, inland up the Yangtse.

At 11.45 am, a new story – not previously listed; a NUPE official who has seen the operations list at Birmingham Children's Hospital has rung, having noted that a private patient (a child) has been admitted to the hospital for an intensive care bed. He suggests that morally this is 'a scandal', with an operation taking place when others are being turned away. Reporter is seeking the surgeon for comment and will record the NUPE man only when the surgeon's view is known.

12.25 pm

Liz Pike is back. Mrs McIlkenny was not at the hospital, but Liz has found out that the new baby is her 14th grandchild. 1.10 pm, still no sign of Kate McIlkenny, but search continues.

2 pm

Consultant at children's hospital agrees to be interviewed about private patient. He is Babulal Sethia, much respected for his work in helping the Birmingham Children's Hospital. Haig Gordon (reporter-presenter) is going with crew; they will then go on to the NUPE man who raised the issue. Expected back about 4 pm. While Haig Gordon is away – and in case he calls in – a hypothetical discussion takes place at top end of newsroom. Owen puts questions:

'Is it stopping others? Did one kid jump the queue? Have we checked with COHSE and Royal College nurses? I can't believe someone's paid money for something they'd have had anyway'. Others reply that the consultant says there was no queue-jumping, and that the hospital won't give the patient's name. Beverley (who located Sethia and set up the interview); 'the nurses are not paid extra for private patients'.
Owen: 'the whole point is, they were using an intensive care bed'.
Simon (chief sub. and script writer): 'we don't want to blacken Sethia, do we? He's been the White Knight so far'.

3.15 pm

Simon is writing a new text for the 'bombers'. He is using the BBC news Ceefax as his source. But it is complicated.

Carol meanwhile has completed her running order, long before the required time of 3 pm. The computer makes quick changes easier. Two uncertainties remain: there is still no contact with Mrs McIlkenny, which affects the length of the 'bombers' story, and it is still unclear whether there was any impropriety about the child private patient at the children's hospital. But Carol says they can revise the plan up to 5.45 or later, simply dropping items from the bottom if necessary. Of the rest she says that there are no problems, apart from the video editing – for 'by definition you go out and shoot in the morning and spend the afternoon trying to get it on the screen'. Owen is thinking: the 'bombers', he says, do not take the affair much further 'but there's so much interest, we'll have to lead on it'; and he's not sure about the private patient story, because he won't know until the reporter gets back whether there was anything wrong or not. 'Sethia's not the sort to abuse the system', so Owen is worried about that story. 'So it's a normal day, really'.

4.30 pm

Haig Gordon is back. A round table discussion takes place with Haig,

Owen, Carol and Simon. How should the story be presented?
Extracts:

> *Haig*: 'It's not an argument about this particular case. It's about
> the basic principal of any private patient'.
> *Simon*: 'The union seem to have a cynical disregard for anyone
> who wants to become a private patient . . . Once a little kid
> becomes private they don't seem to want to know'.
> *Owen*: 'NUPE which is a major union and their head in the region
> covering this hospital – which itself is a massive story – is saying
> "We're cynical about this explanation, we want it investigated".
> We've got the consultant giving a reasonable defence . . . We don't
> want to go head over heels with shots of the dead babies, etc. etc.
> We do it dead straight and we don't lead off with it. A link
> straight into the interviews, drop in a covering shot of the
> hospital, not the ones of the little kids'.
> *Carol*: 'Does he explain at any point what the parents have got for
> their money?'
> *Owen*: 'My deep-throat who works there says that people only pay
> for two reasons. One is better service and the other is jumping the
> queue. He says there's no question of this baby jumping the queue
> . . . This baby has had an operation cancelled anyway. The only
> reason in this case is access to the surgeon, and you can choose
> your own surgeon'.
> *Carol*: 'I still don't think we've got to the bottom of it'.
> *Owen*: 'We've got a duty to give NUPE's view and we'll leave it up
> to people to decide themselves. The NUPE man says that even if
> he hasn't jumped the queue the public perception is bad'.
> *Simon*: 'We can balance it, because we know and people know
> Sethia's been trying to highlight the problem there'.
> *Owen*: 'So, OK. Do it dead straight, Sethia, NUPE, Sethia. And
> [to Carol, about the running order] keep it where it is'.

4.38 pm

Liz on phone to newsdesk. She has found Mrs McIlkenny at her
daughter's house, where she is looking after the previous baby. Where
is the crew? Lurid language from Peter when he hears crew are not
there. Car radio establishes that they have been stuck in traffic but will
be there within minutes. Liz says she will be back in time to be co-
presenter. (Haig would have had to do it if she wasn't.)

4.45 pm

Angry news editor rings Staffordshire police press office. Why has Chief Constable given interview to Press Association when Central were told yesterday and today there would be no interviews? Sergeant says it was not an interview but a statement.

4.55 pm

Carol is giving instructions for editing and 'voiceover' for a Bewdley [Worcestershire] story about 100-year-old's birthday party. The video crew could not get there because it was held back for Mrs McIlkenny; a single-man 'mute' video camera went instead. The item will therefore be short, with the voice commentary over the pictures; a pity, Carol says, because it was a nice story; but it may now be dropped because of the timings.

5.02 pm

Liz is on her way back, having interviewed Mrs McIlkenny. Owen is harassing Haig to get on with editing the hospital. Haig has been making calls to arrange an interview with the Home Secretary tomorrow, but says he has finished the hospital script. Owen says 'I believe Sethia', but of course they cannot say that in the programme.

5.28 pm

Liz back. Owen goes with Carol to supervise edit. Liz goes to make-up. Only half an hour until programme goes on air.

5.40 pm

Peter is briefing reporter for tomorrow morning's funeral of boy who died after a heart operation. He has done a deal with BBC to share facilities, thereby saving £250. (Such deals are exceptional, apart from Royal occasions, but the family had asked that only one camera be used.)

5.45 pm

ITN News on the newsroom monitor. Nobody is watching, so far as I can see. But the headlines indicate nothing that touches Midlands.

5.50 pm

In mini-studio at end of newsroom, the two presenters are in place for brief rehearsal. They are Bob Warman, a veteran at Central though he looks fresh, and Liz Pike who has been there 4 years but is about to move to London. Bob sits upright and speaks with quiet authority; he wears a dark suit, lightly striped shirt, and dark striped tie. Liz also adopts a serious but friendly look; she has fair, shoulder-length hair and is now wearing a plain V-necked coral sweater. During the programme we see very little of Bob or Liz, because the Central News style involves minimum emphasis on presenters.

5.53 pm

Rehearsing the headlines, which pack 3 items into 14 seconds and need exact timing.

5.58 pm

Lawyer who is to be interviewed in first item takes his place.

6.00 pm

On air.

Content Summary

The items finally included in the programme have already been listed, with their duration. Here is a little more detail.

- *Titles*
  These are fashionably acrobatic, with fast-moving computer graphics, symbolic of Central News interests.

- *Headlines*
  Voice over still mugshots of the Birmingham Six – 'Pub bombers' case gets one step nearer the Law Lords'. Then voiceover close-up of porch of children's hospital, with picture closing in further – 'Private operation at Birmingham Children's Hospital: a union says it's wrong'. Then clip of shaggy man looking at singer on tv-monitor, with voiceover – 'And the man from the Midlands who's

a tv favourite in Finland'. Then Bob Warman, in vision close up, introducing the first item.

– *The 'bombers'*
Bob Warman says that permission to take the appeal direct to the Lords has been refused but it can go to a preliminary hearing by the Lords Appeal Committee. Then reporter Stephen Cole outside the Royal Courts, giving more detail. It meant 'a glimmer of hope of freedom for the men and their families'. Next, Liz Pike's interview with McIlkenny, seen in close-up. She does not believe in British justice and is sure they will have to go to European Court of Human Rights. Public pressure, she says, has got them this far. Finally, back to Bob Warman in studio with the solicitor, Ivor Greffen, who says it is too early to celebrate. They have overcome one hurdle, but it will be midsummer before they know whether they can go further. The point of law is whether, with new facts, the judges or a jury should decide the case. He ends by saying that world opinion will force the issue into the open.

– *The hospital beds*
Introduced by Liz, who says that NUPE is calling for investigation of the operation on a baby as a private patient, using NHS facilities. Then to Haig Gordon's voice over a picture, in close up, of the hospital's operations list, identifying Babulal Sethia as the surgeon; and immediately into Mr Sethia saying 'there is absolutely no question of this child jumping a queue'. The child has been waiting for several weeks, in hospital; the medical priority was 'exactly the same' as for any other child in the hospital. The only gain for the parents was in access to the doctors 'out of hours'. The item then cuts directly into NUPE's John Dempsey, who says the public perception is 'how can a private patient manage to get into one of those beds when there are NHS patients waiting'. He says the union is 'cynical' about the explanation. Haig's voice follows, with a statement from the hospital administration that decisions on priorities are taken not by the surgeons alone but by the whole medical team. The item ends with the news of another baby who has been waiting 3 months but has had his operation today.

– *Other news items*
The inquest on the soldier accidentally shot on a firing range in Belize, from Bob, and the unemployment figures from Liz. Then

the longer item on the furniture that catches fire easily, with pictures of a burning settee and the reporter's voice saying that a recent Birmingham survey showed only six out of 46 shops were complying with law; next year the law is to be tightened and meanwhile 'trading standards' lists can be consulted. Next, Liz on the Derbyshire inquiry into the methane gas explosion – an inquiry which some people are calling a 'cover-up'. Angry residents say that fumes are still coming from the dump; and one, now living in a caravan, says she dare not go home. The county council leader says he understands the residents' frustration, but he seems unready to do anything more about it.

The programme then goes into the feature about the Midlands man in Finland and his success in television there. It is picturesque and pleasant, but a rather abrupt change after the painful story preceding it.

The only Midlands item carried on network news that night was the 'bombers'' appeal, and it was carried only by the BBC. Much of ITN's time was taken up by the Prime Minister, in an exclusive interview with Sir Alastair Burnet.

The geographical distribution of items is of interest. Figures are given for the 5 days 17–23 February, together with the comparable BBC *Midlands Today*:

Area	Central News No. of items and time (min./sec.)		BBC Midlands Today No. of items and time (min./sec.)	
General (mainly Birmingham)	14	23.36	14	30.04
South (Hereford, Worcester, Northants, S. Warwicks)	14	22.03	8	15.36
Birmingham	9½	14.27	12	12.08
Coventry area (incl. Warwick)	2	2.18	4	2.27
North West (Black Country, Shrewsbury, Stoke)	12½	22.07	18	10.58
North East (Burton, Leicester, Derby)*	3	7.34	7	13.53

Note:
* For Central News, these are covered primarily in the Nottingham programme.

Use of Language

On the use of language, it is worth noting the way reporters and sub-editors try to write scripts which will catch attention and yet be compact. Each of these three examples was about a quite complex event, and each was a primary item in Central News West on Thursday 18 January 1988.

– (*Headline*): 'The pub bombers' case gets one step nearer the Law Lords'.
– (*Text*): 'The six men convicted of the Birmingham pub bombings have been allowed to take their case another step further to the House of Lords Appeal Committee. Although they were refused permission to take their appeal directly to the Law Lords, the judge left the door open for further legal moves, and it means the case could still end up in the Lords. Stephen Cole reports'.

– (*Headline*): 'Private operations at Birmingham Children's Hospital: a Union says "it's wrong"'.
– (*Text*): 'The Health Service Union NUPE is calling for an investigation into a private heart operation carried out on a baby at Birmingham Children's Hospital. The Union says it was insensitive to use NHS facilities. But the consultant who carried out the operation and the hospital administration say the baby didn't jump the queue for treatment. Haig Gordon reports'.

– (*No headline*).
– (*Text*). 'A long-awaited report into a methane gas explosion which destroyed a bungalow in Derbyshire was published today. But already it's been called a cover-up and a whitewash by local people, and now they're planning to take their case to court, as Alan Taylor reports'.

Again, it can be seen that these were concise, free of needless adjectives, impartial and yet seeking to hold the attention of listeners.

Commentary

To stay strictly with hard news, or to mellow the diet with some homely fare? That is a dilemma for the early evening regional programmes. Another, especially in the Midlands, is how to satisfy all the diverse communities with little interest in each other – the Black country to the north-west, Birmingham itself, wealthy South Warwickshire, Gloucester and others.

As it happened, Thursday 18 February illustrated both dilemmas. There were 3 hard news stories which had to be covered because of their scale and significance, and some smaller ones. For Central News West that left little time for anything else, since the Finland story and *Police Five* had to be carried. As a result, nothing of a lighter or more homely character could go in – even supposing it had been wanted, for there has been pressure from the IBA to stay with hard news. Worse, only one of the 7 items carried that day was from outside Birmingham.

Owen Smith at the end of transmission said the programme had been too short to 'have to the right feeling'. There had been barely 14 minutes of reporting. He had no misgivings about the main elements – the Law Lords had been 'talking heads' but the studio interview had gone well, and the controversy at the children's hospital had been covered 'extremely fairly'. Those were judgements with which I fully agreed. The complexities of the Lords appeal procedure had been neatly unravelled, and Mrs McIlkenny had been articulate though predictable in her criticism of British justice. The hospital controversy had been explored and defused, thanks both to the readiness of the surgeon to reply to questions openly and to the balance of the editing. The NUPE official looked niggardly by the end, but he was given the last word (contrary to Owen's earlier instructions) and undid his own case.

3 short items followed, then the lethal furniture and finally the methane gas explosion. The furniture was of public importance because of the listing of unsafe products though mostly the story was old. The methane explosion was an extraordinary story, well worth its place, and with a strong human element in the anguish of people who were not to receive compensation for their damaged or wrecked homes. It might be criticised for intrusion on personal grief, since it ended with several seconds of a weeping woman who said she could never go back to her home; but most viewers must have felt sympathy for her and amazement at the council's unwillingness to help. Derbyshire County Council may have regarded it as hostile in its presentation, but they appeared to be shrugging off all responsibility. The BBC's *Midlands Today* led with that event, putting the Law Lords

second. For Central News, although seventh in the running order, it was the first item based outside Birmingham.

Because that was the only non-Birmingham item in the news and the only one with a strong human element, it was the more unfortunate that the Bewdley birthday party and the Loughborough–Yangtse vaccine hovercraft were both eliminated. If either the Finland feature or the *Police Five* had been absent, both would have got in – for the programme would have been closer to its normal 24 to 27 minutes. But Bewdley ranked low because it had been shot by a 'mute' camera with only background sound, while the hovercraft was deemed to be visually dull. (The BBC's version included dramatic library pictures of the rapids in the Upper Yangtse.) The Central News decisions are therefore understandable, and it must be admitted that the Midlands tv. man in Finland was theatrical, musical and unusual, so he provided a lighter element.

The geographical imbalance that day, with only one news item from outside Birmingham, was not typical. As we have seen earlier, both the Black Country of the North-West and the wealthy south (with Worcester, Gloucester and Oxfordshire) are fairly well served. Friends in Worcester and Malvern complained that Central News was too 'Brummy', but the figures do not bear this out. The surprise in the week's figures is the poor showing of the Coventry area and the North-East (Leicester and northwards). They were treated almost as if Central News West was willing to look north, west and south but not to the east, close as Coventry and Leicester are to Birmingham.

The issue of hard news v. lighter and more homely fare is to some extent related to the geographical problem. It seems easier to generate the lighter and more human stories from outside Birmingham than from within the metropolis, though there is no evident reason why that should be so. Pressure from the IBA has been a factor in giving preference to hard news in recent years – pressure generated because some regional news magazines tended to degenerate in their second half into poorly produced entertainment. The stiffening was welcome, but something may have been lost.

In Central News West, taking the whole week, there were some attractive lighter elements – but also one that was of questionable value. Among the attractive lighter items were one from within the Ashmolean Museum in Oxford, one from Stratford about a failing organ in the church where Shakespeare is buried, another from Stratford on the steam-driven mini-trains, and the preview from

Herefordshire (with elephants) of Ian Botham's coming trek across the Alps. The 'human' elements were fewer but often good – among them the reactions of Birmingham and Walsall people to a Scottish university survey saying that those were among the worst British towns in which to live, and the firemen planning to sail round Britain in their holidays, having been wrecked last year but having rescued a windsurfer in the storm. The 'light' element which I personally found embarrassing was about a Black Country 'Clint Eastwood': it seemed both silly and to some extent glorifying guns. But others who saw it said it was harmless and amusing.

Central News West provides a strong and efficient diet of hard news. There is little depth to its items, but that can be found to some extent in Central's political programme *Central Lobby* on Thursday evenings and sometimes in its Friday evening *Central Weekend* (on occasions running to a 90-minute debate). Its programmes are well prepared and free from bias, apart from the inevitable 'socio-centralism' of middle-ground broadcasting. Central's biggest problem lies in the disparity and diversity of its huge region, and perhaps in preoccupation with their UK network programmes among the higher management.

People

Liz Pike
From school, though offered place at Bristol University, direct to NCTJ pre-entry journalism course at Cardiff. Then three years with West London local papers. Next to BBC radio news, London, as subeditor; then reporter, BBC R. Medway. From 1982 with Central Television. From mid-1988 with Thames tv. as sole presenter of *Reporting London*, weekly Current Affairs show.

Carol Proudlove
London University, BSc Sociology, 1971. Temping, London, 1971–5. ILR R. Trent, community liaison officer and trainee reporter, 1978. BBC R. Stoke, reporter 1978–81. BBC Radio News, London, 1981–3. BBC Pebble Mill, television, as regional journalist, 1983–7; also periods of producing half-hour current affairs documentaries. 1987, to Central News.

Robert Warman
Walsall Observer, 1967. Chief reporter, *Sutton Coldfield News*, 1968.

Reporter, *Birmingham Evening Mail*, 1969. News producer, BBC Radio, Birmingham, 1971. Reporter-presenter, ATV Network, 1973. Reporter-presenter, YTV, 1976. Freelance presenter, ATV, Southern tv., and Central tv., 1978. Founding partner of tv. production company 1984. Presenter, Central News and other programmes, 1988.

13 Crisis in the Hospitals: *Midlands Today*, 22 February 1988

Content comparison

First, a listing of what *Midlands Today* carried on that Monday, together with the content of Central News. Then the day's activity in the newsroom, leading to transmission at 6.35 pm.

BBC time (min./sec.)	BBC running order		Central News place in running order and time (min./sec.)
2.26	(1)	Land-Rover strike to continue	(3) 3.18
0.30	(2)	700 on strike at Shropshire poultry farm	—
0.16	(3)	Staffordshire textile plant at standstill	—
2.16	(4)	Row over documents found in street with detail of people without tv. licences (Birmingham)	—
2.34	(5)	Inquiry into suspension of doctor on full pay for several years (Derby)	—
—		(Brief headlines and titles to mark splitting of E. Midlands and W. Midlands transmissions)	—
0.22	(6)	W. Midlands police hold 11 people over murder of man (Birmingham)	(5) 0.28

114

0.23	(7)	Public schoolboy from Malvern admits robbery of London taxi driver	—	
0.27	(8)	Listed building that suffered arson attack to be knocked down (Gloucester)	(4)	0.22
0.25	(9)	Staffordshire army sergeant appeals against conviction for bullying recruits	—	
0.24	(10)	Liver transplant on 7-month-old baby from Staffordshire (Birmingham hospital)	—	
0.15	(11)	Coventry magistrates court praised for helpfulness to newspapers	—	
0.14	(12)	Seven Black Country boys accused of making petrol bombs; bailed	—	
0.46	(13)	62 youngsters from Black Country home after charity walk from Manchester	—	
0.27	(14)	W. Mercia police to charge Shrewsbury town player	—	
0.10	(15)	Escape of man charged with murder on way from Telford court to Shrewsbury prison	—	
—		(Pause for link again with E. Midlands)	—	
2.48	(16)	Gloucester firemen build mini-fire engine; to be put on market for other brigades to buy	(11)	1.38
4.26	(17)	Sport	(13)	9.20
0.38	(18)	Weather	(15)	0.52

The first item on Central News was about a disagreement between the parents of the boy who died after a heart operation, Matthew Collier, and the vicar who had preached the sermon at his funeral on Friday. The parents thought it was too political. *Midlands Today* decided not to cover it, as we shall hear. The second item on Central News was on Birmingham health authority deciding to hold a formal investigation into the private heart operation in the previous week, though it said that the child's need for an early operation was beyond doubt. The difference of style and content between the BBC programme and the Central News' on this day is immediately evident, with many more short news items in *Midlands Today*. Over the week as a whole *Midlands Today* carried 74 items, not counting Weather or Sport, while Central News West carried 58. With the major stories Central News on the whole gave rather more of the background.

Narrative, Monday 22 February 1988

The television newsroom has been manned since 5.30 am, but reporter Richard Phillips has been at the gates of Land-Rover in Solihull since just before 5.30. He is joined by a video crew at 5.40. He knew only at 10 pm last night that he was to cover the story both for BBC network and for Midlands programmes. A call from *Breakfast Time* in London at 10 pm told him that they needed a report for the 7 am bulletin. It could well be the lead story (and it was). This was the start of the first strike at Land-Rover in over 7 years. Last night just after 10 pm he had rung two Union convenors to find out what they expected this morning.

With the crew there, he told me afterwards, he checked with the gate that it would be all right to film from the forecourt of the plant. He would also film among the pickets, of course, but he had to have consent to go inside the gates for some of the shots. The crew car had a radio telephone, so he rang London direct to say that it was all OK. By 6 am the pickets had begun to arrive, though even between 7 and 8 am they had never numbered much more than 300.

The first few whom he approached were 'not friendly'. But before long he got 'three excellent interviews – more than enough'. What had he been wearing, I asked, remembering reporters' troubles during the 1984–5 coal dispute. A tweedy overcoat, he said, and a scarf. So he looked middle class? Not really, he replied, because the coat had a black velvet collar. So upper middle or City professional?

It led to a lot of remarks. 'Oh, look, here's a solicitor'. I could say 'No, it's only the coat'. That was a plus, really, so the conversation started. I don't think if I'd been dressed in something downmarket it would have done any good. I got what I wanted.

The cameraman had been immediately behind him, with the camera just over Richard's shoulder while they recorded brief comments.

2 despatch riders are at hand, to take tapes back at 40 or 45 minute intervals. The first leaves at 6.30 am with the interviews, to be at Pebble Mill by 6.50. It is transmitted immediately to London, with a 'track' (voice over pictures) and a piece to camera. *Breakfast Time* will have 5 minutes to edit it, taking the bits they want, and it will be on air at 7 am – as it was, an item of about 1½ minutes after the headlines. As soon as the despatch rider left at 6.30 am Richard again phoned London to tell them that the cassette was on its way and to say what was on it; also to get further instructions. They say they want a different piece for 8 am; so Richard records more. 'Although nothing is happening, you have to give the impression that something *is* happening'. He sends off the second despatch rider at 7.15 am, in good time for the 8 am news.

London – 'news intake' – then wants yet another version for 9 am. So that is recorded, with some vox pops among the pickets, and it goes off at 8.15. But there is a hitch: wrongly, a van has been sent instead of a motorcyclist, and the van gets stuck in rush hour traffic. Instead of 15 to 18 minutes, it takes nearly 40. London news intake is annoyed and says it arrived too late to edit.

With nothing much happening, at 9.25 Richard rings Pebble Mill to say he is coming back. No objections. ITN is still at the plant's gates 'but someone has to pull out first'. They didn't arrive until long after the BBC crew anyway. Richard wants time to put together 'a considered item' for the network 1 pm news, and then a 'deeper' report for *Midlands Today* at 6.35 pm. He may come back to Solihull in the afternoon if anything is moving, or to get some shots at dusk.

At Pebble Mill, 5.30 am

Reporter Graham Simmons and reporter-presenter Kathy Rochford have arrived. Graham was in late the previous evening, writing short news items in readiness for this morning, and since 5.30 am he has been bringing them up to date, dealing with the logistics of feeding tape to London, making the routine calls to police and others. Two stories have come in, by standing arrangements, from BBC local radio – one from R. WM and one from R. Nottingham – and both have been used from 7.15 am onwards. Kathy meanwhile has checked the texts for her bulletins. She will put herself into transmission from a tiny studio, on cue from a London countdown, and at 6.45 am she is in that studio to check with the engineers and others that everything is working. 'Routine', she says, 'but it takes time'. Only stills can be used, not live video, because she has to push all the buttons herself – the only help coming from someone elsewhere operating the caption generator.

Morning conference, 9.30 am

Today it is chaired by Peter Hiscock, who is producing tonight's programme. There is a sound hook-up with Nottingham, so that East and West can both hear what the other is planning. The main items expected today:

– Land-Rover, likely to be the day's biggest event.
– Everest, a Birmingham climber is off to the North-East ridge, hitherto unclimbed.
– Charity walk, schoolboys and girls, age 12 to 18, completing their walk from Manchester.
– Story from R. WM: a pile of documents about unpaid tv. licence fees has been found blowing about a Birmingham street. There are personal details that should not be there. It will be on Ed Doolan show at noon. Alan Towers (one of the regular *Midlands Today* presenters for past 8 years for half his time and contract reporter for other half) is asked to follow it up.
– Court case (civil) being brought by a woman against a golf club which expelled her; a lively story, but her lawyers have advised her to say nothing to *Midlands Today* or others.
– Sport, quite a lot, including Cup draw.
– Nurses at Birmingham Children's Hospital: Clare Harrison, reporter specialising in NHS and related matters, has rung to say there may be an announcement later today of cash for two extra beds at the hospital. There has been a huge response to appeal for extra nurses.
– A tunnel link with the M40.
– The Gloucester firemen who have built their own design of fire-engine, cheaper and quicker. (BBC Bristol covering?)

And from Nottingham, a £10 million superstore being opened in an area where there are already five; and the case of a doctor, suspended on full pay (£30 000) for several years, who wants to get back to work.

A question is raised about the Birmingham girls 'sold' into marriage in Yemen. The Home Office says that they cannot bring their 'husbands' with them if they wish to return, but if they seek divorce the Yemenis will not let them bring their children. This development was in the Sunday papers: is it worth following up? There is little enthusiasm for it. Other possibilities are also discussed.

At 10 am, Richard Phillips is back from Land-Rover. He does not expect much more to happen today. But he will stay with Land-Rover until 6 pm – a very long day.

The morning unfolds

At 10.10 am, early reporter Graham and producer Peter in conversation. There has been a call from Notts police: they have a video of three girls with AIDS. Questions: What's new? Are they the same three who were on BBC 2's *Split Screen* a year ago? What are Notts police trying to do? Graham is asked to ring BBC in Nottingham, suggesting they ring Vice Squad. There is an impression that it's being put up to scare prostitutes. At 10.25 am, news intake in London on phone complaining about late arrival of the last of the Land-Rover tapes. Graham says it went down to London at 8.55, and it could have been used at 9 am if London had had an editor ready, but they didn't. Peter says it's better not to ruffle London by saying so, because they are paying most of the Land-Rover costs today. That means that *Midlands Today* may hire an extra freelance crew today if they need to, which otherwise they could not afford.

At 10.40, Alan Towers is preparing for the tv. licence story from R. WM. The radio station got on to it because a listener telephoned to tell them. She is to be on Ed Doolan's programme at 12, with the person who found the documents and someone who is named in them – though she will probably be anonymous. The kind of detail in the documents is 'Mrs X, husband works away in Somerset; she says she thought he had paid'. Dates of birth and other details are on the forms. The Post Office is embarrassed and stalling.

At 11.20 am, producer Peter says he has eliminated two potential items. The Nottingham prostitutes with AIDS turns out to be a 'rehash' of an old story. And the 'five superstores within five miles' proves to be only three, within 15 miles. So that is dropped. At Land-Rover, all seems quiet.

At 11.30 am, a call from the London office of one of the US big three, NBC. They want the Land Rover tapes – two versions, one with Richard's commentary and one with mute sound track, so that their man in London can dub on his own commentary. Also confirmation from BBC network news in London that they will want a new Land-Rover piece after 6 pm. They want it by mid-afternoon while there is still time to get extra shots if needed.

11.45 am

Clare Harrison, the NHS specialist, is in. She insists that she is not a specialist – only a regional journalist who does her shifts as a sub-editor (she is on late duty today) and as a reporter. She happens to have covered many hospital and NHS stories in the past 9 months and thus to have developed good contacts. That was how she heard this morning about the funds for the two intensive care beds at the Children's Hospital – though the announcement is likely to be delayed until later in the week.

At 12.45 pm, producer Peter sums up the prospects. Land-Rover is still the obvious lead. A crew have gone to a Smallheath (Birmingham) pub where a man was murdered on Saturday night. Otherwise it's all much as before.

At 1pm, the BBC national news has dropped the Land Rover item to sixth place. Gorbachev meeting the US Secretary of State is first; Richard's Land-Rover report gets 1.20.

Adjustments in the Afternoon

At 1.50, another industrial story – 700 workers go on strike at a poultry processing plant in Shropshire. Clare is asked to prepare a 45 second script.

At 2 pm, the afternoon conference with producer Peter again in the chair. (Roy Saatchi as Editor, News would normally chair one or both of the conferences, but he is taken up with other affairs today.) Tonight's presenters are here – Kay Alexander, who is regularly in this role, and Brian Conway frequently.

Peter goes quickly through the provisional running order, saying how the items are to be linked. Kay and Brian will write some of the links afterwards, while sub-editors write others. For both the presenters it is important to know as much as possible about the programme content, especially because of late changes or other last-minute problems. Kay, in answer to me after the conference, says this:

Don't forget that tonight we are Mr and Mrs BBC in the Midlands. People like to sit at home and say 'oh, it's Brian and Kay tonight' or 'it's Alan and Kathy'. They like to know who their people are – who is giving them the news. That persona is important. It's like someone conducting an orchestra . . . You could probably put a computer or robot on the screen, but the personal touch is everything. And, quite honestly, with a live programme where things can go wrong or reports can come in a bit longer or a bit shorter than was originally said, you need a person to keep the audience up to date, to get the programme in on time and out on time, and to give the audience that personal feeling.

As to the running order, Land-Rover stays at the top. 'The most significant story', Peter says. The tv.-licence story, with the papers dropped in a street by a private investigator, is also coming out well. Nottingham is offering the story of the Derby consultant suspended for nearly 6 years on full pay, which is worth running for East and West. (The Notts reporter comes in on the voice link, saying he is due in Derby at 3 pm, should be back at 4.30, and will put the item through to Birmingham at 5.30.)

After the consultant, East and West will each have $3\frac{1}{2}$ minutes for local news (the 'opt outs'). Birmingham hopes to get 7 or 8 short items into that time; Nottingham at present is planning 4. The conference ends with a technical discussion with the director on graphics, captions, seating and other matters. Getting the technicalities right is vital and time consuming.

At 2.45, another consultation with Nottingham. Two men have died at a swimming pool in south Derbyshire. Should the crew on its way to the Derby doctor be diverted? Peter says 'no', and is glad 25 minutes later when he hears that there are no exceptional aspects. One man drowned and the other had a heart attack afterwards. 'A rather tragic happening', he says, but with no implications.

At 3.30, the Environment Minister has decided that the Listed Building in Gloucester harbour, badly damaged by fire last year, can be demolished. By coincidence, 2 young men are in court in Gloucester today charged with starting the fire. That strengthens that story. At 4.25, a 7-month-old baby has had a liver transplant – the youngest ever, it is said. Peter asks Clare for her opinion: is it new? Clare rings someone at the Health Authority, who confirms it. So she says 'yes' to Peter: it is pioneering work. It will make a half-minute item. Thus the list develops, with 2 more short stories accepted in the last hour before transmission and one rejected. By 5.30 Peter has seen and approved every item, though tightening some texts. In studio he is about to record in studio and opening sequence, which is complex. He says it has been 'a quiet night'.

At 6 pm, Central News is monitored in the newsroom. It is leading with the row over the sermon at Matthew Collier's funeral on Friday. Peter had rejected that earlier in the day, believing that with the sadness of the Collier story – the child had never had much chance of survival – it was better to set this dispute aside. Nothing else in Central News draws comment. The BBC's 6 pm national news is also being watched, in case its headlines or opening pictures duplicate those in *Midlands Today*. They do not.

There is a little flurry 12 minutes before transmission, when it seems that Birmingham police are about to make a statement about the city-centre murder: if it comes, the teleprompt text can be changed while the programme is on air since it is controlled electronically from the newsroom. But the police, although telephoned at 10-minute intervals, are still not ready.

6.15 pm

rehearsals in studio and gallery.

6.28 pm

Peter still revising one or two texts, to improve the wording.

6.35 pm

On air.

Content summary

– *Titles*

Almost as acrobatic as Central News': a vortex with the West Midlands 'logo'.

– *Headlines*

The presenters are behind a snake-shaped curving red desk with a blue strip along its front. (It may sound dreadful, but visually the curved desk works well for varied shots; the colour is another matter.) Then Kay Alexander in semi-close-up, against a light blue background; a relief. The headlines are longer than Central News', lasting 32 seconds.

– *Style*
Kay is wearing a v-necked black jacket with silver embroidery and black revers. No jewellery except pearl earrings. Simply arranged fair hair to short of shoulders, with soft fringe. Serious demeanour at this stage; smiles come later.

Brian in plain dark grey suit, striped black and white shirt, grey flecked tie. Neatly cut brown hair. Pleasant, well groomed, clean image. Also serious at this stage, smiles later.

– *Land-Rover strike*
Kay in vision with 'Land-Rover' logo behind left shoulder. She says 6000 on strike, their union say they will stay out until Land-Rover improves its pay offer. Management say they are offering 14% over two years (inset picture of pickets, above bold text 'Management say: 14%'); union says in real terms it's only 8% (extra line added to text 'Union say: 8%'). Kay then introduces Richard Phillips' report on 'first strike in seven years'. Pictures of pickets arriving in dark early morning. Brief interview with T & G chief negotiator, lit in close-up against dark morning background: he says 'ball is in the management's court' and union ready to meet them at any time.

Then daylight pictures, over commentary on pickets trying to persuade office workers to give support – 'some gave it' (picture of girls in van, waving as they turn back, pickets cheering). Pictures of managing director arriving in a Land-Rover: he turns away to use another entry. Next, shots of traffic jams 'at one stage more than a mile long'. Interviews with workers, seen eyelevel in mid close-up. 'We're solid', 'I'm confident we'll get a better deal', 'It will be a long dispute', 'Jaguar are on 25% basic more than us'. Later shots with only a few pickets present. Comment that components companies in the Midlands will feel the effects within a week. Length, 2.26.

Central News, though placing this item third, gave it 3.18. It gives more background, including the company's 'turn round' from loss to profit in 1986. Pretax profits of £3 million were achieved in that year, and £15 million are projected for 1987. The unions (Central News says) see this as a much bigger cake; the company see it as 'only a very small slice' compared with turnover which was £460 million in 1986 and £500 million in 1987. Current thinking in the industry, it is said, considers that profits of at least £50 million are needed before the company will have 'a sound financial footing'. A T&G spokesman is seen saying that they would all like to see higher profits but the company can afford to pay more now. Central News, however, has no early morning pictures and none after most of the pickets have gone.

– *The tv. licence documents*

Alan Towers on pavement of busy street, first in medium long shot and then close-up. The forms were found in a street east of the city centre. For people said not to have paid their tv. licences the forms give name and address, date of birth, date tv. set installed, date of first use without a licence, set owner, personal circumstances (income good, fair or poor), occupation, and 'comments made by person interviewed'. Examples of the last – 'husband works away in Somerset', 'single parent family', 'divorced from wife'. Then a short statement from tv. licence records office in London saying they know of no documents being missing, but if they are 'an exhaustive inquiry will be held'.

Then interview with housewife who is named on one form. She is identified (with her consent) and seen in close-up. She fears burglary as a result of scattered forms. A council road sweeper then describes how he found some forms blowing down the street and more further up the street.

This is an exclusively BBC item, derived from R. WM, as we have already seen. Alan Towers, speaking to me afterwards, says he thought it right to disclose 'the big brother element'. But, he said, many viewers would have no sympathy with those who did not pay for a licence. He had reported without drawing any conclusion in the item.

– *Other items*

Most were short, as noted at the beginning of this section. The Derby micro-biologist suspended in June 1982 on full pay after a disagreement with the administration. The total cost to the health service, including legal fees, now amounts of £610,000; a great waste of public money, he argues, and he still wants his job back. One of the health Ministers has now promised an inquiry. The only other item of any length comes last – the Gloucester firemen who have designed and built their smaller, cheaper and faster fire-engine. They want to make more and sell them to other fire brigades. As demonstrated, it looks a good machine.

– *Editorial decisions*

A final comment from Peter Hiscocks on two of the main items.

To Land-Rover: 'It's not just another strike. It matters because it's large scale. It's the worst we've had in the whole of our region for at least a year. The previous large one was at Jaguar, a short affair. This looks as if it might be longterm. There are lots of political implications. People are saying that the Government is waving a stick over Land Rover, saying "don't give in". It is also about the motor industry which has been extremely important in the Midlands, and people are very worried that the motor industry may be slipping away into Japanese or American hands ... It's also important because if we have 6000 people on strike, they have families – we're probably talking about 24 000 people directly affected'.

And on the Derby consultant: 'For one reason and another, health stories are extremely important in this part of the country. The public perception is that people are dying because of health cuts. We have done our best to get the record straight on that. It's a difficult one to get at. Only in one case has there been any accusation that a person has died as a result of health cuts – that was a child that had to be moved from Birmingham Children's Hospital to Liverpool because they couldn't look after the aftercare of that child, and the child died in the ambulance on the way to Liverpool ... This consultant was suspended on full pay while some irregularity was investigated. He's been paid nearly £200 000 for staying at home. It's another angle on a very long-running story'.

The Hospitals and the NHS

Clare Harrison's role in uncovering the cash crisis in the hospitals and the consequent closing of beds has already been mentioned. Another journalist at Pebble Mill also played a significant part – producer Peter Hiscocks. In the autumn of 1987, as the controversy over hospital finance was gaining momentum in the Midlands, he produced a 40-minute programme 'Hospitals in Crisis'. And, more important, his wife had a baby with a serious heart problem. She (the baby) went on the waiting list at Birmingham Children's Hospital. As a result, Peter had the unique experience of seeing the story from both sides. He saw the hospital crisis from the inside but, as he says, then had to 'pull back' from it.

For Clare Harrison, the story started not in the Birmingham Children's Hospital, which became national news later, but at the Queen Elizabeth in the summer of 1987. The oncology department had to close beds and then developed a waiting list, which it had never had before. At that time, Clare says, she had no sense that it would become part of a national debate or a long-running national story. 'It was just one hospital with one problem'. But cancer cases were involved, and a consultant said 'I have a patient who will be dead in a matter of weeks and I've been told he can't be treated'. It was 'a highly emotive story'. *Midlands Today* took it; network news accepted it as a single story but were not interested in any follow up.

Then there were the first of the Birmingham Children's Hospital cases which were more dramatic, with names and babies. These came in the autumn, when *Midlands Today* ran the story of William Pound on 3 consecutive days, at one point with his father weeping on camera. The father was a very articulate man, and when the baby got his operation, after the delays and cancellations, it was a success. William Pound did well. The reporting on *Midlands Today* made a big impact on people in the Midlands, but was still not national news.

As a local reporter, Clare says, it was difficult to know where the controversy began. She had always been aware that things were happening in Manchester, but she did not know who was first. After William Pound she went back to the Queen Elizabeth and found that things were much worse. Twenty people every month were dying needlessly – cancer patients who would have been in hospital in any other region. They were dying because of lack of resources, and the doctors showed her the names. 'It seemed to me more profoundly horrific than what was happening at the children's hospitals', she said, but at first she could not interest anyone in it. 'Once the children's hospital had become the focus of debate, you couldn't interest anyone in another hospital'.

Again, however, the 40-minute programme produced by Peter Hiscocks had impact. It explored the background to the crisis – why there were empty beds, why some of the hospitals were critically understaffed, and how the new medical technologies had made possible the treatment of maladies which were killers a few years earlier. It was concise and low-keyed at the start but quickly grew into a fierce but orderly debate between medical specialists, mostly professors, on one side and the health administrators and politicians. One of the most devastating critics, however, was the maverick Conservative MP Anthony Beaumont Dark, who said it was 'folly' to have the best balanced budget but refuse to find £12 million to save lives in the West Midlands. No less criticial was Professor Sir Geoffrey Slaney, past president of the Royal College of Surgeons, who said that Britain was maintaining high standards of treatment but denying treatment to many patients. We had been forced into 'health care rationing'. That was happening in other countries, too, but Parliament did not understand that the UK had 'the most under resourced health service in the Western world'.

Two or three weeks after William Pound came the case of David Barber. It was different because David's parents took legal action when his operation was again postponed in October. According to Clare, 'the Children's Hospital became a very sexy story, if you want to call it that. You'd got children rather than adults and you were talking about threatened lives'. That became a national story, taken by *Midlands Today* and network news. But because the children's hospital was the focus of debate 'you couldn't shift anyone into another hospital'. She believed that the five Birmingham distrists were not the most under resourced. The Bromsgrove and Redditch district had a fast growing population and its health resources had not kept pace. It was hard to get anything about that on to *Midlands Today* and impossible to get it on to network. 'The editorial judgements seemed arbitrary. The children's hospital is easy – everybody knows about it. Anywhere else you've got to start from scratch'.

But then the children's hospital became such an 'overkill' that viewers were thought to be bored. The story had become such a snowball that it was working against further reporting. *Midlands Today* did try to cover other events without taking up names, but that was difficult. Then the Matthew Collier story developed in January and that again became news. He died, however, after 5 weeks in intensive care.

Looking back, Peter Hiscocks believes that *Midlands Today* covered the hospital crisis 'honestly'. As someone with an inside view, because his baby was on the list at the children's hospital, he thought that there were times when the perceptions of journalists were wrong. They were sometimes 'manipulated' by the surgeons for their own ends. The core of the controversy was that with new medical technology they could do operations that they could not do 2 years earlier, and the money could not catch up with the technology. The Government's projection of resources was years behind. The nurses and ordinary hospital doctors were 'in the middle of a tug of war', Peter said, while consultants competed with each other for the limited funds.

He is critical also of media treatment of the case of Matthew Collier. *Midlands Today* at first decided – rightly, in Peter's view – not to cover the case because there seemed to be so little chance of a successful operation. But when the national newspaper took up the story, BBC network news in London asked for material. They said that with the nationals making a lot of it, they could not be left out. So the *Midlands Today* team went to work on it. One consequence of the massive national publicity, however, was that the parents began to believe that their child could and would be cured. That was part of the tragedy.

Of her own part, Clare says that when you have been covering an event for 2 or 3 weeks you acquire some expertise. 'You develop contacts and people call you, so you are the first to know'. Since Roy Saatchi had recently come as Editor, News, reporters had been encouraged to follow stories through instead of just being 'at the whim of the rota'. 'It suits me', Clare comments.

> You get more satisfaction, and you believe in yourself as well. It's not just because you acquire an authority on screen. You have greater confidence in yourself – because you know you can understand all the intricacies of the story.

On the day of Matthew Collier's operation, *Midlands Today* set up a live OB (Outside Broadcast) inside the hospital. Because Clare knew all the people at the hospital, she was able to make it go very smoothly. They gave the BBC permission to set up the OB inside the hospital, while Central Television had to do theirs from the steps outside. Matthew's doctor came to do a live interview into *Midlands Today* at 6.35 pm. Although BBC network news had been offered an interview from the hospital for 6 pm, 'they felt they had other things to do'. ITN, however, filmed Clare interviewing the doctor: it went out to the whole country in *News at Ten*. But *Midlands Today*, Clare says, 'had got in first'.

A final comment from Peter Hiscocks: 'sick children make stunning television, but I'm not sure it helps rational argument'.

THE FAMOUS GROUSE

THE SCOTSMAN

LEGGE 5-LEVER SECURITY LOCKS
LEGGE
LOCK MAKERS SINCE 1881

No. 45,158 • Friday, May 27, 1988 Price 25p

Two guilty of rioting and hostage-taking at Peterhead

TWO of the three accused in the Peterhead Prison siege trial were convicted yesterday of mobbing and rioting, assault and taking a prison officer hostage.

The jury at the High Court at Peterhead found Samuel Ralston and Douglas Mathewson guilty of being part of the mob which took over the jail's D Hall in September last year. They were also found guilty of assaulting hostage officers, Mr Bill Florence and Mr Jackie Stuart, and placing them in fear of their lives.

Ralston was also found guilty of continuing to detain Mr Stuart against his will and forcing him on to the jail's roof to the danger of his life. He was further found guilty of assaulting firemen by throwing slates at them.

Ralston and Mathewson will be sentenced today.

The third accused, Graham Duncan, was found not guilty of mobbing and rioting and removed from the dock.

Ralston's mother was in court and as he was being led away, he said to her: "I've been wrongfully convicted again, ma, that's nothing unusual. There's a lot of innocent men in jail."

Mathewson directed his comments to the jury. He said: "Nae wonder you're looking away, you hillbillies. You have thrown my life away."

In his final address, Mr Duncan Antonio, for Mathewson, suggested to the jury that some of the evidence given by hostage officer, Mr Jackie Stuart, was unsafe.

He drew the jury's attention to evidence given by Det Sgt Michael Barron who interviewed Mr Stuart after the siege. "Mr Stuart was able to name those who had assaulted him, but at no time did he mention Mr Mathewson.

"How can he come here eight months later and be categorical in his identification? It's extremely odd and very puzzling.

"Mr Stuart was not in a position to identify Mr Mathewson days after the incident and he is not able to identify him now."

He invited the jury to examine the threads of the Crown case against Mathewson. "You will find that it is threadbare and I ask you to acquit him."

In his charge to the jury, Lord Cowie said they should not be influenced by the publicity surrounding the trial or even by publicity of incidents in other prisons.

He drew the jury's attention, in particular, to publicity "which may in any view have cast aspersions on the truth or reliability of the accused."

He told the jury they should not be influenced by outbursts from the dock or evidence given about prison conditions. "This is not a public inquiry and the accusations which you may have heard are a one-sided account."

He also told the jury that how the prison authorities handled the incident was not a matter for it, in particular how the siege was brought to an end. He said evidence given on that was wholly irrelevant. He told members they should have no prejudice towards the accused because they were prisoners. "For the purpose of this trial they are innocent and remain so until the Crown satisfies you, if they can, of their guilt."

THE DAY THE ROOF CAME OFF — Page 13

TODAY

Can Botham bounce back?
Ian Botham yesterday went into hospital for his "bloody sore" back. Bryan Christie assesses his chances of making a comeback. Page 11

Poetry in motion
A new map guides poetry lovers round Edinburgh. But why is it that the capital so seldom inspires its poets to produce their finest work? Page 13

IN YOUR INTEREST
Eveline Hunter examines the pros and cons of investing in offshore funds following this year's Budget tax changes. Page 21

WIN AN AUSTRALIAN HOLIDAY
Page 10

TOMORROW

Sketches of the road
In tomorrow's colour *Weekend Scotsman* Alexander Maitland takes to the road to rediscover his favourite private places in Perthshire. And in the first of a new series on outdoor activity sports, Eleanor Ironside gets to grips with mountain biking

DIGEST

Patients 'tied up'
Elderly and mentally ill patients are being tied up in hospitals because there are not enough nurses to look after them, the Royal College of Nursing claims. Page 2

Bad debt plan
High street banks plan to end their tradition of customer confidentiality and pass on details of defaulting borrowers to credit information agencies in the next three months. Page 3

Study doubts
A leading epidemiologist yesterday called for a reassessment of the causes of child eye defects and cattle deaths which occurred near the Bonnybridge incinerator plant in Stirlingshire. Page 5

OTHER PAGES

Arts	15
Business	18,19,20,21
Crossword	28
Farming	21
Foreign news	9
General Assembly	6
Home news	2,3,5,6,7,8
Letters	12
Lifestyle	10,11
Parliament	4
Sport	26,27,28
Weather	28

TV and radio Page 14

Leith move to censure Mace-dropping MP

Storm in teacup, says Brown

By WILLIAM PAUL and PETER HANNAM

LEITH'S maverick Labour MP, Mr Ron Brown, is to face a motion of severe censure from his own constituency party at a specially convened meeting next month.

The move to censure Mr Brown, who has already been expelled from Westminster and had the party whip withdrawn, was formally started last night when a motion was tabled at the end of the monthly meeting of the Leith Constituency Labour Party.

The motion censures him for the manner in which he conducted himself over the incident

Mrs Brown in a supportive role last night.

in the Commons on April 18 when the ceremonial Mace was damaged during a debate, and also his refusal to apologise the next day.

It states that these actions have nothing to do with socialism and Mr Brown's comments to the Press served only to heighten to an extreme what was a "regrettable prank" which had little to do with politics and much to do with theatrics.

At a Press conference after last night's meeting Mr Brown, sitting beside CLP chairman Bill Axon, said the matter was "a storm in a teacup" in his opinion but he accepted that party members had the right to express their views and that it should go through the proper procedures.

"I have confidence in Leith Labour Party and they will judge me on the issues," he said. "If you want an execution you will have to wait until later."

Mr Axon said the motion had been tabled and seconded after two hours of discussions on Mr Brown's recent behaviour in Parliament but there had been no discussion on the actual content of it.

"There will be in two weeks time and you will have your story then," he told reporters.

Mr Brown, who has increased his majority in every election in Leith since first winning the seat in 1979, was asked to defend his actions to around 50 CLP members last night. They also heard a report from the party's chief whip at Westminster, Mr Derek Foster, which outlined the MP's allegedly poor voting record since 1983.

Mr Foster's report said that Labour MPs were "incensed" and "clamoured for action" after the Mace dropping incident and his refusal to apologise which rescued the Government from potential embarrassment over the poll tax.

The MPs wanted to show him "they would not tolerate such self-indulgent misconduct that brings the party in disrepute" and to warn others not to be tempted to follow suit.

The report analyses Mr Brown's voting record in Parliament over the last five sessions, showing that he has frequently missed votes without permission from the Whips' office.

This session he has voted on two and three-line Whips (which require attendance) on 104 occasions, been given absence 40 times and missed 31 divisions.

In 1986-87, he voted 75 times, was given absence four times and went missing 37 times. In 1985-86, the figures were 123 votes, 18 approved absences and 58 misses. In 1984-85, 124 votes, 48 approved absences and 25 misses. In 1983-84, 193 votes, 68 absences and 46 misses.

Continued on Page 2, Col 6

Pictures by JACK CROMBIE

In a light-hearted moment after last night's meeting Mr Brown sports an ill-fitting hat borrowed from a reporter. Looking on is Mr Bill Axon, constituency party chairman

Three held after family's 14-hour gunpoint ordeal

By Our Own Reporters

SEVEN members of a family were last night recovering from being abducted from their home at gunpoint and being held hostage for 14 hours.

Three men have been arrested and charged in connection with a series of incidents which began early yesterday. Two men, aged 25 and 20, were arrested around mid-day in Craigton Cemetery, Glasgow, one of them after a police chase.

Soon afterwards, the seven hostages, three women, four men and a two-year-old child, were found in a flat on the fifth floor of a multi-storey block at 29 Broomloan Court, which overlooks Ibrox Stadium. Police later learned that a third man was in a flat on the third floor of the same building in the company of an elderly couple. Police armed and with riot shields surrounded the building.

After more than six hours of police negotiations, also involving a Glasgow journalist, the elderly couple left the flat unharmed and soon afterwards a man, aged 27, gave himself up.

Det Chief Supt John Orr said the three men were now the subject of a report to the procurator-fiscal and it was expected they would appear at Glasgow Sheriff Court today.

The drama began in the early hours of yesterday morning when a family was taken at gunpoint from its home in Summerston, Glasgow, by several men who forced their way into the house.

At the request of the chief constable a news blackout, with the agreement of the media, was imposed during what Mr Orr described as a major police operation. At the completion of the day-long incident, police recovered a number of weapons.

The hostages were taken to the Southern General after their ordeal and a spokesman for the Greater Glasgow Health Board said last night that none was seriously injured. One man had bruising on his face and an elderly woman's high blood pressure gave cause for concern.

After treatment they were taken to Govan Police office where they helped police with their inquiries.

A resident at Broomloan Court earlier described how she heard police shouting and trying to kick down a door as she tried to get out of the building.

The woman, who lives near the top of the block, was one of a number of people caught up in the drama yesterday afternoon. "I just went out to get messages but when I found the lifts weren't working I started to go down the stairs. When I got to the bottom police wouldn't let me out and told me to go back up," she said.

"But as soon as I reached the fourth floor another policeman with a shotgun told me to stop. I was trapped for ages in the stairwell before they finally let me out.

"I could hear kicking and shouts of 'Open the door' and when I got outside the place was swarming with police.

"I never heard any shooting, but there were three ambulances and they went racing off with their sirens blaring. The road was closed to traffic and nobody was allowed in or out of the building."

Principal in call to privatise universities

By ALISON CLEMENTS

PROPOSALS by a Scottish university principal to cut direct links between Government and higher education and introduce a form of privatisation has encountered outrage among lecturers and students.

Dr Graham Hills, Principal and Vice-Chancellor of Strathclyde University, said at a business conference at Gleneagles Hotel yesterday that to get Britain, its universities and its students into a more enterprising frame of mind required some radical changes.

The pressure for change, he said, came from the Government's unrelenting desire to decrease spending on the public sector, of which the universities are a part.

Dr Hills claimed that a system where higher education institutions were funded by fee-paying student customers and by industry would force universities to compete for student numbers and research contracts.

A student, on being accepted at a university or polytechnic, would automatically qualify for a merit entitlement award (MEA). That Government cheque would cover all, or nearly all, of the full economic cost of the course on which the student was embarking.

The student would then choose and pay the educational institution he wanted to attend, thereby using customer power to buy an education fitted exactly to his needs and wishes.

Students would no longer have a free ride, he said, because they would have to find

Dr Graham Hills: No "free ride" for students.

the difference between their MEA and their course fees through a gift, sponsorship, loan or vacation work. That gap could be anything from £100 to £1,000.

Dr Hills said that business itself should take a lead and promote what he believed to be Britain's most promising business, namely the knowledge business. It was the industrialists who must raise the status of business education and of those institutions specialising in it, he said.

Mr Bill Johnston, president of Strathclyde Association of University Teachers, claimed at a Press conference at Strathclyde University yesterday that the speech was "a windy, rhetorical, propagandistic document."

He said Dr Hills was trying to impose a Marks & Spencer retail model on university administration and was approaching businessmen because he had failed to convince universities of the value of his concept. Dr Hills was "out on a limb, flying a kite."

Miss Jennifer Marchbank, president of Strathclyde Students' Association, claimed that the proposals would prevent students from lower income families from entering higher education.

She also criticised the role industry was to play: "If industry is giving the backing they will also dictate the line of research." She added that it would be impossible for universities to plan ahead because their income would not be in a predictable block grant but from an unpredictable flow of student fees.

Mr Johnston said that, just because the idea fitted in with the rhetoric of Right-wing distribution, did not mean it was feasible or productive. The reorganisation suggested by Dr Hills was merely a cover-up for further reductions in funds to universities, he said.

Press considers fightback over Wapping pictures

By JACK O'SULLIVAN

SEVERAL newspapers were last night considering whether to fight a court order that they surrender unpublished photographs of violent demonstrations outside News International's Wapping plant in London.

They feared the ruling could seriously endanger their photographers in the future.

ITN agreed to comply and hand over untransmitted film, which could be used in evidence against policemen accused of serious criminal offences.

A High Court judge ruled in London yesterday that the material should be supplied to aid inquiries into allegations against officers policing the printers' dispute.

Last night *The Independent*, *Observer* and *Mail on Sunday* were discussing whether to apply for a judicial review of the decision.

The National Council for Civil Liberties, representing four freelance photographers, was also considering an appeal.

"One's inclination is to fight this ruling all the way," declared the *Observer's* editor, Mr Donald Trelford.

He said that the safety of photographers could be endangered if those at demonstrations knew that pictures of violence might be passed to the authorities.

"The end result could be that they would not be able to cover certain events and the public would not get a free flow of information. That is a very dangerous situation."

Mr Jacob Ecclestone, deputy general secretary of the National Union of Journalists, said: "The convenience of the State has again been given precedence over the safety and independence of the Press. We are a step closer to State control."

Mr Stewart Boyd, chairman of the UK Picture Editors' Guild, suggested that the only regrettable recourse would be for photographers and cameramen to destroy as a matter of normal practice all unused material.

It would have been contempt of court for the companies in question to have done this once the Police Complaints Authority applied for the court order last November.

The news organisations had opposed the PCA's application on the grounds of safety and that Press freedom and independence would be infringed.

Mr Justice Alliott ruled that the fears were unfounded. He said the over-riding public interest was that the investigators should have access to possible evidence.

Allegations against police officers include assault, wounding, causing grievous bodily harm, indecent assault and perjury. Over 440 complaints about police behaviour during a Wapping riot in January 1987 are being investigated.

A Northamptonshire police team investigating for the PCA has already viewed 500 still photographs and 15 hours of film voluntarily handed over.

The editor-in-chief of ITN, Mr David Nicholas, said last night: "ITN observes the law so we shall comply with the court's order. However, our policy is not to hand over untransmitted material voluntarily . . . It is vital that we are seen to be independent."

Yesterday's decision marked only the second successful application by the police under the 1984 Police and Criminal Evidence Act for the surrender of Press material.

The previous instance was in 1986 when a Bristol newspaper was forced to hand unpublished photographs of that September's riots over to the police. The only picture actually used against a defendant had already been published.

The relevant section of the 1984 Act does not apply in Scotland. Under it the applicant must prove that the evidence is likely to be of substantial value in an investigation of a serious arrestable offence.

A Scottish precedent is the seizure by Strathclyde Police of a Scottish Television video of a fight between players during last October's Rangers-Celtic match at Ibrox Park.

The procurator-fiscal successfully applied for a warrant to search and two players were subsequently convicted after the court was shown material previously not broadcast. The two men are appealing.

In March, ITN and the BBC surrendered film of the killing of two soldiers at an IRA funeral. They had been threatened with proceedings under anti-terrorist legislation.

Editorial — Page 12

Front page of *The Scotsman*, 27 May 1988

RENWICKS
The name to remember
Audi
PLYMOUTH TORQUAY NEWTON ABBOT TRURO

The voice of Devon

12.30 a.m. edition

The Western Morning News

Wednesday, June 15, 1988 — All the local AND national news you need — Still only 20p

TODAY

Argyle highlander

ARGYLE manager Dave Smith finally ended the speculation when he told WMN chief sportswriter Rick Cowdery of his transfer. See back page.

Hands off TSW

South-West TV chiefs have reacted angrily to a suggestion that would base Westcountry television in Southampton — page 7.

Tomorrow

- Selling off council estates to private landlords — how it would affect tenants.
- Money Matters — how to save tax through small investments.
- Ray Thomes on Westcountry.

Unplanned baby case dismissed

TOGETHER: Mrs. Keane, her husband and son James whose birth led to the court action.

PLYMOUTH mother Doreen Keane, who gave birth to an unplanned fourth child three years after a sterilisation operation, left Exeter Crown Court in tears after losing her legal battle with Plymouth Health Authority.

Minutes after Mr. Justice Steyn rejected her plea for damages against the authority, 42-year-old Mrs. Keane wept on the shoulder of her husband James, a 44-year-old machine operator.

Beside them outside the court was their son, James, whose birth in June 1983 — three years after Mrs. Keane's sterilisation — gave rise to the court hearing.

Mrs. Keane, of Wentwood Gardens, Plymouth, claimed that the health authority had a duty to warn her about the small risk of pregnancy following sterilisation, and failed to do so.

She said she was "desperate" to have no more children after her third daughter suffered health problems, and claimed she would not have had the operation had she been warned of the risk.

The judge said that on "compelling evidence" he came to the conclusion that Mrs. Keane was warned of the risk of further pregnancy and probably appreciated it.

He felt constrained to reject the evidence of Mr. and Mrs. Keane on critical points although they did not lie.

The judge said that when the couple first visited a gynaecologist about sterilisation they were given a form relating to the operation, which she and her husband read and realised there was a risk.

At the hospital, a staff nurse obtained Mrs. Keane's signature on the form, said the judge, who was satisfied she was either read the relevant part, including the warning, or Mrs. Keane read it herself.

Mrs. Keane raised no objection and that by itself would be a discharge of the authority's duty.

Mrs. Keane said after the hearing: "I know I was not warned, and I still maintain that.

"I know I told the truth all along. I know the judge said I did not lie, b[ut] that is how I have been made to feel.

"It was not the money, it was j[ust] wrong what they did. I have lost faith [in] the law and in doctors."

But she said she "thought the wor[ld] of James."

And her husband added: "He is [a] beautiful boy, and we were overjoyed [at] having him. But they even turned th[at] against us in court."

A spokesman for Plymouth Hea[lth] Authority said last night: "We sh[all] continue with our policy of advisi[ng] patients both verbally, and on a fo[rm] which has to be signed, of the possibili[ty] that they may not become or rema[in] sterile as a result of this operation."

Two near-disasters in Westcountry involving military aircraft

Jet crash dive near to school

A BRAVE pilot steered his crippled jet clear of a village school and ejected only seconds before the plane crashed harmlessly into a field in the first of two near-disasters involving military aircraft last night.

In the second, unrelated, incident a fuel tank fell off an RAF Jaguar jet and landed only 100 yards from houses at Halberton, near Tiverton.

The Defence Ministry is to investigate both incidents.

Villagers at Ilchester, Somerset, rushed to help as the elderly Hawker-Hunter single seater dived into the ground about 200 yards from the local school. The Navy pilot, who has not been named, landed safely by parachute and was taken to Yeovil hospital for a check-up.

Exercise

A Navy spokesman said the pilot had been flying the Hunter on a target practice exercise off Portland, Dorset and was returning to land at RNAS Yeovilton — about two miles from Ilchester — when the jet developed technical problems.

"The pilot guided the aircraft away from the village and ejected," said the spokesman.

The pilot, who was uninjured, was praised for his bravery by Ilchester town clerk, Mrs Pauline Penn.

"The plane came down just as the children were leaving school — there would have been a disaster but for his skill and courage," she said.

A Naval Board of Inquiry into the accident is expected to meet at Yeovilton today.

Meanwhile, Halberton villagers were outraged by the tank that fell off the Jaguar aircraft near their homes. They say they could have been killed if the 10-ft. long tank had fallen on to their properties.

The tank dropped onto a field near council houses at Orchard View at about 4.30 pm when dozens of residents were at home.

The RAF Jaguar was on a routine training flight from the Empire Test Pilot School at Boscombe Down, Wiltshire.

Mrs Nicky Slater, of Orchard View, said she first thought there had been a road accident. "It was a bit alarming — to put it mildly," she said. "You don't want to think what would have happened if it had landed on houses."

Parish councillor Terry Yendall, also of Orchard View, described the incident as a "disgrace."

"There have been a lot of low-flying aircraft here recently and something like this just isn't on," he said.

A spokesman for the MoD said the drop tank, carried under the wings of the aircraft, was used to extend the Ja[guar's] range.

Last year, in a s[imilar] incident equipment fell [from a] military plane near Cre[...] narrowly missing a house[. The] RAF said then it would ta[ke] necessary measures to en[sure it] did not happen again.

ROYAL NAVY

PICKING UP THE PIECES: Staff from RNAS Yeovilton were soon at the scene where a Navy Hawker-Hunter crashed at Ilchester yesterday.

NEWS IN BRIEF

Rocard to rule France

FRENCH President Francois Mitterrand is asking Socialist Prime Minister Michel Rocard to head a minority government following inconclusive general elections which left him 13 seats short of a majority.

Mitterrand went on television to tell the nation: "France is and will be governed."

He hinted that his comparatively strong powers as head of state would bring an additional element of stability to the minority government.

Brothers obey

A LEFT-WING move to mount a law-breaking campaign among town hall workers against the Community Charge was defeated last night at the Nalgo annual conference.

Turks stay

TURKISH Prime Minister Turgut Ozal has ruled out even a partial withdrawal of his troops from war-divided Cyprus during a visit to Greece.

War peaks

IRAQ says it has captured five strategic border heights from Iranian troops in a major offensive in rugged mountains in the north-eastern battle zone.

Money talks

THE European Community wrapped up a deal to finance the bloc into the 1990s yesterday — but the issue of a single Euro currency is still a sticking point.

Digging in

THOUSANDS of West Germans are backing a Hamburg man who lost a court battle to keep two garden gnomes in his garden.

Pedal power

ROADS Minister Peter Bottomley rode on the back of a tandem through Whitehall and the Strand in London yesterday to launch a booklet aimed at Britain's new cyclists.

Beeb prepared

BBC RADIO is planning to provide listeners with better advance warning about programmes containing offensive bad language or blasphemy.

Troubled Seoul

SOUTH Korean students shouting anti-American slogans demonstrated in Seoul for reunification with the North at the edge of the Demilitarized Zone yesterday.

and finally...

Bear-faced cheek

A SIX-FEET tall black bear went to school in a New York City suburb yesterday — and was fed peanut-butter sandwiches by parents until wildlife officers tranquilised him.

Weather

A FINE sunny day. Details on Page two.

Violence flares again

VIOLENCE flared in Dusseldorf last night as English and West German soccer fans clashed in the streets.

Police were attacked, shop windows smashed and the city railway station was damaged.

Trouble started when West German fans were met at the station by waiting English fans. Fights broke out and the police were overrun by about 300 rioters. Police reinforcements in riot gear were called in.

The Prime Minister yesterday warned that soccer was fighting for its very survival in the struggle to beat hooliganism.

Unless the terrace troublemakers were rooted out, Mrs. Thatcher believed thousands of law-abiding football fans would vote with their feet and quit watching the game.

Amid growing reports of violence and rowdyism in Germany where England are contesting soccer's European Championships, Mrs. Thatcher announced she would meet key Ministers tomorrow to agree a plan of action.

But the Prime Minister was reported to be baffled as to what decisive action could be taken to have any real, long-term impact on the problem.

She was expected to urge the soccer authorities to institute a national membership card scheme which could be used to prevent offenders gaining admission to football grounds.

But football's bosses have already fought one successful action against the plan and last night warned they would do so again.

McVeigh saga shamble[s]

Patrick McVeigh

THE Dublin Government will appeal against the controversial Irish court decision to free top IRA terror suspect and Scotland Yard extradition target Patrick McVeigh.

They announced the move yesterday as Mrs Thatcher, under intense pressure in the Commons, told MPs that Britain was not responsible for the confusion which led to McVeigh's release and put the Anglo-Irish Agreement under further strain.

McVeigh, 37, from Belfast, was freed from the district court at Portlaoise on Monday after Mr Justice Jarlath Ruane complained that British police were not there to identify him.

Mrs Thatcher who was said to have been "utterly dismayed" at the decision insisted that the Crown Prosecution Service expressly asked the Irish whether further identification evidence was needed from the UK. They were "explicity told it was not," she told MPs during Qu[estion] Time in the Commons.

British anger at the shock decision is [...] more pronounced because it was suppose[d to be] the first case involving an alleged terrorist [to be] dealt with under the new extradition agre[ement] between London and Dublin.

In a statement to the Dail, the I[rish] Parliament, Irish Justice Minister Gerry C[ollins] stressed his Government's "deep conce[rn to] resolve the issue.

"An appeal by way of case stated will be [made] to the High Court against the decision [of the] District Justice," he said.

There was said to be some irritation in D[ublin] at what was seen as a "knee jerk" [...] reaction from leading Government figur[es in] London on Monday night to the news.

Filly on the rails

FASHION STAKES: Polish beauty Anne Kropacz keeps cool and lets the train take the strain of getting to Royal Ascot from Waterloo Station.

Shock bid of £90m for Torbay housing

by ADAM SAGE

A PRIVATE firm is among the front runners to buy up Torbay Council's entire housing stock after submitting a shock bid of £90-million — more than double the estimated value of the properties.

The borough council, now almost certain to become the first in the country to attempt a housing sell-off, has been widely expected to deal with only non profit-making housing associations.

Change image

But a confidential short list of bids, seen by The Western Morning News, gives a glowing reference to the private Glasgow-based firm, Quality Street Limited.

The company, backed by the Nationwide Anglia Building Society, is now battling with four housing associations for the right to buy Torbay's stock.

And the consultants appointed by the council to advise on the sell-off apparently favour the private firm. Quality Street is "committed to changing the image of public sector rented housing" they say in a report, adding that "it alone has the vision and resources to do this."

A special meeting of the resources committee is to be held on June 24 to discuss the sell-off and decide which of the bids will be put to council tenants.

As the second highest bid is £56-million, jointly from the Devon and Cornwall Housing Association and the Westcountry Housing Association, Quality Street clearly has far greater financial muscle than its rivals.

Yet Conservative councillors anxious to go ahead with the sell-off, may decide that council tenants would be unwilling to choose a profit-making private firm as landlords.

The successful bid is likely to be put to tenants in a referendum later this year.

Rents fear

The Quality Street offer of more than £90 million includes almost £50 million to build new houses in Torbay and revamp old ones.

Operations director Dick Manson said council tenants should have no fears about the newly-formed company putting up rents to exorbitant levels.

"We hope that our links with the Nationwide Anglia will reassure people," he said. "Building societies are very secure and it is very important for them to protect their image.

"We have offered safeguards to both the council and tenants in our package.

Child abuse soars to record high

EXCLUSIVE
by LIZ HANNAM

CHILD abuse in Devon is soaring by 17 per cent. a year, according to latest figures released by the NSPCC last night.

One hundred-and-twenty-five extra cases came onto the child abuse register last year, taking the total to 874.

The news comes at the same time as national figures for 1987 show an increase of less than half the Devon total, 8 per cent.

"We only reflect the situation; I cannot comment on the national picture. Everyone here is working at full stretch to cope with the situation," said Reg Marriott, manager of the NSPCC's Devon child protection team.

He said it was impossible to find a single cause for the increase but there was evidence that a parent's own upbringing affected whether and what type of abuse occurs.

Also important is the initial child-parent relationship, whether the child is liked and accepted from the beginning.

The increase was greatest in South Devon, where the number of children put on the register increased by a staggering 66, from 215 to 281.

Figures show 5.23 per 1,000 of the child population figure in South Devon is on the register, compared with only 2.15 per 1,000 children in North Devon, where the lowest figures were recorded.

Most of the children come onto the register in the "at risk of serious abuse or neglect" category. Sexual abuse, which seems certain to be highlighted nationally when the report of the Cleveland child abuse inquiry is published, account for a significant proportion of all Devon's cases.

In North Devon, there were 12 incidents of sexual abuse; in East Devon 36; in South Devon 34 and in West Devon 71.

"Many of the cases of sexual abuse are coming to light after the greater public and professional awareness of what it does to children, and the fact it should not happen," said Mr Marriott.

He also pointed to the worrying increase in physical injury, which, after having levelled off three years ago, is now beginning to increase again.

The type of children most at risk depend on the type of abuse. Mr Marriott said babies were more likely to be abused because they could not defend themselves.

He called for more Government and public support for the South West's hard-pressed social service workers.

Reported increases in Cornwall are much less severe. Numbers fell by 35 to 244 from 1986 to 1987. But figures for the end of May, 1987, show a slight increase, bringing the total to 226.

The newspaper with the late, late news that the London papers miss

2. Front page of the *Western Morning News*, 15 June 1988

Coventry Evening Telegraph

City Final

Voted Britain's BEST DESIGNED evening newspaper

Friday February 19 1988

18p

Peter Cordle

CIVIC PAYROLL IS OVER THE TOP

By PAUL DALE, Political Editor

COVENTRY council has admitted it employs significantly more white-collar staff than the average local authority.

The evidence of overstaffing has been disclosed by city treasurer Peter Cordle. In a report to finance committee members he says Coventry had 16 per cent more non-manual staff than the average council.

The disclosure comes in the wake of a recent *Evening Telegraph* investigation which showed how council staffing had jumped since 1979.

The details also come at the time an Audit Commission report criticises the treasurer's department for being overstaffed and costing too much to run ... and coincide with a planned 8 per cent rate rise for Coventry households.

The commissioners, appointed by the government to keep an eye on local government spending, say that compared with towns like Dudley and Barnsley, parts of the treasurer's department at Coventry cost too much to run.

They say the council should move from a "first class" service to an "average" service.

Today Mr Cordle said: "Coventry has a tradition of doing things in a first-class way, in a way of excellence and high standards."

Higher than average staffing levels were caused by the great social problems in Coventry.

Contracts

The most controversial proposal by the auditors is that the council should hire private bailiffs to chase rent and rate arrears, rather than rely on in-house staff. The auditors point out that Coventry's bailiff service is twice as expensive as the contracted-out unit at Dudley.

Coventry was also criticised for sending out too many letters to ratepayers requesting information or giving advice.

Other suggestions by the auditors include cutting rating office staff, changes in the way rate bills are collected and a crackdown on arrears.

The council is also advised to collect cash for facilities like sports halls and community halls in hand rather than sending out invoices.

City treasurer Peter Cordle has rejected some of the criticisms, although some suggestions have already been adopted. Cuts in staff have been made, although Mr Cordle admits that at March 1987 full-time white-collar staffing levels for the whole council were 16 per cent above average.

Mr Cordle added in a report

It's the cost of '5-star service'

on the commission's findings that the treasurer's department gives a caring service with a "firm but human touch" which would be endangered if all the recommendations were implemented.

Staff asked to collect money for the use of council facilities would be placed at risk of attack and general levels of service would fall.

Mr Cordle added that all council departments were being encouraged to seek better value for money, with £2 million already saved and the prospect of cutting back a further £1.2 million.

M-F boss in move to Rover

By KENNY FARQUHARSON
Industry Reporter

THE MAN who axed 800 jobs in a ruthless cost-cutting drive at Massey Ferguson in Coventry has resigned.

Managing director John Towers, who took up the post 10 months ago, is to become manufacturing director at Land Rover.

Today about 6,000 workers at Solihull-based Land Rover were preparing to strike from Monday in a dispute over pay.

Mr Towers, who has a reputation as a tough hatchet man, will take up his new post at the end of the month.

Wages cut

In a statement he said: "M-F clearly has a bright future and I leave in the knowledge that the employees at Banner Lane are determined to continue to build upon all the advances they have made in recent months."

Within six months there, Mr Towers had overseen a jobs cut of 800, a £30 wage reduction and the introduction of radical new working practices. Production rose by 40 per cent in 1987.

And in December M-F announced it had crawled out of the red for the first time in a decade.

Towards the end of last year MF took 30-per-cent of the world tractor market, the first firm to clinch such a proportion for more than 10 years.

Mr Towers: took M-F into the black

Rape suspect jumped to death

By GILLIAN GRAY

MAN who jumped from a multi-storey car park was depressed and worried about being held over a rape charge.

An inquest heard that Lawrence Thorneywork, who died after plunging 75 ft, had spent five months in a police cell

last year on a rape charge which was later dropped.

He jumped from the fifth storey of the Tavistock Street car park in Leamington on Sunday, the day after his 22nd birthday.

He stayed with his sister in Crown Way, Lillington, and worked part-time as a labourer on a Warwick district council scheme.

endon Avenue, Leamington, was held at Bedford last year accused of rape, but the charges were dropped in November for lack of evidence.

"He maintained he had done nothing wrong and said he was going to commit suicide."

Denise Sawbridge told Warwickshire coroner Allan Dixon that her brother had been depressed and bitter.

Speaking after the inquest,

she said she was convinced the episode played a major part in her brother's suicide.

"He had a difficult time as an adolescent and became involved in petty crime, but all those were minor offences. He had moved to Northamp-

Turn to Page 2

Weather P4, Chris Arnot P6, You Write P7, Family Notices P24, TV P28-29, Business P30, Sport starts P52

Front page of the *Coventry Evening Telegraph,* 19 February 1988

TUESDAY May 17 1988

Daily Record

22p   FORWARD WITH SCOTLAND   No. 30,862

MEET OUR MODEL LOVELIES

IN THE PAPER WITH STYLE

IN COLOUR

A-Team doomed in new telly clamp

SIR WILLIAM

HOLLYWOOD is on the hit-list of a new telly watchdog.

And among the shows likely to come under fire is the violent kids' favourite, The A-Team.

Sir William Rees-Mogg was named yesterday by Home Secretary Douglas Hurd as chairman of the Broadcasting Standards Council.

And he admitted last night that the A-Team is one of the shows he thinks should never have been seen here.

He said: "It is violent and aimed at children. This is the sort of combination that should not be allowed."

Chiefs

Sir William also revealed that his council, of which he is so far the only member, will also be demanding that broadcasting chiefs allow them to vet imported programmes before they are screened.

Despite the fact that the appointments are still up for grabs, Sir William did veto one person – TV clean-up campaigner Mary Whitehouse.

He said: "Broadcasters tend to ridicule her but she says some sensible things. However I don't see her joining."

His appointment came under fire in the Commons and also from Channel 4 boss Michael Grade.

Sir William dismissed accusations that he has been appointed as a Government censor.

The Record tackles the BIG issues

BARRED!

Kids caught in the storm over Catholic schools

THESE are just three of 44 Scots kids caught in the middle of a religious row.

The Creighton sisters – Emma, seven, five-year-old Louise, and nine-year-old Suzanne – and their schoolmates pose a simple question:

WHY are they barred from the school nearest their homes?

But the answer isn't so simple.

It's put the youngsters at the heart of the biggest storm to hit Scottish education since separate schools for Roman Catholics were set up.

Their own non-denominational school is being closed down. The nearest school is a Catholic one, but Church authorities fear "back-door integration" if the 44 children are enrolled.

Strathclyde can't find the solution.

Meanwhile, Emma, Louise and Suzanne and their pals wait for the grown-ups to solve an age-old problem . . .

RECORD VIEW – PAGE 2   **A BITTER LESSON – PAGE 7**

---

4. Front page of the *Daily Record*, 17 May 1988

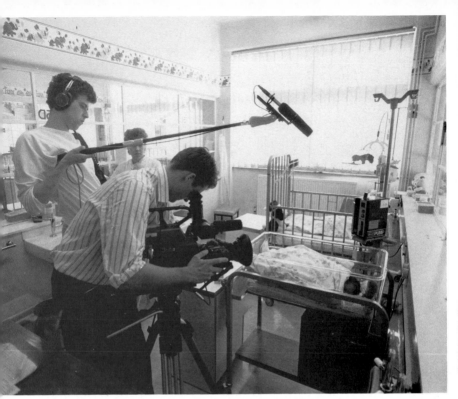

BBC, *Midlands Today*, at Birmingham Children's Hospital, November 1988

BBC, SW (Plymouth) *Spotlight*: (*left to right*) presenters Chris Slade and Juliet Morris; (*far right*) weatherman Craig Rich (June 1988)

7. Judith Stamper, co-presenter of BBC *Look North*, introducing the report on the National Union of Miners' ballot (see Chapters 3 and 5) (25 January 1988)

8. *Look North* display of the voting figures for the NUM Presidency, 25 January 1988 [Plates 7–11 are a sequence from *Look North* that day.]

9. *Look North* interview from Westminster with Energy Secretary Cecil Parkinson, 25 January 1988

10. *Look North*: pithead interview with a miner in West Yorkshire, 25 January 1988

11. Judith Stamper in *Look North* studio interviewing Mr Arthur Scargill, 25 January 1988

12. BBC, SW (Plymouth) *Spotlight*, June 1988

Commentary

As with Central News, so with *Midlands Today* – the dual dilemmas.
To stay strictly with hard news or to mellow the diet? And how do you
satisfy the diverse communities with little interest in each other – from
Worcester and Gloucester in the south to the Black Country and the
Potteries in the North?

Roy Saatchi, as Editor, News, has no hesitation about the hard news.
It must be the top priority. That has been the policy at Pebble Mill for
some years. To the question whether audiences can stand a whole hour
of hard news between 6 and 7 pm, with the national news followed by
the regional news, he replies by pointing to what he sees as good
audience figures, with *Midlands Today* well above the BBC's 6 pm news
– though the ITV soaps at 6.30 do better still. But he also wants 'all
sorts of shades' in his programme. He adds that the lighter items are
often 'more difficult' to produce than straight news; 'they involve brain
power'. 'When they work well they are terrific; when not they are
terrible'.

With the last comment I absolutely agree. In the past there have been
too many shoddy second halves in regional magazines, which is partly
why the IBA and BBC have tried to cut short the early evening series.

The lighter items, when well done, are worth keeping. In the week of
our study, one was memorable – a competition to raise funds for a
Herefordshire theatre. At £1 a time, people were invited to take little
plastic ducks on holiday and to photograph them, with prizes for the
one that went furthest. Ducks were seen – over suitable music and a
running commentary – on the Devon coast, in Leningrad, in Zim-
bambwe and elsewhere. The winner was on the Great Wall of China. It
was brilliant.

Like Central, Pebble Mill seems less ready to look east than to look
west, north or south. The Coventry area again comes out exceptionally badly, in spite of its comparative prosperity. The north-east,
too, receives a thin share of attention. But the disparity of interests
between the industrial and commercial centre of the region and the
more rural areas makes a news schedule that will interest everyone the
harder to put together.

The presenters are clear, competent and of suitable variety in
character. The two principals – Kay Alexander and Alan Towers –
combine authority with friendliness. Alan Towers as a reporter can
have a severe demeanour, but he modifies it as a presenter. Both Kay
and Alan appear to prepare carefully for interviews and put their

questions with precision. Of the other regulars – Brian Conway, Kathy Rochford and Sue Beardsmore – I found all three congenial to watch and efficient in their approach. As Kay Alexander said people sitting at home like to know who is presenting the news. Many indeed, like to feel some common identity with them. *Midlands Today* is wise in keeping to a limited number of presenters and letting them appear for several days at a time.

What was clear, given the comparatively limited staffing and reports available to *Midlands Today*, was that interesting and efficient programmes were being produced. Faced with the disparity of interests between the urban centre of the region and the more rural areas, that is an achievement.

People

Clare Harrison
St Hugh's College, Oxford (graduated Politics, Philosophy and Economics 1979). Postgraduate journalism course, Cardiff. 2 years with Plymouth Sound. 18 months with BBC R. Leeds. Then regional tv. BBC Leeds, as reporter and presenter. To Birmingham Easter 1987.

Peter Hiscocks
King Edward VI School, Bath. Then *Wiltshire Times, Western Morning News* (Plymouth), *Bristol Evening Post, Western Daily Press* (Bristol). Freelance work with most national dailies and Sundays. Producer, BBC R. Leicester 1974. BBC tv. South (regional journalist) 1979–84. Since 1984 Assistant Editor, BBC tv. news and current affairs, Pebble Mill.

Roy Saatchi
Essex University. IPC Business Press. Radio City (ILR, Liverpool) 1974–8. BBC Newcastle 1978–81. Assistant Editor, Midlands 1981 then tv. news London; R. 4; and later senior producer documentaries and features Pebble Mill; programme organiser, R. WM; Editor *Midlands Today* from autumn 1987.

Alan Towers
From school to *Liverpool Echo*, later to *St Helens Reporter* and *Slough Observer*. Into tv., 1968, full-time freelance reporter-presenter for news and sport. Senior presenter, *Midlands Today*, 1979–88.

14 Eleven in One: *Coventry Evening Telegraph*

Takeovers, Death and Humanity

There cannot be many local or regional newspapers with a political staff of 4 – to cover local and national events – plus a shared lobby correspondent at Westminster. Nor can there be many with up to 11 editions every weekday, to cover an area extending little more than 10 miles from its centre. The *Coventry Evening Telegraph* has 100 journalists and expects to generate over 150 stories each day. It is a prosperous newspaper, selling about 96 000 copies each weekday in an area with some 750 000 people.

It has one of the most complex editorial systems to integrate its various editions. To indicate its scope, here are the titles and timings of the editions on a typical day, Friday 19 February 1988; 4 are for the Coventry area and the others for surrounding communities. The timings are the 'off stone' times for the final page – the 'off stone' term being derived from the days of hot metal printing, now replaced by electronics. The front page headlines are also quoted.

10.45 am *Coventry Evening Telegraph*, 'Lunch' edition
'Land Rover Deadlock: strike is on'

1.00 pm *Nuneaton Evening Telegraph*
'"90 More Go" sours news at Sterling'
('Sterling' is the Sterling Metals Company at Nuneaton, which had just escaped a take-over bid)

Bedworth Evening Telegraph
Same headlines and front page as for Nuneaton

1.10 pm *Leamington and Warwick Evening Telegraph*
'Strike Mars "Victory" at Pottertons'
(Pottertons is a Warwick industrial company which, like Sterling, had been subject to a take-over bid by a bigger company)

Stratford-on-Avon Evening Telegraph
Same headlines and front page as Leamington edition

1.15 pm *Rugby Evening Telegraph*
'Escape from a Takeover turns sour'

1.40 pm *Coventry Evening Telegraph*, 'Late City' edition
'Overkill on city staff is admitted'
(That is a report to Coventry City Council on non-manual
staffing, a matter of recent controversy)

2.15 pm *Coventry Evening Telegraph*, 'City Final' edition
'Civic Payroll is Over the Top'
(Same text as at 1.40, but revised headline)

4.15 pm *Coventry Evening Telegraph*, 'Night Final'
The 'city centre' edition, maintained in case of major late
news in the afternoon

For the 5 primary editions there are changes on up to 6 or 7 inside
news pages. The Nuneaton, Leamington, Rugby, Bedworth and
Stratford titles are published every day, with 2 further editions
specially flagged for Kenilworth and Hinckley. The Bedworth and
Stratford editions have extra slip pages 3 days a week.

Narrative, Friday 19 February

About 6.45 am Alan Kirby arrives – he is News Editor and Assistant
Editor. He goes through the overnight copy, having left at 5.30 pm
last night. In practice 5 or 6 of the inside news pages will have been
prepared and made up the previous evening, but will probably be
revised before midday. That leaves 6 news pages to be filled, including
the front, by 10 am or soon after for the 10.30 edition.

The earliest reporters arrive at 7.45 am, others at 8.30. They work
until 4–4.30pm. The editor and deputy editor, Geoffrey Elliott and
Roger Monkman, come in at 8 am. At 8.15 the morning conference is
held in the editor's room. Some of the opening comments will give a
taste of it.

Kirby: There's a very good story out of an inquest yesterday in which
it was revealed that a young Leamington man, who jumped from the
top of a car park in Leamington, had in fact been held by Bedford

police for three months on a charge of rape and the charge was later dropped. The kid – not surprisingly – became very depressed over this and decided to kill himself. We spoke last night to his sister and his father and got a 'pick up' picture of him. It will depend really on what the police tell us, because I can't quite understand why they should drop the case without its going to trial, but that's what they did.

Elliott: He was actually charged with rape, was he?

Kirby: He was charged with rape and detained for three months but the charge was later dropped without going to trial.

The Land-Rover dispute is obviously a good story. Last night's talks on that failed and it looks like an all out strike on Monday at Solihull, so we'll obviously be looking at that and giving full details of what the dispute's about.

The Blue Circle bid for Birmid failed last night – you may have seen last night's story which said that they were re-counting the votes.

There was a suggestion that they may have double-counted some of the shares and that's exactly what happened, and it means that the bid can't be reinstated for at least a year: That's obviously good news for the two local firms, so we'll be getting reaction to that.

Elliott: When was that announced last night?

Kirby: I don't know. I learned about it this morning.

Elliott: But it's still new, is it?

Kirby: Sure, sure and it affects two local firms of course – Sterling Metals and Pottertons.

The little boy from Nuneaton who's undergone a heart op. yesterday, he's in intensive care this morning – we're obviously doing a condition check on that; and it's the funeral in Birmingham this morning of Matthew Collier, which I would have thought would make a picture piece for us.

It's quite an interesting court story which we're covering again today – it's a running trial, a Stratford man who went berserk and stabbed his wife eight times. She recovered – he then tried to commit suicide and he's in court this morning accused of attempted murder.

Rugby council set its rate yesterday – the borough rate which is 5.9 per cent – but it doesn't mean a great deal in as much as you can't tell people what the Warwickshire rate is and until you can do that nobody can calculate how much they've got to pay ...

Elliott: I suppose we can say what percentage of their rate that represents?

Kirby: Sure, sure. And I think if we point out to the public that it could be anything say from 14 per cent to 18 per cent – the Warwickshire County rate – then people can try and calculate what they might be in for ... It'll make something for the front of Rugby but it won't make a lead.

So the discussion continues, with the conference lasting about 20 minutes. Of the events mentioned in the early part of the conference, nearly all made the front page in 1 or more editions, and when not on the front they were well placed inside. Apart from the Land-Rover dispute, none had been on television news the night before; nor was the failure of the Blue Circle bid for Birmid in the national newspapers that morning.

Mid-morning – 10.30 am

Paul Dale, head of the politics unit, is working on the Audit Commission report on Coventry City Council. It is interesting, he says, because the Audit Commission 'are virtually saying that Coventry should stop providing a first class administration'. It means that Coventry 'is doing too much, trying too hard'. It is not an embargoed document, so it could be used today or tomorrow. In the end it becomes the front page lead in the later editions.

At the same time another member of the politics unit is seeking local reactions to a Commons statement on school managements. The chairman of Coventry Education Committee 'is fairly steamed up' because it seems to mean that schools will not have money for swimming lessons or individual music tuition or coach trips unless they charge for them.

At 10.50 am, a mini-conference round the newsdesk. Decisions are taken to lead the Nuneaton and Bedworth editions with Blue Circle v. Birmid (the alternative being the further heart operations needed by little Lee Allsop, but he has been on the front page twice already this week); to lead Leamington with the lad who jumped to his death from the car park (though that is changed half an hour later); and Rugby will probably be the rate rise, because nothing better is in prospect. The reasoning behind these decisions is explained to me afterwards by News Editor Alan Kirby.

– Nuneaton
'Blue Circle v. Birmid was not a routine takeover. It's dramatic.

Blue Circle seemed to have achieved a takeover earlier this week, with something like 50.5 of the shares. But last night there was a recount, because the brokers felt that they may have made a mistake – they may have counted some shares twice. That's exactly what had happened. It was revealed last night, too late for the national press. It's a relief for the people of Nuneaton who are employed there. The story will be used in Coventry as well, because it's of tremendous interest'.

– *Leamington*

'It's a very human story – a young man who took his own life, which is tragic in its own right. But he took his life for a very unusual reason – he had become depressed, having been detained by the police for three months without trial, accused of rape. He obviously denied it. Having considered the evidence it was decided to drop the case. He left prison – his sisters told us how he became depressed . . . We would not normally give prominence to a suicide, but the circumstances are so unusual that we feel it's of interest to the public and something that people will read'.

– *Rugby*

'The difficulty with the rates is that although the borough council-has set its rate we can't calculate precisely what the whole rate increase will be, because Warwick County Council who take the major proportion of rates haven't taken a decision and won't until March 1st. What our political editor is now doing is to calculate what it will mean to Rugby residents if Warwickshire goes for the lowest rise and if it goes for the highest'.

For the front page, when the main Coventry edition comes, Alan Kirby sees the funeral of Matthew Collier as 'no more than a picture story'. His tragedy had made him a national figure, but he was not from the Coventry area. Over the next hour, he says, they must find something stronger. Unlikely as an audit report seems, it is a possibility 'if we can relate it to the public's interests'. At this point the editor, Geoffrey Elliott, appears in the newsroom having written two leaders. He wants to be brought up to date with the news.

At 11.25 the Birmid story takes 'a completely new twist' (Alan Kirby's words). Having won its battle to prevent takeover by Blue Circle – a cause for celebration at Sterling Metals in Nuneaton and Potterton's in Leamington – Sterling Metals has announced that 90 people are to be made redundant. 'So the celebration has turned completely sour'. The immediate source is Kenny Farquharson, the acting Industrial Editor. Soon after 11.00 am he had had a call from one of the district reporters to say there was going to be a strike, but the reason was not clear. Farquharson rang the public relations office at the parent company, Birmid Qualcast, but 'as usual' they said they knew nothing about it. So he tried Sterling Metals, and they said that 90 redundancies were coming. 'They always announce redundancies at this time on a Friday because they think they can get away with it', he says.

There was, however, enough time to give 'a new nose' to the story for the Nuneaton edition – although the copy deadline was just coming up – and to rewrite the story for Leamington. Farquharson was being assisted by another man on the industry desk, because they had to make other calls about the strike. It was, they said, 'an exciting forty minutes'.

Further intense activity came soon afterwards for the industry desk, making front page news for the main Coventry editions. The managing director of Massey-Ferguson in Coventry was now moving to Land-Rover in Birmingham. So, again, calls had to be made and a new story written – 'the man who masterminded a jobs cut of 800 and a drop in wages for Massey-Ferguson is leaving to join Land-Rover'. And Land-Rover's 6000 workers at Solihull were expected to go on strike on Monday, because of their pay dispute. The 'tough hatchet man' who had made Massey-Ferguson profitable was to move within two weeks. As Kenny Farquharson said, 'it's part of the job to have contacts who produce tip offs such as these'.

For the 2 final editions, however, the front page lead came from the head of the politics unit, Paul Dale. It is the unembargoed Audit Commission report which he was working his way through at 10.30 am. A dry subject, you might think: but it confirms the findings of a recent *Evening Telegraph* inquiry into the staffing of Coventry City Council. The civic payroll is 'over the top', with a larger white-collar staff than other comparable cities. At 12.30 Roger Monkman (deputy editor) and Paul Dale are in discussion about how to treat the report, and they are joined by Geoffrey Elliott, who is delighted that the *Evening Telegraph*'s findings have official confirmation. The staffing has been a factor in the high level of rates, they say. And, no – they are not making it the front page lead because it fits the paper's policy: it's still, they say, the strongest story of the day.

Specialist Staff

Among the specialists are the political, industrial, health, education, crime, women's, arts and entertainments staffs. The crime reporter on that day (19 February 1988) provided lead stories for two inside pages – one on measures to train young people on newspaper delivery rounds on how to protect themselves, and another on West Midlands Police revision of its crime prevention units. The political and industrial desks each provided a number of items in addition to their front page stories. The Health Correspondent, Melanie Knight, had a leader-page feature on safe and unsafe tranquilliser pills and three substantial news reports which took up much of page 9 in all editions.

As she explained, all three were 'follow-up' stories derived from the previous day's monthly meeting of the Coventry Health Authority; 2 days earlier she had been able to provide reports based on the agenda for the meeting, and on the previous day (Thursday) one story for the front page and three for inside pages. The front-page story reported the proposal by the Health Minister, Tony Newton, that the Walsgrave hospital in Coventry should take children's heart surgery cases to relieve the crisis at Birmingham's Children's Hospital. Yet the Walsgrave hospital, as Melanie Knight reported in the longest of the Friday 'follow ups', already had patients occupying some of its corridors. The hospital manager was quoted as saying that in spite of the existing pressure and some complaints from patients, treatment was being carried out safely; but he made no comment on the Minister's proposal. The newspaper, Miss Knight said, was taking care 'not to build up hopes' among parents with children whose operations had been delayed or cancelled.

Both Melanie Knight and Kenny Farquharson had come to their first jobs, at the *Coventry Evening Telegraph*, in the summer of 1985 – one from the postgraduate course at the City University and one from the Cardiff journalism course. With less than 3 years experience, both were in specialist posts. Paul Dale, head of the politics unit, had longer experience, with some years with the *Oxford Mail*.

Court Reporting

The *Coventry Evening Telegraph* is unusual – possibly unique – in its treatment of court cases. Although the Editor says that he 'does not like to see papers like ours full of court cases', a number are reported every day. Some appear as individual stories, prepared by reporters as in other newspapers, but with the general brief from Geoffrey Elliott to 'look for the serious, the unusual, and for anyone that's prominent in our own area'. In addition, however, there is every day a listing from the magistrates' court and, when sitting, from the crown court of almost every completed criminal case – simply with the name, age and address of the accused, the charge and the fine or punishment awarded. The lists appear 2 or 3 days after the finding, because they have to be compiled from the court registers. An exception is made for minor motoring offences – parking, speeding and careless driving – but there is no exception for drink driving or reckless driving or forged tax discs or driving without insurance. Similarly there is no exception for 'social crime' such as television licence dodging or litter offences or dog nuisances.

One aim of these listings is to equalise the publicity for such cases rather than publishing some and omitting others. It has been made possible in Coventry as a result of long negotiation and because the court authorities believe it to be in the public interest. Similar arrangements are said to have been made in Portsmouth and in Great Yarmouth, though with slightly different exceptions. It appears to be a sensible arrangement which ought to be followed in other areas.

Sport has the biggest count, with 5 pages to itself on each of the 3 days and brief previews at the front of the paper. That apart, the *Pol. A* (political and social) category for the Coventry area rightly comes at the top. National and international news items of the day are treated only in short stories – but on those 3 days the major national events were not of commanding strength. *Stars* remain a low priority, and *S & S* at nil. Agriculture is also at nil, whereas the countryside (*Env.*) element is substantial: February is not, of course, a time of high agricultural activity, nor were there any shows to report.

Commentary

When choosing the *Coventry Evening Telegraph* as one of my targets in the Midlands, I knew next to nothing about it. My object was to see whether there were marked differences of character and operation between newspapers at the centre of a region and those at a distance from the metropolitan heart. Coventry and Huddersfield, in quite different ways, proved to be perfect examples of this. Both have strong local interests of their own. Both are served by highly efficient

Content by Categories: *3 weekdays, Wednesday 17–Friday 19 February, 1988, taken together*

Category*	Total space (sq. cm)	No. of items
A&S	6683	(34)
Crash	610	(14)
Crime	4431	(48)
Env.	1670	(9)
Health	1140	(15)
Health A	2153	(17)
Human	6764	(62)
Int.	315	(9)
Money	2084	(18)
Pets	619	(5)
Pol.	1554	(21)
Pol. A	10056	(60)
Sport (3-day total)	18939	
Stars	1571	(17)
S & S	nil	
Terror	170	(5)
War	138	(3)
Weather (3-day total)	585	

Note:
* For explanation of categories, see pp. xi–xii.

newspapers, with a broadly liberal approach. But whereas Huddersfield has a single edition at midday and a second edition only when there is strong late news to call for it, Coventry has up to 10 or 11 editions each day, with variations to cover the city and its surrounding communities.

As must be clear from the Coventry narrative, production of so many editions calls for intricate and integrated decisions. That production is made easier by the introduction of electronic equipment. Stories can be stacked in word processor 'baskets', and alternative versions can be prepared simultaneously. Editors, news editors, sub-editors and picture editors all have access to the texts in preparation, without interrupting whoever is working on them. Even so, there is need for talk and brief debate before decisions are taken. Hence the mini-conferences and consultations described in the narrative.

The influence of the editor and the deputy editor is greater than may appear from the narrative. Geoffrey Elliott runs the 8.15 am conference and monitors the character of the primary stories. Then Roger Monkman, as deputy, takes over the 'minute by minute' supervision of the newsroom. The final decisions are made after the editor returns to the newsroom around 11 am, and later for the later editions.

Elliott himself was a trainee at the *Coventry Evening Telegraph* after leaving school. He became deputy editor at the age of 27, left to become editor of the *Kent Messenger* from 1979 to 1981, and then returned to Coventry as editor in 1981. That was a difficult year, with depression in Midlands industries, and the only year in which the paper lost money.

Since 1981 he has made a number of changes in the style and priorities of the paper – in particular, encouraging reporters to become semi-specialists, creating the political unit, revising the layout (which has won the paper a series of design awards), and insisting that attention should be given to 'people' and to the effects of events on individuals. That accounts for the high level of 'human' stories in the content. He writes a weekly 'bulletin' for distribution to every member of the editorial staff, commenting on the week's papers and giving news of staff changes or other internal events. Personally he is a quiet man, unlike the cinema stereotype of the shirt-sleeved editor.

As to news priorities, the summary of contents shows the top rating of regional and local 'politics' in its widest sense – including the industrial, economic and social wellbeing of the community. For any serious newspaper, that must surely be the top priority. The reporting is concise and factual, without evident bias, and there is economy in the use of adjectives. The background provided by the feature articles is substantial, and good use is made of specialist knowledge among the staff. Altogether, the *Coventry Evening Telegraph* is an impressive operation.

People

Paul Dale

Reading Chronicle, then *Oxford Mail and Times* (public affairs correspondent). Midlands Journalist of the Year, 1985, for investigation into delays in cervical cancer tests. To *Coventry Evening Telegraph* 1986.

Geoffrey Elliott

From school to trainee reporter, *Coventry Evening Telegraph*. ('Broke his mother's heart', he says, that he didn't go to university.) Deputy editor at 27. To *Kent Messenger* as editor, 1979. Invited back to Coventry, as editor, 1981.

Kenny Farquharson
Aberdeen University (Hons English) 1984. Postgraduate journalism course. Cardiff 1984–5. To *Coventry Evening Telegraph* as reporter, 1985. Acting Industrial Editor from February 1988.

Alan Kirby
Joined two-man weekly at age 16. Later to *Chronicle and Echo*, evening newspaper Northampton; then freelance. To *Coventry Evening Telegraph* 1973 as reporter. Then to newsdesk; 3 newsdesk roles, last as news editor. Assistant Editor from 1987.

Melanie Knight
Durham University, English degree, 1984. City University, postgraduate journalism 1984–5. To *Coventry Evening Telegraph* as reporter, 1985. Community relations-race relations reporter 1986–7. Health Correspondent from September 1987.

15 Olympics, Business and Ethnic News: The *Post*, Birmingham

To try to produce a serious morning newspaper with only one daytime reporter and two specialists is an almost impossible task. It is made no better by having so few sub-editors that nobody can be spared to revise a badly written Press Association report which is intended to lead an inside news page. That was the position at the *Post* in Birmingham on Tuesday 23 February 1988.

At that point the *Post*'s fortunes were possibly about to improve. The paper had just been bought – along with its sister, the *Evening Mail* – by Mr Ralph Ingersoll II of Princeton, New Jersey, already reputed to be the owner of 37 dailies in the United States and 150 weeklies. (Some of these, however, appeared to be joint enterprises with other US companies.) Hitherto American publishers had been unwilling to invest in the UK because of union restrictions and what was seen as a weak economy in Britain. By 1988 the union problems had been cracked and the economy was believed to be 'on the up and up'.

The *Post* was in urgent need of rescue. It had been severely injured by bad judgement of its management in preceding years and by being starved of resources. In 1975 it had suffered from a 10-week dispute with its journalists, during which 'an apology of a paper' (as one of its staff of that time described it) was put together by the editor and a handful of others. In 1978, in common with nearly all other regional newspapers in England, it was hit by a further 8-week strike of journalists. By 1980 its sales were down from a peak of about 80 000 to no more than 33 000; and 2 years later, when the management decided to merge the *Post* and the *Evening Mail* into a single all-day newspaper, there was a further fall to below 30 000. In 1986 the two papers were separated, though still sharing some services.

A West Midlands morning newspaper suffers, of course, from the proximity of London and the consequent competition of the national morning newspapers. It suffers also from the lack of a common identity in the communities of the region. As already noted, people in Wolverhampton or Coventry or Stoke seem to have little interest in the affairs of Birmingham, nor are Brummies much concerned with what is happening in the neighbouring cities. Thus the *Coventry Evening Telegraph* and the *Express and Star* in Wolverhampton can reach towards sales of 100 000 or beyond, concentrating on their own areas and secure in their profits, as to an extent the *Evening Mail* does in Birmingham. But the lack of community in the West Midlands as a whole is not, in itself, enough to explain the poor sales of the *Post*. Weak management and inadequate editorial staffing must be to blame.

Narrative, Tuesday 23 February 1988

Only a brief account can be given here. The paper has 2 editions, one at 11.45 pm and the other about 1.30 am. Planning, however, starts at 11.45 am with an editorial conference which has a chatty run-through of the prospects for the coming evening. First comes the 'Business and Finance' section – an 8-page pull-out in the centre of the paper, regarded as important in a trading city. Later comes the main list: today with the second day of the Land-Rover strike, a court case where a senior tax officer is charged with fraud, and Eddie Edwards of Cheltenham ski-jumping tonight in the Winter Olympics at Calgary in Canada.

The staff shortage today means that only one general reporter is working from 11 am and one more coming at 5 pm, but the news editor is using two of the specialists for general duties. The single reporter is trying to follow up an early morning story of a fire in a hotel in Bulgaria where 6 British skiers are said to have died. People from Birmingham are known to have been in the hotel. She is trying by telephone to gather information from the British Embassy staff in Sophia, from travel agents, and from the ski resort.

The *Post* has access also to all the work done by reporters for the *Mail*. But its policy is not to give too great prominence to anything covered in the evening paper. Also there is too little time, and there are too few sub-editors to revise or rewrite items for the morning paper.

At 5 pm the main conference is held. Day and night senior staffs are there. It is sharper and less chatty than at 11.45. The paper is by now clearly taking shape. After the conference the night editor gives me his reasons for his choice of priorities, endorsed by editor Peter Saunders. For the front page, probably:

1. *Eddie the Eagle*: 'If he makes his jump! If he kills himself, it's the splash. If he does well, it's still a great story. There's so much interest in the guy – he must go on page 1 whatever happens. He's something of a super star. In these Winter Olympics he's the only star we've got. There's no Torvil and Dean this year'.
2. *Tonight's Wolves v. Torquay football match*: Wolverhampton fans are 'notorious' for their bad behaviour. The Devon police are to have checkpoints on all roads into Torquay and will turn back cars with West Midlands numberplates. 'If they go round tearing things up and smashing – that's why they've been barred. If they get through and carry on like that, it's one of those stories you have to put on the front page because of its Midlands interest'. (In the event, there was no trouble. Devon police said that they had turned back a few cars, but so far as they knew no Wolves fans got into the ground. So it became a back page story.)
3. *Ulster*: with the Army's decision to take back a man who had served three years of a life sentence for killing a Catholic, coming on the same day as the funeral of another shot dead on the border – and with Cardinal O'Fiaich at the funeral speaking of the 'deplorable' record of the armed forces in his archdiocese. 'It's the major national story of the day, so far. It hits you as a good story'. He hoped the PA would pull it all together, because 'we don't have the staff to do it'.
4. *Land-Rover*: The second day of the strike, but there was 'not a lot that's new'. As a business paper, the *Post* 'must give prominence to a major industrial story'. Also Mrs Thatcher had been speaking in the Commons.

More unusual are three or four items which night editor David Ransome-Wallis expects to place on page 3:

1. *Genealogists* 'fighting a daily battle' for use of microfilms in Birmingham's Central Library: with a booming interest in ancestry, the scuffles and arguments between professionals and amateurs had become so bad that the librarian had decided to make sure that ratepayers came first. 'It's a nice light story'.
2. *A tribunal at Rugby* hearing a case against Rugby School and its

headmaster brought by a religious studies teacher who had been made redundant: 'It's one of the top schools in Britain. It's the first time they've had an unfair dismissal case. It's unusual'.

3. '*Twitchers*' – a court case in the north of Scotland against two Coventry bird watchers charged with disturbing rare black-throated divers while photographing them. 'Bird watching and rambling are the sort of things a lot of our business readers do in their private life. There's a lot of interest – seeing someone fined for watching some birds. If they had pleaded not guilty it would have been the first case of its kind'. (They pleaded guilty were fined £50 each under the 1981 Wildlife and Countryside Act.)

4. *The lady golfer*: 'It's a beautiful story – everyone is reading it. It's about a woman being kicked out of a golf club because of her so-called behaviour. She's being accused of cheating, wearing short shorts and brief briefs. A lip-smacking story ... We have a lot of golfers. She's an excellent golfer, county rated. She's suing the club for reinstatement and claiming damages for an injured reputation. She says there's been a lot of petty jealousy. Unfortunately we didn't have a reporter to send today, so we're having to rely on PA'.

As to sources, the *Post* had to depend on news agencies for cover of the Calgary Olympics. For the Wolves – Torquay match, the warning of police roadblocks came at first through the sports staff, and the late reporter obtained his information by telephone calls to the police in Devon. The various aspects of Ulster were all Press Association copy. Land-Rover was a combination of the staff man in Parliament, PA, and the business staff in Birmingham. The genealogists in conflict at the city library came initially from a friendly phone call and had been followed up by the social services correspondent, on secondment to general news that day. The Rugby School hearing was covered by a district reporter, working for the *Mail* and the *Post*. The 'twitchers' story from Scotland was PA; and the golfing lady was also PA, though on earlier days it had been covered by a staff reporter.

A final comment from the night editor, David Ransome-Wallis. 'I like making decisions – "we'll use this, we won't use that". We have a few arguments, but we hope it comes out as a good production'. About 7.30 pm he is joined in the newsroom by the editor, Peter Saunders. They talk through the plans for pages 1 and 3, with a look also at the main UK stories for pages 8 and 9. They are agreed, and there are no 'arguments' tonight. The big uncertainty is Eddie

Edwards – whether he will jump, what will happen, what time they will hear, and whether there will be pictures. Already Saunders and Wallis are sketching out two or three alternative plans for the front page, depending on what pictures they receive. But for the first edition, Northern Ireland is the lead with a picture of the coffin and mourners at the Tyrone funeral of an unarmed man shot by the army.

At about 11 pm, when an element of nail-biting was beginning, news came at last from Calgary – not from the Press Association, as expected, but from an enterprising freelance. He provided enough copy to let the *Post* report that two men from the West Midlands had 'captured Olympic glory'. Eddie the Eagle had jumped 71 metres, a British record, though far behind the Olympic leaders; and a Birmingham man had won the gold medal in the 500 metre speed skating.

1 hour and 16 minutes later, in time for the City edition, the PA copy came. For that final edition there was a big spread across the front page, with pictures of a triumphant Eddie and his fast-skating countryman, Wilf O'Reilly. The 'paste up' was somewhat behind time, but not enough to upset Birmingham distribution.

Ethnic Issues and Yemen

Within the West Midlands, there are large communities whose origins are in Pakistan, India or the West Indies. Peter Saunders admits that covering ethnic issues is 'very, very difficult'. He believes that within those communities there is a prejudice against the press – 'possibly justified'. Whereas the *Post* used to have a reporter who specialised in these matters, at present it had nobody for that role. However, both its social services correspondent and one of its feature writers took an interest.

The social services man, Jonathan Leake, said that dealing with organisations in the ethnic areas was easy but contact with individuals was difficult. He had chosen to live in Handsworth (scene of the riots in north-west Birmingham in 1985) when he first came to work for the *Evening Mail* in 1984 – not because it was an ethnic area but because he had the chance to share a house with friends there. He had been a user of the pub where the riots started. The ethnic element was only around 30 to 40 per cent, but the area was one with many very old, very big houses which were cheap. He thought that the *Post* was not particularly interested in stories about people who did not read the paper, so he had to 'sell it hard' if he wanted to get anything of that kind in. With emotive issues such as child abuse, though the numbers involved were small, it was easier to get stories into the paper.

(Leake himself was a marine biology graduate of Liverpool University and had come straight from there to the *Evening Mail*. He had moved over to the *Post* in 1987. He thought his science training had given him some advantages over Arts graduates, because he understood the figures which were involved in many stories, local government and others. 'The science method is quite similar to the ideal journalist's method'.)

Another with an interest in ethnic issues is the feature writer, Thomas Quirke. He was the primary source of the series of reports – major national news for some months in late 1987 and in early 1988 – on two Birmingham girls whose father sold them into marriage in Yemen. That had happened in 1980, when the girls were children. They had been there ever since, now with children of their own. Their mother, estranged from their father, had tried to get them back but the Foreign Office had said it could not help.

Quirke had heard of the story through one of the *Post*'s industrial reporters, working in Hansworth. He had approached it cautiously, with disbelief, but had spent 2 days talking to the woman. He had become convinced that she was telling the truth.

In 1980, after the girls had been taken to North Yemen, the mother had written to the Foreign Office and had gone to London. As a working class woman dealing with experienced officials, she made no progress. They said there was nothing they could do. (Quirke saw the letters, which she still had.) Her MP received the same reply. Then in 1986 she was hit by a car and received £8000 in compensation. Part of this she used to visit Yemen and find her daughters. She made a tape recording of the elder daughter describing the way they had been raped, forced into marriage and had to live in the mountains. Still with strong Birmingham accents, they said they wanted to return home. The mother made this tape in order to send it to the director of Defence of Children International, in Geneva, which she did.

Quirke then telephoned to Geneva, from the *Post*, and asked for the tape to be played so that he could record it. It removed any doubts that he or others at the newspaper had. 'Once you'd heard the tape there was no doubting', he said. 'It was a galvanising tape. It was clear that what the mother had told us was true. It was a heart-breaking tape'.

The father, still living at Sparkbrook in Birmingham, had warned the mother that if she went to the press the girls would immediately be taken across the Saudi border to where they could not be found. There seemed a real risk that they might be killed. The *Post* therefore adopted a strategy of preparing for publication on a Friday morning (27 November). Beforehand it briefed Roy Hattersley (deputy leader of the Labour Party and MP for Birmingham Sparkbrook), and he arranged to see the Foreign Secretary, Sir Geoffrey Howe, the day before publication. The *Post* expected the story to be picked up by national dailies on the Saturday and then by the Sunday papers, since it would have provided all the detail on its front page and its main feature page, and with a transcript of the tape recording on page 7. It also expected that, being in possession of all the details before publication, the Foreign Office would send a jeep from the embassy in to collect the girls from their village.

In fact, whether because of concern over legal hazards or for other reasons, the national dailies did not carry much on the Saturday. The *Observer*, having been given early warning by Thomas Quirke and having had the chance to study the documents, made much of it on Sunday and sent their own reporter out to North Yemen. The Foreign Office made no move.

In ensuing weeks most of the national newspapers took up the story, some sending reporters to Yemen. Some made offers to the mother for exclusive rights in the daughters' stories when they came home, one going as high as £20 000. These offers were refused. The father, in an interview with Thomas Quirke published in the *Post* in the following week, admitted that he had married off the daughters in a secret Islamic ceremony in a house in Birmingham, before they went on their 'holiday' to Yemen, but the girls had known nothing of that until they arrived in Yemen.

The selling of the Birmingham girls is an extraordinary story, and the *Post*'s persistence in establishing the facts is much to its credit. Publication, however, was not popular with some of the ethnic communities in Birmingham, because they thought it damaging to their reputation – in itself, an illustration of the difficulty of dealing with ethnic issues.

Content by Categories:

4 midweek days. (Tuesday–Friday) and counting only the news pages (Not included are the arts review and arts features, books, boats and caravan show, general features, holidays, leaders and letters to the editor, and motoring.)

Category*	4-day totals	
	Total space (sq. cm)	No. of items
A&S	1 354	(9)
Ag.	595	(3)
Crash	2 370	(15)
Crime	2 201	(30)
Env.	617	(7)
Health	232	(3)
Health A	1 395	(11)
Human	3 645	(31)
Int.	2 574	(25)
Money	28 444	(189)
Pol.	3 970	(30)
Pol. A	5 479	(37)
Terror	1 840	(10)
Sport	21 836	(122)
Stars	967	(10)
S & S	25	(1)
War	1 139	(8)
Weather	790	(4)

Note:
* For explanation of categories, see pp. xi–xii.

The importance to the *Post* of financial and business news is abundantly plain, taking up over one third of the total news space. Sport comes next in the paper's priorities, and *Pol. A* (regional and local political, economic and social news) comes third, with one quarter of the space given to sport, and incidentally only two fifths of the space given to that category on average by the *Coventry Evening Telegraph*. The figures for *Health A* are also low when compared with other regional newspapers at that time.

Commentary

To judge the *Post* as it was in February 1988 could be unjust to a hard-working staff. With the Ingersoll takeover, better resources may eventually come. But, as the paper was at that time, its staffing and resources were sadly inadequate. A serious newspaper cannot be run with as few reporters and sub-editors as were then available. Perhaps rightly, the main effort appeared to be concentrated on business and financial news. Front pages which consist mainly of Press Association and other agency news, and inside pages also heavily dependent on non-staff sources, give a drab impression – even if, as with the *Post*, the page make-up is often skilled and the pictures well chosen.

The *Post* faces serious competition from the Reed *Daily News*, distributed free of charge in much of the city of Birmingham. The *Post* remains far ahead in its finance and business news, both for the West Midlands and nationally, and its sports cover is both more extensive and more attractive. But the main news pages of the *Daily News* have a briskness and bite that the *Post* cannot match while so short of staff.

The features and the Arts pages in the *Post* are readable and competent. The letters to the editor are mostly dull, though with an occasional spark on local issues. But it is the main newspages which, above all, need rejuvenation.

16 Populists in Coventry: Mercia Sound

Mercia Sound's newsroom is unashamed about its character. It is ILR's version of a popular tabloid newspaper, but without the page 3 girls. It aims at the popular market – according to its head of news, Colin Palmer – and it 'must be realistic about that'. Its news is pitched towards crime, human stories and events in the city of Coventry. Its audience is mainly in the city – where it claims a weekly reach of over 60 per cent – while it attracts listening percentages only in the 20s and 30s in the surrounding rural areas or in the more academic environments of Kenilworth or Warwick. As one critic from those areas said, 'they treat Warwickshire as a rather "twee" place full of farmers'.

An indication of its news priorities can be found in its 1 pm bulletin of Friday 12 February 1988. The headlines at 12.58 am, preceding the national news from IRN in London, covered three items.

- 'Seven Leamington policemen are commended for bravery in tackling violent gangs of bikers'
- 'A heart operation on a Warwickshire baby is cancelled for the third time'
- 'And there's a warning about door-to-door salesmen peddling smoke alarms'

In the background to this is drumming rock music, faded down a little while Colin Palmer reads the headlines at a lively pace, then faded up for 2 or 3 seconds, and then faded down as the national news begins (with no mention that it is coming from IRN) and finally out as the newsreader in London gets into his stride. As it happens, the network news opens with a West Midlands story: an MP in Parliament accuses the Government of letting children die in the West Midlands 'because it won't put more cash in the Birmingham Children's Hospital'. Six items are covered in the three minutes from IRN. The Mercia news follows immediately, delivered by Colin Palmer. It includes 6 items and the weather forecast, with recorded interviews in 5 of the 6 items.

151

Taking 5 Mercia news bulletins – 3 at 8 am, 1 and 1 pm and 1 at 5 pm on different days that week – we find that of 44 items 13 are in the *Crime* category, 12 *Human*, 12 in *Pol. A* (a wide mixture from Coventry bus fares to a pub landlord who will employ a vulgar pop band already banned elsewhere, and including Lord Young at Warwick University), 4 in the *Health* category (all concerned with children's heart operations), 2 in *Arts and Science* and 1 *Crash*. These counts exclude the IRN national news elements from London. Compared with BBC WM in Birmingham, the *Pol. A.* count is lower while the *Crime* and *Human* categories are proportionately higher. Palmer says that Mercia's success is based on its 'parochialism'.

All but one of the 6 local items included reporters' recordings of the people concerned, and all of them had been obtained that morning. With a limited staff, Palmer thought they had done well. Of the 10 journalists, 1 had to be detached each day to work at Coventry Cable, providing their bulletins with material fed from Mercia. Another looked after sport. That left Palmer himself and 6 others, of whom one came on duty at 5.15 am, another at 7 am, 2 at 10 am (if nobody was sick or on holiday) and 1 at 3 pm. Two had been out this morning, each producing 4 stories or variations of a story to be used later in the day. With Lord Young at Warwick University this morning, for example, they had recorded a rebuttal of rumours in some of the national newspapers that Mrs Thatcher was about to shake up the Industry Department, merging it with Employment. He had sent that to IRN at noon, and it had gone out from IRN on the printer service to all ILR stations. He had retained for Mercia's own use at 1 pm the friendly comment from Lord Young about the new management course at the University of Warwick, because it was more local, and there was a third story for use at 5 pm.

Though his staff is small and mostly young – and not so well paid as BBC local radio, he says – the enthusiasm of 'the kids' is great, and they are willing to work long hours without extra money. His own background is newspaper journalism (the *Birmingham Mail*) until 27, then 3 years with BRMB in Birmingham, then 3 more with Viking Radio in Hull when it started, then to Mercia. Palmer says that in the first 18 months of Viking he trained 10 radio journalists who then took better paid jobs with BBC radio stations. Personally, he did not want to work for the BBC because he thought it 'stuffy'.

The style of news at Mercia is conversational and fairly fast, but not too fast and free from slang. I thought it odd, in that Friday 1 pm bulletin, that in reporting the cancelled hospital operation no reference was made to the preceding IRN report from Parliament on the problems at the children's hospital. Admittedly time was short, but to have slipped in an extra half sentence would not have been difficult. It was also evident from the *Coventry Evening Telegraph* an hour later that Mercia had missed an even stronger story on its doorstep – a Coventry child, aged 2, who had just had his heart operation postponed for the eleventh time.

With the coming of BBC's R. Warwickshire in the autumn of 1989, Mercia will face stiffer competition. It expects to lose some of its audience in the areas outside Coventry itself, but expects to 'hold the city'. By the autumn of 1989 it will have some advantage through operating split frequencies – with sport having priority on MW at the weekend, for example, while disc jockeys and popular music take the FM transmission. The MW (medium) programmes may be a little less brazenly raucus then. Other changes may follow from the management merger of BRMB in Birmingham and Mercia Sound in Coventry, but probably not many while Mercia's profits remain strong.

17 The South-West of England: 'Ships, Celts and the *Wednesday Walk-in*'

England's south-westerly peninsula stretches some 150 miles into the Atlantic. In the far west, Cornwall has a Celtic tradition and remnants of the Celtic language, with some of the oldest Christian settlements in the British Isles. Devon is bigger, more wealthy, based largely on farming and with the cathedral city of Exeter as its capital. But by far the biggest city of the region is Plymouth, with Europe's largest naval dockyard and a nautical history that does back many hundreds of years. Edward I once gathered 325 seagoing ships there, and it was from Plymouth in 1588 that Drake set out to defeat the Spanish Armada. Much of the city centre was destroyed by bombing in 1941, but some of the old buildings and the splendour of the seaward view from Plymouth Hoe remain.

For broadcasters and for the region's only morning newspaper, the *Western Morning News*, the area extends further. TSW (Television South West) transmits well to the east of Devon, reaching far into Somerset and Dorset in competition there with HTV based in Bristol and TVS based in Southampton. BBC South West – competing with TSW within the region – can also be seen in parts of Somerset and Dorset, but it has amicable agreements for the exchange of news and videotapes with BBC Bristol and BBC Southampton. It also has transmitters in the Channel Islands.

For the *Western Morning News*, with 5 editions every night, the territory is much the same. Proudly it says at the foot of its front page every day 'The newspaper with the late, late news that the London papers miss'. That is a justified claim. But its strength lies in the extent of regional reporting. Its first edition, going to press about midnight, is aimed mainly at Exeter and East Devon while also reaching

Taunton in Somerset and Yeovil in Dorset. The second goes to Torbay and mid-Devon, the third to North Devon, the fourth to Cornwall (but soon to have separate West Cornwall and East Cornwall cover), and the last to Plymouth and its environment. It sells 56 000 copies a day on average, which is good going in a scattered area with only 2 million people.

The diversity of interests within the region creates problems for broadcasters and newspaper journalists. So does the inflow of tourists, holidaymakers, people with second homes, and retired people. Quite often, while in the South West, I was told that Devonians are not much interested in Cornwall and the Cornish not much in Devon – and that both groups are 'against' Plymouth and even more 'against' the incomers. Yet, coming there as I did after a period in Birmingham and the Midlands, I thought that there was a greater sense of community in the South West than in the areas covered by Pebble Mill, Central Television and the *Post* in Birmingham.

Here, however, are some comments from journalists in the South West. Ken Doble, a senior member of the staff at the *Western Morning News*, is a Devonian and the third generation in his family to work for the paper. While agreeing that Devon and Cornwall ought to have a strong community of interest, he said that there were 'very vocal' people in Cornwall who would rather have nothing to do with Devon. Their current campaign to have a separate Euro MP instead of sharing with Plymouth – doomed to failure because of population numbers – was an example. They took the Tamar river as 'an inviolate boundary'. They were Celts on their side, while the Devonians were Anglo–Saxon. They had their Gorsedd, their Gathering of the Bards, their links with Brittany and were orientated to a Celtic tradition which the people of Devon did not share. In addition, because Cornwall was more sparsely populated, they were finding greater difficulty in coping with the numbers of people retiring there or with second homes – people 'with alien ideas and more money'. Devon was bigger and could cope.

David Atkins, head of news and current affairs at TSW, was brought up in the Midlands but shares some of Ken Doble's view. In an ideal world, he says, Cornwall would merit a broadcasting organisation of its own because of its roots in Celtic tradition and its 'very firm' Cornish identity. But, looking ahead, he says that the make-up of the South West is changing.

We did a story the other day which revealed that two out of every three homes over a certain price range in the South West are being bought by people from the home counties. We are becoming almost a commuter market. You will find regular commuters in Weymouth, Yeovil and Exeter travelling to London. We actually did a story about people living down in Cornwall who catch the plane from Newquay every day up to London.

Thus, he says, there are tremendous differences of allegiance and interests between people in the region. But with the loss of their mining – formerly the biggest industry in Cornwall – he believes that for some people in Cornwall tourism is an alternative industry to be embraced. 'You still get protestors, you know, "no grockles" – we don't want you down here, etc.'. So although there is a deep-rooted suspicion, he suggests that they may be a declining group. ('Non-grockle' was evidently a popular sticker on Devonshire cars at one time, and 'Non-emmet' can still be seen in Cornwall, perhaps as a bad joke or perhaps to tell traffic wardens that these are locals. An 'emmet' is an ant.)

By chance, while I was in the South-West a Central Statistical Office survey was published ('Regional Trends 1988'). It showed that the region had the second highest population growth between 1981 and 1986, the fastest being East Anglia, and that in the 10 years 1976 to 1986 it had the highest growth of home owners (15 per cent). Many of these, however, came from the home counties – and the proportion of pensioners had risen to 21 per cent. Some 70 per cent of houses were owner-occupied and only 18 per cent rented from local authorities. The region also had the highest ratio of car ownership (73 per cent of households) but many were old ones needed for getting to work in rural areas. The pupil–teacher ratio was among the best, with 23 to 1 in primaries and 17 to 1 in secondary schools. The survey was reported on an inside page of the *Western Morning News* on Thursday 9 June and given prominence by BBC SW's *Spotlight* that evening. The BBC's reporter Keith Blackler summed it up this way:

So perhaps we educate our children quite well, even if many will need old bangers to get to work and will have to compete with wealthy retired people from other regions to buy a house.

A neat example of how to give humanity to statistics.

For TSW, BBC SW and the *Western Morning News* it is of course essential that they serve all the divergent groups within the region.

The daily sales figures speak for the *Western Morning News*, and the JICRAR figures for television. It was notable that during the 1987 General Election the early evening news programmes of BBC SW and TSW were consistently among the top performers, in percentage terms, in the whole of Britain in spite of having fewer resources than broadcasters in bigger regions.

The radio broadcasters have a narrower remit. BBC R. Cornwall, based in Truro, is concerned with Cornwall alone. Plymouth Sound, the ILR station for the Plymouth area, reaches 20 or 25 miles outwards from there, into East Cornwall and West Devon, though it can also be picked up quite well in parts of West Cornwall. BBC R. Devon is based in Exeter but with a presence in Plymouth, and good transmission over most of the county. And ILR's DevonAir is also based in Exeter but effectively covers only South Devon.

Again, though, the radio producers have to take account of their inflow of people from the South-East of England and the Midlands. Mike Hoskin, station manager at BBC R. Cornwall, and himself Cornish, says that no more than 40 to 45 per cent of people living in Cornwall are native Cornish – though he adds that 'the people who settle here are no less enthusiastic about being "Cornish" than the people born here'. R. Cornwall has the highest audience of any BBC station on the British mainland (excluding, that is, the 3 Scottish island stations and R. Foyle). Its daily average is a reach of 24 per cent of people in its area, and a weekly reach of 50 per cent. But, he says, the only way to run his station is to recognise that it is 'not English'. BBC R. Devon, he believes, has a harder time since Devon is becoming 'Surrey moved west'.

Plymouth Sound is unusual among ILR stations in carrying above average speech. It has a flexible schedule so that it can move over immediately to significant news in the Plymouth area or to topical discussion. It has become known in the trade as 'the upside-down station' because it carries so much more speech than is normal in ILR. It has a 2-hour morning phone-in, 5 days a week, normally run by the station's Controller of Programmes, Louise Churchill. It has the *Wednesday Walk-in*, from 2 to 3 pm every Wednesday, in which listeners can come to the studio and express their views live. Anyone who turns up by 1.50 is guaranteed a chance to go on air that day – provided they do not break the laws of libel, indecency or contempt – and when necessary the *Walk-in* runs beyond the scheduled 3 pm. Plymouth Sound has an exceptionally small staff – as broadcaster, only Louise Churchill, 5 journalists, 5 presenters and a handful of clerical and other assistants.

So the south-western peninsula, with no more than about 1 800 000 people in a strip of land over 150 miles long (and with an estimated 600 miles of coast), has a rich record in broadcasting. It has the *Western Morning News* as its one daily paper reaching the whole region; the *Western Morning News*'s sister (*Evening Herald*) for the Plymouth area, evening papers also in Exeter and Torquay, and a number of small weeklies (some good, some disappointing). Let us look at the main sources of news and information in greater detail.

Analysis and Commentary

Consider the quality of reporting and explanation to people in the South-West. Taking the week of June 6–11 1988, one event stood out before all others – the loss of jobs at Devonport Royal Dockyard, which by 1990 would bring it down to half the number employed before privatisation of its management. Since it is the biggest employer in the South-West and vital to the Royal Navy, this was a bitter blow. A week earlier there had been hints of bad news to come, after three national newspapers (*Guardian*, *Independent* and *Telegraph*) had had a facility visit to the yard. Then midweek, on Tuesday 7 June, the *Western Morning News* in a front page 'splash' forecast that between 1500 and 3000 jobs were to go, on top of the 1500 already lost since DML (Dockyard Management Ltd) took over in 1987. When confirmation came at midday on Friday 10 June, the figure for further losses was 3300. From a peak of above 13 000 during and after the Falklands war, the jobs were to come down to 6000.

On the evening of the *Western Morning News*'s 'splash', TSW's *Today* also led with 'Bracing for the shock: 1500 losses?' It was the longest item in the programme, running to about $4\frac{1}{2}$ minutes. The report said that the problem was the reduction of Royal Navy work and that the unions believed the Government had always known the rundown was coming. Dr David Owen, as MP for Devonport, was interviewed live from Westminster and said that the losses might now be as much as 2500 because the navy budget was under pressure, refits were being postponed, and the fleet was smaller. He said that Plymouth was doing well in new industry, though with jobs mainly for women, and that more male jobs were needed. The BBC SW programme *Spotlight* carried nothing that evening, because it could obtain no firm confirmation of figures and because in previous weeks it had already carried reports of a coming rundown.

On the Friday DML called a press conference for mid-morning (11.30 am), to be taken by its managing director. He announced that a further 3300 jobs would have to go, that the new Royal Navy programme of work would support only 4500 of the remaining staff, and that the staff could be maintained at the new figure of 6000 only if other outside work could be obtained. TSW got the bare bones of the statement into its 11.25 am news bulletin, having arranged beforehand to get the figures at 11.15, and carried a longer version with pictures into the 1.20 regional news. BBC SW carried the main points at its first available outlet, at 12.55. Plymouth Sound, BBC R. Devon and R. Cornwall reported the news and union reactions at 12 noon, 1 pm, and in later bulletins. Plymouth Sound extended its 1 pm bulletin to run for 40 minutes. In the early evening, TSW's *Today* led with a report almost 11 minutes long. Because the BBC's *Spotlight* was committed to a live broadcast from the Royal Cornwall Show, it was able to give only 4 minutes to its report.

As to content, both programmes began with the essential figures and a summary of reaction. TSW's reporter said 'Workers, unions and local politicians say they're saddened, shocked and even staggered by the news'. The BBC's man was more restrained, saying that the scale and timing of the job losses had brought 'surprise and depression' in the yard. Interviews with the managing director of DML followed, including admissions from him that morale in the yard was low and would be difficult to restore. The TSW man asked whether the company had been 'stabbed in the back' by the Government, getting the reply from the managing director that he 'would not go as far as that' – though his face was far from happy. Replying to the BBC, he said that the company had been 'trying for some months' to get a clear picture from the Ministry of Defence of its expectations. Both programmes also carried clear and concise interviews with the leading trade union spokesman.

TSW, however, with more time available, was able to include live interviews with the Minister for Defence Procurement, Tim Sainsbury, and the highly critical Conservative MP for South East Cornwall who said he was 'flabbergasted'. It also carried recorded interviews with Dr David Owen, who said that the Government had been 'totally duplicitous' and had deserved the 'dusting down' it had received from the Audit Commission and the Public Accounts Committee; and interviews with two other Conservative MPs for Plymouth, Janet Fookes and Alan Clark, who were more restrained but nevertheless 'shocked'. It had street reactions from workers and a brief talk with one man's family at home.

The high point, however, was the TSW interview with the Minister. The co-presenter of the programme, Chris Rogers, is also TSW's political editor. While courteous, he gave the Minister a hard time. Mr Sainsbury's case was that there was 'more scope for efficiency' than had been envisaged earlier, that the Navy's 'core programme' for refits had been reduced because less servicing was needed with gas turbine engines than with steam, and that the dockyard must be more competitive in seeking outside work. Chris Rogers came back at him twice over with 'You must have known this for some time' and 'You knew that from your projections! You must have known this for ages?' To which he got 'No, No' and 'Absolutely not' – vigorous, but wholly unconvincing when privatisation had occurred only just over a year before.

BBC SW also carried recorded interviews with the critical South-East Cornwall MP Robert Hicks and with Dr David Owen. Both were brief, though to the point. Neither had the bite of the Rogers–Sainsbury debate. The *Western Morning News* next morning, not surprisingly, led with the dockyard story, giving it much of the front page (but shared with Princess Margaret and the Royal Cornwall Show). Page 3 also contained further detail. It carried brief quotations from the Minister, Mr Sainsbury; from Neil Kinnock and the new Shadow Defence Secretary, Martin O'Neill; from Janet Fookes, Alan Clark, David Owen; and from City councillors and economists.

If the BBC's *Spotlight* ran second to TSW's *Today* in reporting on the dockyard, it won by some lengths on the next biggest story of the week – the single-handed Trans-Atlantic yacht race. Nearly 100 yachts had crossed the starting line outside Plymouth Sound on Sunday afternoon. There were daily reports of their progress and of the misfortunes of some, though only the better equipped vessels were in regular radio contact. In terms of editorial priorities, the race had next to no political or social significance. But it had all the elements of excitement, human endeavour, the unexpected, and sporting competition. Since the South-West has many thousands of yachtsmen, with vessels of many sizes in almost every harbour or creek, it was an event of strong interest.

To cover the race, the BBC in Plymouth had been preparing since January. In charge was Tony Byers, normally a *Spotlight* producer. He had been involved in reporting the previous single-handed race in 1984, and the Fastnet disaster some years earlier. For the Sunday start of the race he had been able to organise 4 cameras – 1 in a helicopter, 1 with him on a motorboat, 1 on the start boat, and 1 on shore beside the 'start gun'. He did this by negotiating shared costs with French television, BBC Bristol and BBC Southampton, plus a last-minute contribution from network news in London and *Grandstand*. Small video cameras were also provided for three competitors – 1 in a large trimaran, 1 in a medium-sized monohull, and 1 in a small catamaran. The tapes from these were to be used in a documentary in the autumn.

For *Spotlight* on the Monday evening after the race began, there was more than 6 minutes of superb photography. The leading yachts had been followed far out to sea in late afternoon and were seen from the air and at sea level. The latest positions were reported. One of the three with amateur video cameras – the Marine, Pete Goss – had thrown his first cassette to the motorboat. The 'aggressive' start of the leading British competitor, Tony Bullimore, was seen. TSW's *Today* also had a variety of pictures, from sea and air, in an item running to about 4 minutes, but they did not take the audience far beyond the start. And, though good, they were no match for *Spotlight*'s.

Both programmes maintained daily reports through the week, with two rescues by Spanish trawlers directed by Nimrod aircraft – one after his yacht was attacked and sunk by whales, and one after falling overboard – and a variety of other incidents. Both had radio telephone talks with some of the competitors. When one of the best known skippers, Chay Blyth, turned back to Plymouth a BBC cameraman spotted his yacht in the early morning; and he was interviewed exclusively by *Spotlight*, whose report was also used by BBC network news. *Today* had one misfire when it reported that another famous name, Robin Knox–Johnston, had turned back because of trouble with his pump. That was not entirely *Today*'s fault, in that a relative told TSW that Robin was having trouble and later a radio 'ham', usually reliable in his tips, misinterpreted a message he had heard and said that Knox–Johnston had turned back. That was corrected in the next day's programme, by which time Knox–Johnston had in fact turned back.

The *Western Morning News* also provided daily reports, and on the first day a front-page picture of the start. But static black-and-white is no match for a moving coloured picture. Someone in a hurry in the morning could, of course, quickly find the positions of the leading yachts and the news of rescues or other incidents. Midweek the *Western Morning News*' page 5 story had the headline 'Mystery as Chay Blyth stays silent', noting his radio silence and his handicap in having sailed with a leg in plaster, after breaking it some weeks earlier. On the morning when that was published his yacht was already in Plymouth Sound, as *Western Morning News* reported next day – with a big cheerful picture of Chay and a comment from him on having twice slipped and fallen into the boat's safety netting.

News judgements are inevitably subjective. Reporters, news editors and others have to take instinctive judgements hour by hour. Without that pressure, looking back at that week, I would place third in news values a story about kidney transplants in Exeter. It was a straight exclusive for *Today*, although the programme did not claim it as such. Indeed, out of caution it put the item third in its running order. It was the work of one of TSW's two Exeter reporters, Shirley Lewis, and it came about through good contacts with the Royal Devon and Exeter Hospital there. The *Western Morning News* also carried the story next morning, with greater detail, so strictly speaking TSW had a 'beat' rather than a 'scoop'.

It was a hard news event, with human drama and implications for the National Health Service. *Today* split the story into two separate elements, one following the other, because it had been asked to do so by the hospital and the surgeon in charge. The *Western Morning News*' 'splash' had no such reservation, leading with the headline 'Boy's gift of life to others'. TSW's version opened with a report that the parents of a teenage boy killed in a road accident in Devon the previous day had agreed to the child's organs being used for transplant operations. Then, without a direct link, it went on to the Exeter hospital and an appeal by the surgeon for more renal transplants because there was 'a critical shortfall'. In fact that item, by sheer coincidence, had been recorded the previous day. It went on to a moving interview with a patient, a girl aged 24, who had had a kidney transplant 4 years before but had suffered a rejection 2 years later. She was one of 60 in Devon waiting for transplants, 'endless waiting', as she said, on dialysis 3 days a week. Of the hope of another transplant she said 'It would be the best thing that could happen to me. It would be . . . I can't put it into words'. To which the presenter added, closing the item, 'Let's hope she does so soon'.

Seeing it on transmission that night, I was at first puzzled. Was there a link or not? The presenter's closing words were a hint. In fact the operation was about to start when the programme went on air, one of two at Exeter that night, both successful. Next evening TSW reported it with the opening words 'Good news!', repeating part of the interview with the girl. The *Western Morning News*, on the morning between the two programmes, gave no names. But to anyone who had watched the link was plain.

Among other substantial items carried by one or both of the two television channels and the *Western Morning News* that week, I counted 15 relating to the South-West – not including the 'briefs' of a few seconds only or the extensive cover given to the Royal Cornwall Show by BBC SW and the *Western Morning News* (two thirds of Friday's *Spotlight* and 3 or 4 pages in the newspaper, with detailed results). To list all 15 here might be tedious, but let me mention some. An analysis of the priorities will follow later.

- A US company's proposals to dump rubbish in a disused mine in Cornwall (and in one in Cheshire), and possibly to build a methane power station on the site. This had been a running story for some time, but opposition from a group of MPs and Cornwall County Council's intention to impose 'strict rules' brought tv. coverage midweek and front page reports in the *Western Morning News* on two days.
- Dartmoor prison, with manning problems and an attempted escape (almost successful, and the first for some years). *Spotlight* had items on 4 days, *Today* on 2, and *Western Morning News* on 3.
- The future of West Cornwall's hospitals, with threatened closure of the Penzance maternity unit (which would mean 40-mile drives for women in labour). A 'peace plan' proposed by the health authority was covered by all three.
- The Central Statistical Office report on population, summarised by the *Western Morning News* and *Spotlight* as already noted.
- Questions about the future of the RAF air–sea rescue service based at Chivenor in North Devon; and items about the use of the Devon police helicopter for rescue and medical calls, and about the privately-funded Cornwall air ambulance.

These and the others in my list of 15 all seemed events or issues of interest and concern to people in the South-West. And lest it appears that these leading media of the region are stodgy or parochial, remember their extensive cover of the trans-Atlantic yacht race and the lighter items with which both *Today* and *Spotlight* usually end their half-hours. In that week those included preparations of various kinds to celebrate the 400th anniversary of the Armada, reports on the competition to design a new fountain for Plymouth city centre (with excellent pictures), the sale of an extraordinary collection of vintage cars which had been hidden away for 30 years, and a variety of others. The *Western Morning News* was also running a daily 'news report' from the Armada, which I found fascinating, with (early June) the fleet already in trouble through shortage of water and fresh food, with the commanders scared of telling the truth to their king.

Content by Categories: *the* Western Morning News *Wednesday 8–Saturday 11 June 1988*

(The figures here are for news only, excluding feature articles, leaders, etc. Business news and 'money' matters are included. The farming pages, sports pages and the Royal Cornwall Show pages are not included. The 'sports' items appearing in the news count are almost wholly the trans-Atlantic yacht race, which for convenience has been treated as a South-West event.)

Category*	SW totals (sq. cm)	No. of items	Non-SW totals (sq. cm)	No. of items
Ag.	603	4	—	—
A&S	2813	23	46	5
Crash	834	6	96	5
Crime	2358	32	389	9
Crime C	355	4	180	2
Env.	1801	16	110	2
Health	—	—	623	3
Health A	2068	20	—	—
Human	2036	25	1270	7
H/women	96	1	—	—
Int.	—	—	1274	58
Money	1985	15	4056	47
Pets	199	1	87	2
Pol.	—	—	1693	29
Pol. A	3672	36	—	—
Pol. Ed.	798	3	160	2
Terror	—	—	304	4
Sport	779	5	—	—
Stars	343	3	786	8
S & S	—	—	342	1
War	—	—	64	1
Weather	—	—	800	4

Note:
* For explanation of categories, see pp. xi–xii.

For the television programmes, the categories are the same, but since *Today* and *Spotlight* report only on events in their own region there are no national or international elements. Which does not, of course, mean that events within the region were of no interest outside it: the dockyard, the yacht race, the transplants and other events were reported nationally.

Tuesday 7–Friday 10 June 1988

Category*	TSW Today		BBC SW Spotlight	
	Total time (mnin./sec.)	No. of items	Total time (min./sec.)	No. items
Ag.	3.45	2	8.7	3
A & S	7.23	4	4.55	6
Crash	2.42	2	1.55	6
Crime	2.29	4	4.55	6
Crime C	0.20	1	0.45	1
Env.	11.19	6	10.25	5
Health A	9.18	5	4.25	4
Human	4.40	3	5.02	5
Pets	0.35	1	—	—
Pol. A	28.12	12	14.21	10
Pol. Ed.	2.53	2	4.00	2
Sport	13.01	7	14.04	6
Stars	1.56	2	2.52	2
War	2.50	1	4.32	2
Weather	9.30	4	8.12	4

In that week *Spotlight*'s content varied from normal because of the outside broadcasts from Weymouth and from the Royal Cornwall Show, 'OBs' being available to BBC SW only about once every 6 weeks (with an OB unit from Bristol). It was partly because of those two OBs that *Spotlight*'s reporting of the dockyard was less comprehensive than *Today*'s. And the BBC's higher figures for Agriculture/ farming is because of the Cornwall Show. 'Sport' in both cases consists mainly of the trans-Atlantic yacht race and the Weymouth trials for the sailing crews in the coming Olympics. The 'Stars' in both cases are Princess Anne at the Olympic trials and Princess Margaret at the Royal Cornwall Show. The 'War' elements were retrospective:

first, the senior RN Surgeon in Plymouth who had been in command of the main casualty unit in the Falklands, objecting to parts of the controversial BBC television play *Tumbledown*; and, second, concern because of a US dump of 1944 mustard gas apparently still existing in a corner of Dartmoor.

Overall, the *Western Morning News* in 4 days carried 194 stories about events in the South-West (not including, as already noted, the farming and sports pages), and 187 stories of UK or International content. The latter figure is proportionately a little higher than the figures for the *Yorkshire Post* or the *Post* in Birmingham. TSW's *Today* carried 56 South-Western stories and BBC SW's *Spotlight* 60.

The most important figures, however, are for *Pol. A* – the local and regional political, economic, social and industrial news, including employment. In broadcasts, *Today* was well ahead with 12 items taking over 28 minutes – and, it must be said, of high quality. *Spotlight*, restricted by its OBs, carried 10 items in 14½ minutes – again at a high standard, though less thorough on the dockyard. The *Western Morning News* carried a total of 36 items, with the most comprehensive reporting of the Royal Dockyard and a wide range of other political and social topics. Since the news in this category has important implications for peoples' lives, the high figures suggest that the region is being well served.

One criticism: on television, some of the short stories tell you so little that they might well be dropped. TSW, for example, carried a 16-second item about a Torquay woman who had been murdered in South Africa, having lived there for the past 7 years. She had been stabbed and was found hanged in her garage. The BBC gave it 20 seconds, telling us that the murder occurred during a spate of rioting near Pretoria – which at least made it more comprehensible. But was it really worth a place in either programme?

18 Choice, Priorities and Decision: *Spotlight* (BBC) and *Today* (TSW)

BBC SW in Plymouth has 19 journalists, including those in Exeter and West Cornwall – less than the 21 for BBC in the Midlands but more than the 17 for *Look North* in Yorkshire and Humberside. TSW has 20 – far below the staffing of Central Television, with 84 to cover the East and West Midlands and Thames Valley, and also below the 35 for YTV's *Calendar*. TSW's *Today* is nevertheless at least as good as the others, and in some ways better.

For cameras, BBC SW has 3 PSC ($\frac{3}{4}$ in) 'sound crews', 1 each in Plymouth, Exeter and St Austell; and 3 single-man Betacam ($\frac{1}{2}$ in), 1 each in West Cornwall, Torquay and Exeter. Its studio crew can also go out up to 4.30 pm. TSW has four Betacam crews – 1 each in Plymouth, Exeter, Yeovil and West Cornwall; and 4 single-man cameras (for 'actuality' – one each at or near Taunton, Barnstaple, Torbay and RAF/RN Culdrose (for West Cornwall). TSW has a big advantage in operating entirely on the Betacam $\frac{1}{2}$ in standard, whereas BBC SW has to combine three standards, and much of its equipment is old.

The working routines in Plymouth are similar to those in Leeds and Birmingham. We shall look at one day with each programme, though without the hourly detail of the preceding studies. It will again be seen that, while some of the news is originated by public authorities or industry at times to suit themselves, at least as much is generated by the initiatives of journalists.

Spotlight **on Wednesday 8 June 1988**

The day was governed by the 'OB' from Weymouth. Both BBC
Plymouth and BBC Southampton were taking parts of it, though with
the South-West team running the show to project itself into south-
west Dorset. The occasion was the Olympic yacht trials.

Spotlight's final running order at 6.35 pm began from Weymouth
with helicopter scenes and 6 brief previews (duration 1.30). The trans-
Atlantic race followed, with two competitors rescued by Spanish
trawlers after Nimrod aircraft searches (1.40). Then a report from the
Cornwall Health Authority meeting trying to avoid a row over
hospital closures (1.41). A breakout from Dartmoor prison – 'a
few hours of freedom' for one man (1.00). A fire at a Dartmoor farm,
property of the Duchy of Cornwall, with arson suspected (.26). Then
the 7 items from Weymouth – the Olympic trials (3.25), Princess
Anne's visit (1.02), the Weymouth–Portland rescue helicopter (2.37),
redevelopment of the old town and an interview with the editor of the
Dorset Evening Echo (3.36), the village of Abbotsbury and the swan-
nery (3.56), weather forecast from Weymouth beach (1.40), and
windup with a series of helicopter shots and music (.56).

As to sources, these were a typical variety. *Spotlight* and its midday
news had early warning of the breakout from Dartmoor Prison
because of the tip-off to its Torquay cameraman, Don Proctor. When
asked later whether the phonecall to his home had come from inside
the prison or outside, he laughed and said he was not answering that.
The fire at the Dartmoor farm was covered because Don Proctor
spotted it while filming police activity on the moor; the health
authority was a 'diary' item, in that the meeting had been notified
beforehand and the problem over West Cornwall hospitals was a
continuing story which had been running for some months, but of
great concern to people in Penzance, St Ives and their neighbourhood.
The trans-Atlantic race is being covered by Tony Byers, with help
from others.

The morning conference is at 9.30 am in the newsroom. Tony Byers
is there but already being called away because of messages about the
race. At 10 am, through ringing Valencia (in the south of Ireland), he
has news of one yachtsman whose vessel has sunk. An RAF Nimrod is
out searching. At 11.05 am there is a radio-telephone call from
cameraman Don Proctor, on his way to Dartmoor. Two prisoners
escaped from prison half an hour ago. This is confirmed by R. Devon
and at 11.30 am by police, though they believe one has been recap-

tured. No names available. At 11.35 am a call from cameraman who has just completed shoot at school in north-east Plymouth of item for tomorrow, but could be used tonight if needed. He is leaving for Exeter. He is told to watch out for roadblocks or other activity round Dartmoor. Later, reporter Phil Fairclough talking to Home Office – the prison's press office. They have not heard about the escape. Tavistock police don't have names and prison won't give them. Phil wants them for 12.55 bulletin. Home Office says it will find out (and does – call back about 12.30). At 12.25 am Don Proctor is on radio telephone from a police roadblock on Dartmoor. Police helicopter has just passed over 'winging back to Exeter', he says. So it looks as if the search has been called off. At 12.35 am Proctor again: black smoke coming up above trees nearby, and fire engine has just passed. He is following it.

By the afternoon Byers has news of two searches in the Atlantic. Reporter Phil is working with him, trying for radio telephone interviews. Phil is also updating the Dartmoor story. One of the prisoners who tried to escape fell from the wall back into the prison and broke a leg; the other is believed to have been captured some distance away, but that still has to be confirmed. And the fire observed by Proctor at the farm is a stronger story than an ordinary fire because the firemen are having to wear masks for protection against toxic fumes from chemicals in the farmyard. Through the morning and afternoon there is regular contact with Weymouth; despatch riders are bringing tapes to be edited in Plymouth.

By mid-afternoon producer Charles Wace has the running order ready, subject to late changes (which can be up to a few minutes before going on air). The yacht race and Atlantic rescues are top of the list, with information still coming in. The reporter at Truro for the health authority left there at 3 pm, having got a good interview after the meeting. Over the Dartmoor escape, the prison authorities are embarrassed because only yesterday a delegation from the Prison Officers' Association had complained about short-staffing, which makes it a stronger story.

A little excitement at 4 pm. Reporter Phil, having made contact with a Spanish trawler through Valencia Radio, bolts down to dubbing suite to record an interview with the Netherlands yachtsman Roal Engels. Engels says he was 'rudely awakened' when his yacht ploughed into some metal object. After having to abandon his ship, he was 'bobbing up and down' in his liferaft until the trawler picked him up, though he had been relieved when the Nimrod came overhead.

The links to Weymouth are ready half an hour before transmission. The two presenters will insert their pieces live from there. All the rest of the material is at hand in Plymouth.

At 6.35, on air. Afterwards, producer Charles' verdict is that the programme was 'passable'. It had nice pictures, he said, but the lack of wind at Weymouth had removed the central theme – the Olympic trials. There had been a flaw at one point when the sound from Weymouth went down during a presenter's link, but they had got out of that 'reasonably well' (in fact, by just going straight on with the item that was being introduced). OBs, he said, 'can go horrendously wrong'. This, on balance, had been 'a good one'.

Commentary

That day was not typical, because of the outside broadcast from Weymouth. The OB as such was a success, providing a change of pace and location for the programme and some delightfully artistic pictures. It was justified as an exceptional exercise by BBC SW. But the price was a loss of hard news. It missed the latest stage in the controversy over dumping US rubbish in Cornwall, an important story carried both by TSW and by the *Western Morning News*. It also missed – though perhaps unavoidably – the kidney transplants about to take place in Exeter. On the plus side, it covered the Atlantic rescues well and it reported the latest placings in the race. It provided a clear and compact report on the West Cornwall hospitals, again a running story but important. And, because of its Torquay cameraman's tip, it had the best pictures from the Dartmoor search and the farm fire.

The two young presenters, live from the beach and streets of Weymouth, had the right touch of informal cheer and were dressed accordingly. For one – Juliet Morris – it was her first week as a regular presenter. She had been plucked from the Falmouth radio journalism course, having been on attachment to *Spotlight* at Easter, because her predecessor, Jill Dando, had moved to BBC *Breakfast Time* in London. For someone new to the job, she did very well indeed. Having lost both its regular presenters in the previous winter, *Spotlight* probably made the best choice it could. But generally it is a tactical mistake to have two young presenters, even when both are as competent as these two were, because together they cannot carry the impression of experience and authority that a mix of young and more mature can offer.

Today **Thursday 9 June**

An average day, but with good results. At its fifth day, the Atlantic single-handed yacht race was again dominant; but for variety the programme led with two fires in Somerset – one where an elderly lady died, with arson suspected; the other destroying a factory (2.12). Then the yacht race, with a third 'Mayday' rescue and more sighting of whales (2.00, OB); next, RAF Chivenor's rescue helicopters seem to be saved from transfer to Wales (3.41). Fourth, 'Good news!' Exeter patient featured yesterday has had kidney transplant. Then 5 brief stories (shortest 0.12, longest 0.38). Others – Alan Beith brings the SLD leadership battle to Cornwall (2.27). Royal Cornwall Show, with cows, bulls, horses, steam engines and rain (3.22). Auction of vintage cars, hidden away for 30 years (2.27), weather (2.11), design competition for fountain to go in Plymouth city centre, 'high tech.' winner (2.05). And, at last minute, Knox–Johnston has withdrawn from Atlantic race (premature, as it turned out) – 0.17.

As to sources, the oustanding initiative was in Shirley Lewis's pursuit of the Exeter transplant operations. The reports of the Somerset fires followed from routine telephone calls, and the Atlantic 'Mayday' story was developed by a reporter after the early warning from a friendly contact. All the main stories other than the Exeter transplants were carried also by *Spotlight*, which had greater detail of the third Atlantic rescue and also had Chay Blyth in its studio. Its race report ran to 4.46, compared with *Today*'s 2.08. *Spotlight* did not have either of the Somerset fires; but it did have the Central Statistical Office report on population, which is presented well with graphics. The Chivenor helicopters, the visit of Alan Beith, and the design competition for a fountain were all 'diary' items, but all three were of substantial public interest – and the design competition had excellent pictures and commentary in *Today*.

Some items from my notebook that morning.
(1) Yesterday a sub-post office was raided but the police withheld all information. Worth pursuing today? Decision – no, too small, unless someone comes up with new information.
(2) Alan Beith campaigning, will have to be covered in St Austell or Truro. Plymouth crew and reporter will have to go, because West Cornwall crew at Royal Cornwall Show.
(3) Shirley Lewis, Exeter reporter who did the transplants story, rings for instructions on how to treat it today – and to discuss two other items.

(4) Mid-morning phone call from the family of a trans-Atlantic competitor, Devon residents, to say that another competitor in one of the big trimarans has put out 'Mayday' because of damage to his yacht.

At 12.45 am a 'running order' meeting. Producer Brian Pedley sees the Chivenor helicopters as the strongest story – a deputation (civilian) is in London trying to persuade the Defence Minister to leave them there. But the 'Mayday' story looks 'very promising' – the strongest human story yet from the Atlantic race. He's worried, however, about whether the crew (delayed by other work in Plymouth) and reporter will catch up with Alan Beith. There have been two fires in Somerset – one a suspected murder – and one of the Yeovil reporters is there.

Notes from the afternoon:
(1) Nikky Parr, 'programme journalist' recently recruited from R. Cornwall, is editing the material from Exeter on the hospital transplants. The pictures are taken from yesterday's item, but with a new soundtrack from Shirley Lewis. Discussion with Sue King, who is revising the script as presenter. Decision to start with 'very good news' – the young woman seen last night pleading from her hospital bed as she waited for a vital transplant operation had within hours received donated organs. From Sue's introduction they would then go to Shirley's voice over the pictures selected by Nikky.
(2) Mid-afternoon: reports on the two fires in Somerset (video tape and voice) are being taken on line from Yeovil by remote control from Plymouth. The reporter in Yeovil is having to go straight on to Exeter – another long drive – to interview the Assistant Chief Constable about police troubles with violent youths.
(3) Reporter Alan Cuthbertson on phone from Truro. The crew arrived half an hour ago, having been held up by traffic, but he has recorded the interview with Alan Beith. The despatch rider should be back in Plymouth by 4.45.
(4) At 4.15 Sue King, having finished all her links half an hour ago, is off to have hair wash and make-up (half hour needed). Co-presenter Chris Rogers is still writing his links. Both must be in studio soon after 5 pm for rehearsals.

Meanwhile producer Brian has recast his running order. There are legal complications over one of the Somerset fires – the suspected murder cannot be mentioned – but he will lead with that rather than the Atlantic race. The race looks good, though, and a radio interview is expected soon with one of the yachtsmen in mid-ocean who has been having trouble with whales. There is a complication with the Chivenor story: a Westminster studio is booked at 6.05 pm (cannot be booked earlier because ITN have it) to talk to the North Devon MP who has led the delegation to the Defence Ministry, so he has to be slotted in then. Chivenor cannot go first in the running order (and in the end goes third). As we talk, Brian is called to the dubbing suite to hear an interview with the Canadian rescue centre over the race. And at the same time Nikky, having completed the transplants edit and other things, is about to edit the Beith interview. That is completed at 5.40 pm, 20 minutes before going on air.

On air at 6 pm, with the items already listed. The Westminster live interview is successful. There are two little slips on transmission – one when an item comes up without sound, and the other when an item is dropped but the cameras come on to the wrong presenter. Both are quickly covered by Sue King and Chris Rogers. Brian's verdict afterwards: 'A good day – very busy'.

Commentary

This was a brisk programme, well presented, and with a pleasing mixture of hard news followed by lighter items towards the end. It was enhanced by having two of the most competent presenters whom I have encountered. Both were BBC trained but had eventually gone to independent television.

As to news priorities, the only substantial item not taken up was the Central Statistical Office report on population. The politics of whether North Devon would be allowed to keep its rescue helicopter squadron was properly covered and Alan Beith's sortie into the South-West was given locally relevant attention. The successful kidney transplants in Exeter were rightly welcomed, with the bonus of having been foreshadowed the previous day. I would have placed that item higher in the running order both because it was such good news and because it reinforced the surgeon's plea for more people to carry donor cards. As always, these judgements are individual; but in terms of responsible choice this must be seen as a reliable programme.

My only serious doubt was whether the two fires in Somerset were worth the top place in the running order. That came about because there was an implicit murder story behind one fire and the need to fill time before going to the Westminster interview. Once it was known that for valid legal reasons the murder aspect could not be developed the story lost some of its bite; and the good news of the kidney transplants could have been moved up.

The headlines, like the links between the items, had been written by the presenters to fit their own style. They gave an attractive and intelligible lead to what was coming. The presenters Chris Rogers and Sue King carry an impression of competence and reliability, with a serious but not too formal approach at the beginning of the programme and a more relaxed freedom later. Altogether, a confident performance which gives confidence to viewers.

Finally, one plus point both for *Spotlight* and for *Today*. They take the weather forecasts seriously and do them well. That is right for a region with a huge coastline and much farming.

People

BBC SW *Spotlight*

Tony Byers
Message boy, *Daily Express*. Bristol University 1967–70. Mirror Group training scheme. Plymouth, freelance for BBC regional radio. Then BBC staff; Assistant News Editor. Developed interest in maritime matters, including trans-Atlantic races. Reports for network news, *Grandstand* and others.

Phil Fairclough
Zoology degree, University of Bristol 1980; while there, worked on student programme for BBC R. Bristol and freelanced. Cardiff postgraduate course 1980–81, radio journalism. Briefly with *Glasgow Herald*, summer 1981; then 18 months with *Birmingham Post and Mail* (NCTJ certificate). Then to BBC Plymouth, *Nationwide* researcher. Then 'Regional Journalist', TV.

Chris Wace (producer)
Milton Keynes Gazette. Then BBC R. Solent. Reporter and producer *South Today* (Southampton). From 1986 'senior production journalist' with BBC Plymouth, and one of two regular producers of *Spotlight*.

Annette Williams (researcher)
Portsmouth Polytechnic, degree in Cultural Studies. Cardiff post-graduate course in TV production (not journalism) 1986. Then BBC Cardiff 18 months. To BBC SW February 1988. (In charge of editing Weymouth tapes on Wednesday 8 June.)

TSW *Today*

David Atkins, Head of News and Current Affairs
School in Elstree and Stafford. Then in succession *Stafford Advertiser*, *Stoke Advertiser*, *Stafford Evening Sentinel*. Then Raymond's news agency, where he 'did learn a lot'. On to BBC R. Sheffield as music producer and presenter, three years, with R. Leeds on Saturdays for sport. 6 years with BBC Plymouth – in newsroom, reporting, present-ing and sport. With BBC Pebble Mill *Midlands Today* 9 months. Then BBC Wales, Cardiff, producing *Wales Today*; then editor tv. news 1984–5, the year of the miners' strike ('a fabulous year', up at 4 am finish at 9 pm). Then a call to TSW – 1 year as editor of nightly programme, then Head of News and Current Affairs since late 1986.

Alan Cuthbertson, (reporter)
Bristol University, MSc Chemistry. Forces Broadcasting Service, Cyprus, 2 years. BBC R. Humberside, presenter, then newsroom ('old style newsroom where everyone had done 20 years before the mast on newspapers, so a great experience'). To Grimsby and Scunthorpe as freelance (no other freelance there 'so made a fortune'). To Brighton, BBC R. Sussex, 4 years ('too long'). Attachment to BBC SW tv. newsroom but staff man came back so there was no job. Had already applied to TSW: reporter there since autumn 1986.

Sue King (presenter)
Left school at 15½. Secretarial course. Encountered BBC crew filming her father (horse dealer). Was offered job with BBC children's programmes; 6 years there. Then BBC Plymouth, 1979, to news programmes. To TSW winter 1988.

Nikky Parr, ('programme journalist')
A levels at school; then BBC production secretary, London then R. Sussex. Always wanted to be a journalist, but realised BBC was not going to train her. So London College of Printing, radio course, 1983 4. BBC R. Cornwall 1984–7. TSW since summer 1987.

Chris Rogers (political editor and presenter)
Electronics engineering, Lanchester Polytechic, Coventry, 1970–3
also freelance for BBC R. Oxford. Station Assistant, BBC R. Carlisle
1973 (when it opened) to 1979. Border tv., as reporter and presenter
1979–82. To TSW as reporter, presenter and political editor from
start in 1982.

19 The *Western Morning News:* 14–15 June 1988

Until he became Editor of the *Western Morning News* in 1985, Colin Davison had never lived or worked in the South-West. As a child he had been on holiday in Torquay and Ilfracombe, but he knew little of Devon or Cornwall. His experience as a journalist was cosmopolitan, with spells in Yugoslavia, Brussels, Yorkshire, Darlington and Lincoln before being appointed to Plymouth at the age of 36. Since 1985 he has rightly wanted to promote the interests of the public whom his newspaper serves, both by thorough reporting and by critical analysis of the region's character.

He likes to tell the story of Mrs Thatcher's summer holiday in North Cornwall. It was when, because of international currency instability, almost the last of Cornwall's tin mines was about to close. The redundant mineworkers thought of lobbying the Prime Minister; but then, because she was coming on holiday, they decided not to. 'How terribly polite', he says. 'But where is that famous fighting spirit that made so many men, almost every man along this coast shipwreckers or smugglers?''

Campaigning for the well-being of Devon and Cornwall is one of his paper's duties, as he sees it. The *Western Morning News* maintains, nevertheless, a restrained courtesy of its own. It deals in serious news, not in sex or scandal. It does not fabricate sensations; and it is pragmatic in deciding whether to give priority to regional or national events. In the week of 6–11 June it led with South-Western stories on 4 of the 6 days (twice with the rundown of the Devonport Dockyard), and in the following week on only 2 days. It justified its claim to carry 'the late, late news which the London papers miss' most notably in the second week, with 2 major stories that came too late for the national newspaper editions reaching Devon and Cornwall – the IRA bombing of a charity 'fun run' in County Antrim which killed 5 soldiers; and

the unexpected midnight resignation of Labour's Shadow Defence
Secretary, Mr Denzil Davies.

The Routine and the Decisions

This is what happened on Tuesday 14 June 1988, in preparing the
morning paper of Wednesday 15 June.

At 8.30 am Andy Gough, one of two Assistant Editors, arrives
having already looked through the nationals and heard some of the
early radio news. He is followed soon afterwards by one of the
assistant news editors and two reporters on the daytime shift; and at
noon the news editor comes. Today, abnormally, there are only two
reporters on the day shift in Plymouth, but also available are almost
all of the 22 district reporters. They are located from Penzance to
Taunton because of the 'massive patch' that must be covered. One of
the two Plymouth reporters is a young journalist who has been with
the *Western Morning News* for only one month, but, as we shall see,
she is responsible for two of the main stories of the day.

The Editor arrives about 1.45 and others of the staff in mid-
afternoon. The main news conference is at 4.30. By then an 8-page
newslist has been put together, the longest I have seen. It is a
compilation covering 'Regional News' (the major events which are
candidates for all editions, plus a short London list), together with
separate lists for Exeter and East Devon, South Devon, North Devon,
Cornwall, Plymouth, a pictures list, and an Arts and reviews list. The
conference is agreeably relaxed, with tea and chocolate biscuits for
everyone present. It lasts 20 or 25 minutes.

5 editions have to be planned. The first is due 'off stone' (with all
pages fully made up) at 11.30 pm but nobody seems to expect it to go
earlier than 12.15 pm. It is for Exeter and East Devon. The second
edition, called the '12.30 edition', is for Torbay and mid-Devon with
changes mainly on page 3. (There is an almost completely new page 3
for each of the 5 editions.) The third is for North Devon. The fourth
or '2 am edition' has the subtitle 'The voice of Cornwall'. For that,
changes to pages 1, 3, 5 and 7 are common, and possibly also page 2
which carries national and world news. The fifth or '3 am edition' is
for Plymouth and its environment. By the time this book appears,
however, Cornwall will have two editions instead of one, with East
Cornwall having its own.

At the 4.30 pm conference Andy Gough (Assistant Editor) said it was 'a fairly quiet day' though with some interesting stories. He mentioned in particular the NSPCC annual figures for child abuse, which for Devon were up by 17 per cent. This, he said, would be an 'exclusive' for the *Western Morning News* because the national figures were embargoed until 10.30 am next day but after long and hard negotiation with the NSPCC they had agreed to let the newspaper carry the Devon (but not the Cornwall) figures in the morning. It had been put to them that if they wanted publicity, release of the Devon figures at least would be in their own interest.

He also spoke of the Exeter Crown Court case in which a Plymouth mother who had had a sterilisation operation to prevent further pregnancy, nevertheless had a further child. She had sued the Health Authority but had lost her case. That news had been in the evening papers and would probably be in the regional television news; but *Western Morning News* had found a fresh angle for itself. The woman and her husband had been distressed by the judgement and had hurried away from the court without speaking to anyone. The newspaper had left it until the afternoon 'to give them a little time to settle down' but they had then agreed to an interview at their home, and, as well, a photographer was on his way there to take a picture of the couple and the child, now 4 years old.

Among other events mentioned were a statement by the Devon Director of Education that there was not enough money to build the schools that would be needed in the 1990s, with a growing population, and that their schools were already underequipped. That was a strong candidate for the front page in the first 3 editions. As a possible substitute for the last two editions there was a report on the way Cornish artists were being put out of business by Taiwanese copies of their paintings, which were being imported and sold at knock-down prices. (Nobody, apparently, knew that this had been covered the previous Friday by TSW's *Today*, with good colour pictures.) A further 4 possible stories were mentioned; as was another 'exclusive' which would lead the sports page, about the manager of Plymouth Argyle Football Club moving to Dundee.

Of those mentioned above, the 'unplanned baby' case, the child abuse figures, and the Taiwan 'wreckers' copying Cornish art all made the front page for some or all editions. Also on page one were an RN jet trainer crashing near a school in Somerset, of which the first news came soon after 5 pm; an agency story about violence among English, German and Dutch soccer fans in Dusseldorf, and a report on a legal 'shambles' over extradition of an IRA man in Dublin. Also there was a trailer for the 'exclusive' on the back page on the Argyle manager moving to Dundee – a story resulting from close relations between the sports staff and the Argyle club. Thus 3 out of 7 front page items were the direct result of initiatives by *Western Morning News* journalists.

Page 2 was given to national and international news, plus weather, cattle markets, exchange rates, and (a pleasing item for visitors and others) RN ship movements expected that day. Page 3 – the page which changes almost entirely with every edition – is local, and page 4 is for leaders and features. (As it happened, next day there was vigorous evidence of the *Western Morning News* maintaining South-Western interests in a leader attacking the Independent Practitioners in Advertising for wanting to see TSW merged with TVS in Southampton to provide a bigger advertisement market.)

After the 4.30 pm conference, and 3 hours before final decisions were taken, Andy Gough said he expected the child abuse figures and the sterilisation case to go on the front page. On the latter he believed that *Western Morning News*'s tactics of letting the couple return home and 'settle down' before the newspaper approached them had worked well, and they now had an interview which almost certainly nobody else had. Whether it went on the front page, he said, would depend on the picture. If it was good, with the parents and child, it could just tip the balance. It was a long-running case, 'and there's very much a human element there'. On the NSPCC figures, he thought these worth the front page both because of the increase in reports of child abuse and because the *Western Morning News* was, in news terms, getting 'the first bite at the cherry'. The topic was much in the public eye, with the Cleveland report in the North-East due in the next 2 or 3 weeks.

At 5.15 pm the first news of the Ilchester air crash came through Somerset police. It is on the edge of *Western Morning News* territory, and no reporter was anywhere near there at the time. Soon afterwards the Somerset News Agency offered a report and pictures. The pilot had avoided the village school before ejecting and was unhurt. At 6 pm Editor Colin is watching TSW's *Today* when it leads with the air crash; it says it hopes to have pictures on screen later – which it does at 6.20 through transmission from its Yeovil office. Colin is delighted by another TSW item, an interview with the Argyle manager, recorded earlier in the day. 'He's signed since then', Colin says, and *Western Morning News* has the story.

Meanwhile Night Editor Alan Lake is preparing some preliminary layouts for the inside news pages. He expected to have them all planned by 8 pm, apart from the front page which would be discussed with the Editor about 9 pm. Phil Stoneham, night chief reporter, keeps in touch with the Somerset agency which sends text and pictures about 7.45 pm. And reporter Liz Hannam – with the paper for only a month – has completed the child abuse 'exclusive' and is finishing the 'Bananas' story which will lead page 3 in the later editions.

Here is Liz Hannam's account of her day. Actually she had started work on the Bananas night club yesterday, having seen the planning application for the building to be turned into an office block. Bananas is a well known night club at Plymouth Hoe, and the council had taken action against it on grounds of 'sex on the steps' and other 'unsavoury' incidents. The council lost its case; the proprietor was now retaliating, a month later, by applying for planning consent to demolish the club and build a five-storey block with offices and flats. Liz had read the cuttings on the earlier 'sex on the steps' court case. This morning she had started 'door stepping' because it was essential to get the proprietor's words on the planning application. He had been unavailable then; and she had been diverted on to trying to persuade the NSPCC to give the *Western Morning News* the Devon and Cornwall figures. In the end, in the afternoon, the NSPCC had agreed to release the Devon figures, and she had obtained an interview with the head of the Devon child protection team. That had taken her to 5 pm. Then she had gone back to Bananas and had met the proprietor. That had turned out to be a very good story. Having won his case in court, he had not re-opened the club. But if the council turned down his application for the offices and flats, he would do so. 'If the plan is turned down' he had said, 'the night club will be there forever – or certainly the next 25 years'. She was just finishing the story at 7.45 pm. It seemed to me, reading it later, that if the *Western Morning News* had been a popular tabloid that story would have been a strong candidate for page 1.

At 9.10 pm Night Editor Alan Lake is planning the front page in consultation with the Editor. As to priorities, Colin Davison said this. He thought it right to lead with the air crashes, because they were unexpected.

It's not the first time this has happened. There are a lot of military flights over the West Country, so it's of general interest and we have an interview with a neighbour who saw what happened.

He had looked at the national list and found nothing to displace it. The explosion in Wales had been running all day, and there was really

nothing on the Dusseldorf hooligans story. As to the woman who had
a baby after her operation to prevent pregnancy:

> It's something that's close to people's everyday lives. Everyone cares
> about pregnancy, parenthood and doctors ... We never thought she
> would win, but it's interesting that she took the trouble to go this far.
> And the child is $4\frac{1}{2}$ – one wonders what he's going to think about it.

He also thought the NSPCC figures a sound choice for the front page,
because there was 'a big awareness' of child abuse, because the figures
showed an increase in the reported cases, and because 'it's likely to
generate quite a lot of debate here tomorrow, and in the national
newspapers the day after'.

An hour later, after further reading of copy and discussion, the
page 1 plan is finally ready. Downstairs a small army, mainly of
women, are setting the type through word processors. Nearly all the
NGA typesetters had taken redundancy money and left in late 1987.
The paper is supposed to be 'off stone' at 11.30 pm, but tonight, as
seems usual at present, the last page is not ready until 12.15. (The
Editor reports that by September 1988 production was regularly on
time.)

Commentary

At 12, 14 or 16 pages, on early days of the week, the *Western Morning
News* seems slender beside the 40-page nationals. Yet it provides a
fairly thorough account of events in the South-West of England,
together with a compact summary of the national and world news. Its
effective cover of such major matters as the loss of jobs at the Royal
Dockyard, the transplant operations at the Exeter and Devon Hospital, and the trans-Atlantic single-handed race have been noted in the
early part of this chapter. The diligence of *Western Morning News*'s
newsdesk and its reporters were evident on the random day taken for
our study, particularly through its 'exclusives' on child abuse and on
the departure of the Plymouth football manager, and in its thoughtful
approach to the family involved in the unplanned baby case. As to
accuracy, its staff appeared to be scrupulous about checking their
information so far as possible; and its decision to do nothing about
the possible nuclear waste dumping, at least until it had some
confirmation, was to its credit.

My only criticisms are that its style of writing is poor and that it is short of features. There are in its columns few items written with a flow of language that makes them a pleasure to read. The 'Armada 400' series, with daily reports from the Spanish fleet of 1588, was an exception; and there was occasional brightness in the headlines, as in 'Argyle highlander' over the football manager's move. The lack of features follows from a limitation in pages, because the level of advertising is or was inadequate to support more editorial space. The features as such were readable enough, and relevant to the South-West.

That said, if I were to live in Devon or Cornwall I would find the *Western Morning News* essential daily reading; and while I should miss the nationals for their political analysis and arts features I would not be too disturbed at having to do without them for a while.

Staffing

22 district reporters in 14 district offices
9 reporters in Plymouth
5 specialist writers
5 'newsdesk journalists' (News Editor and others)
16 'production journalists' (sub-editors and others)
2 photographic staff (most pictures coming from freelance contributors)
5 secretaries, typists and assistants.

People

Colin Davidson, Editor
Slavonic studies, Nottingham University. *Yorkshire Evening Post*, 1969–72. British Council scholarship to study press in Yugoslavia, attached to Politics Studies, University of Belgrade 1972–3. UPI, Brussels, one year. To *Evening Despatch*, Darlington (Westminster Press) 1974–8, as deputy news editor, then news editor, then deputy editor. Editor, *Lincolnshire Chronicle* series (weeklies) 1978–83. Then *Lincolnshire Echo* (Northcliffe) as Editor, to 1985. To Plymouth, as Editor, 1985.

Andy Gough, a Deputy Editor
At 17, trainee reporter in weekly paper, Tamworth, After 4 years, to *Walsall Observer* (W. Midlands Press) – chief reporter for 3 years. Won Midlands Journalist of the Year award (for series of 'digging' stories) 1980. Short spell on *Daily Mail* in Manchester. *Express and Star*, Wolverhampton, for 5 years. ('Good training, and paper was always ahead of the field with equipment, working on screen and the like'.) To *Western Evening Herald* as assistant news editor, when deputy editor of *Express and Star* appointed editor of *Western Evening Herald*. Then, after three years, to *Western Morning News*.

Liz Hannam, reporter
Birmingham University, English and Communications. Postgraduate journalism course at Cardiff 1985–6. *North Devon Journal* (weekly) 1986–8. Then to *Western Morning News*, summer 1988.

Alan Lake, Night Editor
Birmingham Evening Despatch, until it was taken over by *Birmingham Mail*. Freelance in Kingsbridge, Devon, for 7 years. *Western Morning News* for 15 years.

Phil Stoneham, Night Chief Reporter
Harlow Technical College, one year course 1975–6. Weekly newspaper, latterly as news editor. Wanted 'more action', so reporter *Western Evening Herald*, 1 year. Then to *Western Morning News* as night reporter.

20 BBC R. Cornwall and ILR Plymouth Sound

Radio Cornwall

Radio Cornwall is one of the smallest and most successful of the 35 or 36 BBC local stations in England. It is a classic example of how communities with a strong identity need and appreciate a service of their own. It opened only in 1983, when the services to Devon and Cornwall were separated. It is based in Truro, with a small purpose-built headquarters close to the town centre. Its broadcasts are mostly speech-based, with a staff of 10 journalists plus a news editor, a station manager, 3 presenters and others, bringing its total staff to about 26. One of its 10 journalists is based in Penzance to the west and another in Liskeard to the east, again because of the great distances and slow roads in the county.

It has as we have seen the highest audience figures of any BBC mainland station – an average reach of 24 per cent daily, and 50 per cent weekly within Cornwall. Mike Hoskin, the station manager since it opened, says that that is because Cornwall people are 'determined to follow their own way' and will therefore listen to their own station. Hence his comment, quoted earlier, that Cornwall is 'not English'. Most of the staff are young and were new to Cornwall when they came; they work hard, with long hours.

The station broadcasts from 6 am to midnight, with its own output from 6 am to 6 pm and then from 6 pm onwards programmes produced collectively by Cornwall, Devon, Bristol, Solent, Glouceser and Wiltshire. At 6 am only 3 of the staff are present – a producer-reporter (Wendy Pascoe on 6 June), a presenter (Chris Blount) and a secretary, Wendy and Chris having been there since 5 am. Another reporter (Mark Ashton) arrives at 7.20 am, and further staff from 8.15 onwards. There is a general meeting at about 10.15 to discuss that day's and next day's prospects.

On air from 6 to 9 am is *Coast to Coast*, with news, travel and topical features punctuated with a few music discs. From 9 to 10.30 there is a lighter diet, with more music; then from 10.30 am to 1 pm back to current affairs, but with debates, a 'soap-box', possibly an outside item, features and still some music. The afternoon brings a phone-in shared with Radio Devon, and successful in holding a fair audience; and from 3 to 5 pm more music, but with competitions that include difficult questions. From 5 to 6 pm, there is a 'solid' current affairs programme. As to news, on every hour from 6 am to 6 pm bulletins carry a mix of 4 or 5 national items and 4 to 6 Cornwall stories – with the exceptions that at 6.55 am and 7.55 am the local news comes first, for 5 minutes, with the Radio 2 news following on the hour; and at 1 pm and 5 pm there are 10-minute or 15-minute bulletins. Headlines are provided at every half-hour. The system is flexible because, by their nature, the programmes following the news do not have to start at strictly controlled timings.

To non-Cornish people the content of news may be unusual. One of the 7.55 am bulletins I heard began its opening item thus:

> British Telecom has denied rumours that Black Magic rituals have been carried on at one of their telephone exchanges in Cornwall, but they have revealed that an engineer has been censured for practicing astrology on Telecom property. Steve hardy reports – 'The rumours centred on the Mevagissey telephone exchange when strange markings were found on the floor of a room which had been locked. Inside was a drawing in chalk of a circle with four points of the compass and a sail-like device in the centre of the circle'.

On the morning of my visit to Radio Cornwall, Monday 6 June the bulletins were less surprising but of interest. The 6.55 am to 7.55 am broadcasts began with a telephone interview with Greenpeace headquarters in Washington, with critical comment from there of the proposed dumping in Cornwall of rubbish from New York, said by Greenpeace to be toxic. Then an East Cornwall man who had fallen from a train, apparently because he thought it was about to stop, but had survived; next, in West Cornwall an almost doubling of rates arrears in the past year, with a possible explanation of why that had happened; then the resignation of the mayor of Wadebridge, because of a conflict of interest on property development – and so onwards to 3 more such items. For a Monday morning it seemed a quite strong diet.

The programme also included a weather forecast, live from the Plymouth weather centre, an interview with the sports editor of the *Dundee Courier* about the possible transfer of Plymouth Argyle's manager to Scotland, and a longer report about 460 people being marooned on Saturday night on Lundy Island. The marooned people had been taken there by the paddle steamer *Waverley*, but because of bad weather it had not been able to take them off until early on Sunday morning, and there were some outspoken interviews on the subject. The feature items included a 4-minute interview with Cornwall's Euro-MP about what might be done to get aid for redundant dockyard workers, one about a facility visit for tourism writers from London which some county councillors thought a waste of money, and one about success in raising extra money to keep the Cornwall air ambulance going. These, too, provided a solid diet.

These and other material had been left overnight, for Chris Blount and Wendy Pascoe to consider between 5 and 6 am. Later, in time for the 9 am bulletin, Wendy and the reporter Mark Ashton generated 4 new stories. The previous evening a girl walking in Truro had been shot in the buttocks by an airgun fired from a passing car and was now in hospital. The police headquarters at Camborne had at first been unable or unwilling to confirm the story, but shortly before 9 am, answering a further call, they had the description of a car in which they were interested. The Falmouth coastguard had yesterday dealt with a total of 34 callouts – the highest figure this year, brought about by the bad weather. In addition, there was an interview about the effects of acid rain in Cornwall, related to a report published this morning; and a story of discovery of a car stolen from outside a hospital while a Cornwall child was undergoing heart surgery.

The 10.15 am meeting, with the news editor and 5 journalists present (when not taking calls), discussed how these and other stories might be developed. The reporter Mark Ashton was sent off in the radio car to RAF Culdrose, where at noon one of the helicopter crews of 705 squadron was to receive for the fifth consecutive year the top award in the UK helicopter competition. The reporter was sent, it was said, not so much because there was much news value but to improve relations with Culdrose, which had a new public relations officer and could be important when there were big rescues or other events. There was discussion altogether of about 18 items to be pursued that day or later in the week.

Looking back over the past few months, News Editor Steve Hardy said that the topics which had had most attention were the tin mines and the consequences of the 1986 collapse of prices; the Devonport Royal Dockyard, which employed many people from East Cornwall; and the various activities of Peter de Savary who, whatever you thought of some of his initiatives, was bringing the jobs and stability that Falmouth and West Cornwall needed. He also said that covering the county council and the 6 district councils inevitably took time: Radio Cornwall could not have someone at a 3-hour meeting if it was going to produce only one story, but with the committees in particular it was possible to pick up information after a meeting and to get people into a studio then.

One criticism that I heard from an experienced broadcaster now living in Cornwall was that, at times, some of the younger reporters adopted an unduly aggressive approach in their interviews. He thought it out of place, especially coming from what sounded like sensible girls. In a fortnight of intermittent listening, I heard no such falsely 'hard' reporting. Another Cornish resident confirmed that there had been cases of that kind 2 or 3 years earlier, but thought that they were exceptional.

A random fortnight is too short a time for an adequate assessment. But on the evidence of that time, together with the audience figures and the apparent appreciation of Radio Cornwall within the county, it can be said to provide a welcome and worthwhile service.

People

Steve Hardy

Eastern Counties Newspapers (Norwich and Ipswich) 8 or 9 years ILR, Ipswich; IRN London; then back to Norfolk, newspaper 18 months. BBC R. Norfolk. To R. Cornwall 1987, as News Editor.

Mike Hoskin

Newspapers, Nottingham, Birmingham, Bristol; then London, *Daily Mirror*. Freelance radio and tv., Midlands. To BBC R. Nottingham 1968 (at its start). News Editor, R. Leeds; then R. Lancashire. Programme Organiser, R. Lancashire. Station Manager, R. Cornwall, from start in 1983.

Wendy Pascoe

London College of Printing, business studies and journalism. 'Temp' in London 1 year. *Sunday Independent*, Plymouth, $2\frac{1}{2}$ years. To BBC R. Cornwall October 1986. Producer since April 1988.

Plymouth Sound

While Radio Cornwall is small, Plymouth Sound is even smaller – probably the smallest, in staff, of any full-time station in Britain. It has just 5 journalists to provide hourly and half-hourly bulletins from 6 am to 6 pm on weekdays, and more restricted cover at weekends. Between 5 and 6 pm it puts on longer news features, usually 2 or 3 intermixed with music and other information. Its scheduling throughout the day is flexible, so that, for example, on the Friday of the Dockyard announcements it carried a half-hour special programme at 1 pm – only 90 minutes after the press conference had begun – and it brought in interviews with Defence Minister Tim Sainsbury, Dr David Owen, other MPs and trades unions spokesmen.

To do this with only 5 journalists, plus a freelance to help on Sundays, is strenuous. 3 of the 5 have newspaper backgrounds and long experience. 2 are young people in their first jobs, having recently completed the Falmouth radio course. Unusually, 2 of the seniors are a husband and wife team – Malcolm Carroll, the head of news, who has been with Plymouth Sound since it started in 1975, and his wife Susan.

In spite of the small staffing, the journalists are working out of the office for as much time as in it. On Wednesday 15 June, when I was there, Malcolm Carroll was in the office as anchorman virtually all day. One of the young reporters was in at 5.30 am for the early bulletins; the other, Catharine Bayfield, was away for most of the day covering the Princess Royal's visit to the RN training centre at Torpoint, on the far side of the Tamar estuary. She had taken a portable telephone with which to provide hourly reports at midday (of surprisingly good sound quality) and a portable recorder with which to gather material for a feature to be used at about 5.15 pm. She was back in the office from about 3.30 to prepare that. Sue Carroll was away for the day, though she came in later. The other senior was out on two stories, again recording and gathering information – one a strike starting that afternoon at British Aerospace in Plymouth, the first ever experienced there, and one the Greenpeace vessel denied access to a commercial marina in Plymouth.

Since Devon County Council meets alternately in Exeter and Plymouth, there is an arrangement by both stations. They can use the 24-hour IRN line to exchange voice reports, since they are at the extreme end of one of the IRN links. Plymouth Sound, like some other ILR stations, also tries to get at least 2 different stories out of each event it covers – one of immediate news, and another looking forward to what follows. Thus on 15 June it had a report on a Council Committee's debate on the future of a school for use in the early afternoon and a separate story, with different voices, for use next morning about the next stage of the parents' actions. Such stretching of resources is essential with a small staff.

That stretching does, however, have a negative effect. The use of different voices in the school story next morning gave it a fresh polish, but it was unmistakably still yesterday's story. Similarly, the NSPCC figures for child abuse in Devon where still running in Plymouth Sound's bulletins at 4 and 5 pm, having first appeared in the *Western Morning News* 'exclusive'. The one 'plus' for Plymouth Sound was in getting the Devon NSPCC officer to attribute the high Plymouth figures to the armed forces' presence and to some of the council housing estates.

The station concentrates on Plymouth and its immediate environment. Apart from the IRN national and world news, almost everything in the bulletins and news features is about events within 10 miles of Plymouth or about Plymouth people. That must be one reason for its very high audience figures within that area – a weekly reach of 57 per cent among a population of 300 000. Its two BBC competitors, R. Cornwall and R. Devon, cover very much larger areas. The other reason, according to Programme Controller Louise Churchill, is that Plymouth Sound carries a much higher proportion of speech than is usual in ILR stations: not the 70 per cent common in BBC local radio, but probably towards 50 per cent. In this, it runs contrary to the general ILR philosophy and has thus earned its 'upside-down' title.

As already mentioned, its *Wednesday Walk-in* seems a brilliant innovation, likely to be copied elsewhere. The day I was there, the queue of people waiting for their turn in the studio was out in the sunshine enjoying the sun. There is no restriction on topics, provided the laws of libel, contempt and other essentials are not breached and the words do not offend against IBA regulations. Politicians are discouraged because they get plenty of other opportunities; so are councillors, unless they want to speak about some 'pet project'. Political and social balance can always be restored – and is – by inviting others to respond in next day's *phone Forum*, which they can do either by telephone or by coming to the studio. The phone-in is on air every day from 10 am to 12 noon, and Louise Churchill chairs it herself 5 days a week.

The Programme Controller also attributes success to the flexibility of their schedules. That permits the immediate response to events – as on the day when the Dockyard redundancies were announced, since they were able to put on the special programme after the news at 1 pm, and keep it running until they ran out of relevant material at 1.40. Flexibility also makes possible the guarantee to people in the queue for *Wednesday Walk-in* that anyone there by 1.50 is sure to get on air, even if it means keeping the *Walk-in* on air until 3.30. More often it finishes before 3 pm, and the presenter then goes on to something else.

Plymouth Sound is profitable, though the margin is not large and was, for some years, minimal. In the year 1986–7 it had a pre-tax profit of £91 000, its highest ever. About two thirds of the revenue is from local advertising, and the rest from national sources. In 1987 Plymouth Sound was taken into the GWR Radio Group, with Wiltshire Radio based in Swindon and Radio West based in Bristol. The Group profit in 1986–7 was £486 000 before tax, and in the half-year to March 1988 was up to £354 000. That puts it in the top group of ILR companies.

That Plymouth Sound satisfies many people in and around the city of Plymouth is certain. That it achieves a small miracle in maintaining a lively service of news and related programmes with only 5 journalists, 2 of whom are really trainees, must be respected – though the thinness of its resources shows from time to time. Some of its items are trivial; many are more substantial. And the *Wednesday Walk-in* looks like being a brilliant invention.

21 The News in Scotland

Scotland is different. It has its own legal, educational and religious bodies. The Church of Scotland is democratic in ways that the Church of England is not. Scotland had 4 universities when England had only 2, and Scotland still has some of the strongest universities in the UK. Its legal system is in many ways more advanced than England's – for example in requiring that anyone arrested and held must be brought to trial within 110 days or freed. Its banks operate throughout the world. Politically it differs from England, as in the 1987 General Election when it returned 50 Labour MPs, 10 Conservatives, 9 Alliance members and 3 from the Scottish National Party (SNP).

Within Scotland there are differences, too. Central Scotland – a narrow belt across the Clyde and Forth valleys – contains four fifths of the country's people, and most of its industry. The north-east, with Aberdeen, includes good farming land (though with a rugged winter) and most of the offshore oil bases. The Highlands have half of Scotland's land and less than one-twentieth of its people. The Western Isles and the northern isles of Orkney and Shetland each have strong characters of their own, retained in part because of their remoteness. And Southern Scotland, with the Borders, is a mixture of hill and lowland farming together with textiles and fishing and a rich history of its own.

The Scottish newspapers, although serving smaller populations than those in the English regions, have higher sales and generally a broader view. The *Daily Record* has the top sales of any UK daily in relation to its distribution area, with 1 copy per every 7 people – far ahead of *The Sun*'s 1 copy for every 13. Next highest in sales of morning papers outside London are the *Glasgow Herald* and the *Dundee Courier*, with 127 000 and 125 000 a day, while England's highest is 92 000. In broadcasting, the ITV company Scottish Television is among the middle-sized of UK companies. It serves Central Scotland and parts of the south-west Highlands. Grampian Television covers the North-East, most of the Highlands, the Western Isles, and Orkney and Shetland. The south of Scotland is served by Border Television, based in Carlisle, though that may change in 1993.

R. Clyde, in west central Scotland, is one of the most profitable ILR companies in Britan and arguably the most original. 5 other ILR stations serve other parts of Scotland, including one of the smallest, Moray Firth in Inverness. The success of R. Clyde from the day it opened in 1975 shook the rather complacent BBC into esablishing R. Scotland 3 years later, and after a troubled start it has become a highly competent service operating for the whole of the country. 7 smaller BBC stations provide part time broadcasts (1 to 6 hours a day) which are much valued by people in the remoter areas. A strong Gaelic service also comes from the BBC in Inverness and Stornoway.

As Author I admit to a prejudice in favour of things Scottish, but I have no doubt that any impartial assessment would confirm the judgements of quality recorded here.

Staffing

Unusually, BBC Scotland is better off than its ITV rival, Scottish Television. For *Reporting Scotland*, its early evening news programme, it has 39 journalists – and a further 16 work for the weekly current affairs *Left, Right and Centre* and related programmes. Of the 39, one is the Parliamentary correspondent based in London, 3 are reporters in Edinburgh, 2 are in Aberdeen and 1 in Inverness, 1 is the Arts reporter and 1 sport. Sc. tv. also has 39 journalists, 4 or 5 of the reporters being normally in Edinburgh, but their 39 have to cover the current affairs programmes as well as news. Grampian television, of course, has Aberdeen and beyond so there is no need for Sc. tv. to place people there.

Of the newspapers, the *Daily Record* has a staff of 170, mostly based in Glasgow but with district people in Edinburgh, Aberdeen, Dundee, Dumfries and London. The *Glasgow Herald* has a total of 140 journalists, again mostly in Glasgow but with 10 in Edinburgh, 11 in London (including 3 in Parliament and 2 specialists), and 1 in Inverness. *The Scotsman* has 124 journalists, with 14 general and specialist reporters in Edinburgh, 7 in Glasgow and 5 district men. It has 5 feature writers; and in London it has a total staff of 11.

In Radio, BBC R. Scotland has 43 journalists, including researchers, and 5 trainees. Of the reporters, 3 are in Edinburgh, and 1 each in Aberdeen and Inverness. (In addition, R. nan Gaidheal provides the Gaelic news with 5 journalists and 2 trainees.) R. Clyde has 18 journalists in its newsroom and 2 or 3 on other work –

probably the biggest journalism team among ILR stations outside London. Among the smaller ILR stations, Moray Firth claims $5\frac{1}{2}$ news journalists in Inverness, the 'half' having other duties as well.

Perspectives, North and South

To indicate the extent of interest in Scottish affairs on two sides of the Border, two tables are of interest. Each is based on 4 midweek days in May 1988. (Excluded from this newspaper count are sport, City news (finance), leaders and letters.)

Newspaper and Broadcast Coverage: *4 midweek days, May 1988*

Newspaper	No. of items (Scottish)	Total (sq. cm)	Av. daily sales in Scotland
Daily Mail	3	107	30600
Daily Record	136	21972	769000
Daily Telegraph	37	2029	27000 (est.)
Glasgow Herald	166	27993	125000
The *Guardian*	6	949	16750 (est.)
The *Independent*	9	1239	16200 (est.)
The Scotsman	172	25638	91000
Scottish Daily Express	65	5385	156000
The *Sun* (Sc. edition)	72	5922	262000 (est.)
The Times	2	94	15750 (est.)

	No. of items	Duration (4 days' total) (min./sec.)	Audience in Sc. areas (daily av.)
BBC 6 o'clock news	1	1.16	736 000
ITN 5.45 news	nil	—	695 000
BBC *Reporting Scotland*	52	97.00	720 000
Sc. Tv., *Scotland Today*	68	106.40	728 000

These figures show the extent of Scottish news in newspapers and television over 4 midweek days, 17–20 May 1988. While those days did not include any dramatic news from Scotland, there were events of potential UK interest. Among them were:

– Lord Young at the National Engineering Laboratory at East Kilbride, indicating probable privatisation

- Scottish Office Minister, Michael Forsyth, rejecting RC plea to limit the number of non-Catholics in RC schools
- Law Society of Scotland tightening discipline
- Sacked NUS crewmen picketing off-shore supply ships, then being fined
- Gruinard island 'all clear' of anthrax
- Isle of Pabay (off Skye) for sale
- Critical reaction in Church of Scotland to Mrs Thatcher's planned address to General Assembly
- Scottish Development Agency under fire from Audit Commission over its cost estimates for Glasgow Garden Festival

All of these were covered by *The Scotsman* and *Glasgow Herald* and most of them by the *Daily Record*. The *Daily Telegraph* covered four of the eight, the *Daily Express* four, the *Independent* three, the *Guardian* two, the *Sun* two, and *The Times* one.

As to network television news (measured in the following week) only one item appeared on the BBC's 6 o'clock bulletins – the Church of Scotland deciding not to invite the Prime Minister to its Assembly next year.

ITN's 5.45 pm news carried no Scottish items. Very little, indeed, appeared on either programme from any part of the UK apart from the South-East of England. The only substantial cover, by the BBC alone, was for the report of the inquiry into the murder of an Asian boy at Burnage High School in Manchester – a report which the city council did not want published. That said, let us now look at the news as presented in Scotland.

22 A People's Paper: The *Daily Record*

Of the popular taboid newspapers sold in Scotland, the *Record* is both the most Scottish and the most successful. Not only is it far ahead of the *Sun* in sales – at 770 000 a day against 265 000 – but it has the highest proportionate sale within its distribution area of any daily newspaper anywhere in the UK. Its 770 000 daily average represents 1 copy for every 7 people, while the *Sun*'s UK average of 4 150 000 represents 1 copy for every 13. The *Daily Record* is also one of the biggest money-makers among Mr Robert Maxwell's *Mirror* Group newspapers.

Its editor, Endell Laird – who is also editor-in-chief in Scotland – emphasises the importance of its Scottish character. He prefers a Scots story for his front page, though he will always take whatever seems the strongest story of the day, whether Scots or not. He likes also to project an image of the Scots as 'proud, helpful people'. He wants hard news, campaigning whenever possible, and with a heavy emphasis on 'exclusives'. He quotes an old Scottish maxim, 'comfort the afflicted and afflict the comfortable'. He is a Forfar man, from rural Angus; he planned to go to university but after 2 years in the RAF thought it would take too long before he earned any money, so he took a job with the *Dundee Courier*. Since then he has worked for the *Scottish Daily Express*, the *Record*, the *Evening Times* (Glasgow), back to the *Record* as deputy editor for 8 years, then editor of the *Sunday Mail* for 7, and back to the *Record* on becoming editor-in-chief in the spring of 1988. (All three of his children are graduates.)

Two changes in the paper were quickly evident after he took over. 'page 3' girls disappeared – almost, but not entirely – and colour pictures were used more extensively for news. Laird says that there were virtually no letters of complaint from readers when the 'page 3' girls were displaced, although the office receives between 650 and 750 letters a week from readers. In 3 weeks from mid-May to early June 1988, only 5 dollies not related to news or features appeared – none naked or near naked and only 3 on page 3. Instead, the colour pictures on that page included such items as Prince Harry going back to school after a hernia operation, Rangers Terry Butcher at the Glasgow Garden Festival, Scots fans behaving well at Wembley, and 2 school-girls with a child whom they has rescued from a fire. There were compensations, however, such as a centre-spread of 'undies' to 'make women sexy' and other pages on the same theme.

The front page stories in those three weeks, typically, were mainly on crime, human events, personalities or sport. The nearest to the political or social categories were two campaigning stories on 'killer' motor bikes, one on initiation rites at a Scottish prison, and one on deportation of a Pakistani married to a Scots wife. One front page 'splash' gave Mr Terry Wogan a thumping because of the money he was making through his 'swanky car firm' to carry his guests to and from his BBC chat shows – a case of Laird's 'afflicting the comfortable'. Matters such as the controversy between Mrs Thatcher and Mr Lawson on exchange and interest rates or progress in the nuclear disarmament negotiations were given only brief treatment on an inside page.

The 'splash' story of 17 May, however, had political and social implications as well as a strong human element; and it was an example of news generated by ingenuity, quite properly. Hard news was short that day, at least as seen by the *Record*. (*The Scotsman* that day led with the 'soaring' pound and the *Glasgow Herald* with a row over enforcement of the poll tax.) At the midday conference on the 16 May, when the newsdesk list looked unpromising, Endell Laird had drawn attention to a letter in the *Glasgow Herald* about the reaction of the Catholic Church to a request by a group of non-Catholic parents in Glasgow's Townhead to send their children to St Mungo's RC primary. The writer, a Catholic parent, said he had 'squirmed with embarrassment' over the Church's negative response, when it ought to have been 'flattered' by the request. He also noted an 'exclusive' on *The Scotsman*'s front page, an interview with Father Lynch, the Church's representative on Strathclyde Region's education committee, saying why the hierarchy wanted a percentage ceiling on non-Catholics in their schools. Laird wanted the whole background to be explored.

At the main news conference at 5 pm the prospects were still seen to be bleak. The strongest offer was the return that day from Khartoum to Aberdeen of a Quaker relief worker, 3 of whose colleagues had been killed by a bomb just after he left. The next best was a so-called 'shoot out' in Sutherland, where an enraged crofter riddled a mooring buoy and boat equipment belonging to a neighbouring land owner (the round-the-world sailor John Ridgeway).

Faced with this choice, Laird believed that, properly presented, the Catholic school could be a better lead. 3 reporters and a photographer had been at work. The copy was 'excellent', but it should start not with the dilemma for Strathclyde Region, instead it should start with 'the kids who are being barred from the school nearest their homes'. It was a subject 'too good to be let slip'.

A final decision was delayed until 6.30 pm. Meanwhile almost a whole page was planned for inside the paper (page 7), and provisionally a big picture of 3 non-Catholic children excluded from the school was proposed for page 1. Laird also decided to change the intended leaders for that night, and to have a single one on the lessons for Strathclyde Region in the school controversy. Strathclyde, he said, had 'strayed into a minefield' and was now running scared. The Catholic Church was unhappy because it saw the prospect of more non-Catholics in its schools as a step towards 'back door integration'. The way out was for the Church to accept the 44, and then to sort out the future by talks behind the scenes.

The main text on page 7 – written by a senior reporter, Bill Hyndman – set out clearly the background and the conflicting views. Since 1918 the Catholic Church in Scotland had had the right to separate schools, within the state system. In the Townhead area of Glasgow, now carved up by motorways and heavy traffic, the Protestant primary school had a capacity for 500 children but only 48 were still there. The Catholic school had about 100. Strathclyde Region wanted to bus the 48 to a school a mile and a half away; most of the parents disliked this because it meant that the children could not come home for lunch, and there was anxiety lest economic pressure might lead to the bus service being withdrawn. Father Lynch wanted non-Catholics to be restricted to not more than 40 per cent. These and other factors could not have been better set out by a 'heavy' newspaper – indeed, would probably not have been so readable and direct.

For the front page picture there were 3 sisters – aged 5, 7 and 9 – peering through the railings of the school which was not ready to let them in. But it was in black-and-white, because there had been no thought of the front page when the photographer was first sent out. So at 6.30 he was sent out again, to round up the same children if possible. The colour picture was too late for the first edition but ran in all the later ones.

Following the 6.30 pm decision to lead with the school story, at 7 pm Laird and others looked at alternative front page layouts. A 1-word bold headline was proposed, to go above the picture. Laird changed it from 'BARRED' to 'BANNED'. It was not strictly accurate, since the question of a quota had not been settled – and indeed Sc. Tv. on the previous Friday had shown Protestant parents being allowed to fill in registration forms at St Mungo's. But the headline was a powerfully dramatic summing up. Laird asked Assistant Editor Tom Brown to write the short text to go under the picture – not easy, with only some 150 words and the emphasis essentially on the 'kids', not the politics.

The *Record* is not slow in blowing its own trumpet, so above the 'BANNED' headline is stripped the words 'The Record tackles the BIG issues'. And next day, to extend the story, almost the whole of 2 pages in the centre spread were given to reports on 2 schools which were part of the way to integration and 2 already wholly integrated (1 in Aberdeen and 1 in Renfrewshire). The headline: 'WE ARE UNITED'.

Another aspect of the *Record*, a popular approach to social issues, was evident in the centre spread of 17 May (the day of the 'BANNED' front page). Its bold headline was 'TAKE FOUR GIRLS . . .', with the secondary line 'There's more style in the *Record*!' Its bold coloured pictures showed 4 girls – all unemployed and 'from the dole queue' – first in their own dresses and then, with hair restyled by a top Glasgow salon, modelling fashionable clothes. It was the work of the *Record*'s fashion writer, Fiona Black, and a staff photographer.

This was the result of a joint initiative of the Scottish Woollen Publicity Council, the Manpower Services Commission and the *Record*. In April the Wool Council had approached the newspaper, wanting to promote wool garments at the Glasgow Garden Festival. Fiona Black wrote an article in the *Record*, 'Do you want to be a model?', after arrangements with the MSC to collect replies from unemployed people at Job Centres. There was a huge response. In the end 20 were picked, all unemployed for over a year, and given free training by a model agency. They then went on to take part in shows at the Garden Festival – with the prospect, at least for some, of permanent jobs afterwards.

The success of the *Daily Record* must lie in a combination of a popular approach to news – with emphasis on human aspects, as with the 'kids' of Townhead – a strongly Scottish character, simplicity of presentation (not always easy to achieve), prominent 'exclusives' (not

all of which are exclusive), and initiatives such as 'Take four girls . . .'
Also, of course, extensive cover of television and its stars, cartoons,
and at least 6 pages of *Sports Record* every day.

When Mr Robert Maxwell bought the *Mirror* group from Reed
International in 1984, staff in Scotland believed that he wanted to
merge the *Mirror* and *Daily Record*. That was strongly resisted by the
journalists in Glasgow at the time, and their resistance saved 'Captain
Bob' from what could have been a disastrous mistake. The *Daily
Record* remains not only the most popular and profitable newspaper
in Scotland, but the most successful operation in his newspaper
group.

Staffing

The *Daily Record* has 170 journalists, of whom about 80 are writers
and 90 'production journalists'. There are relatively few women. Most
of the staff are based at Anderston Quay in Glasgow, but there are
district staff in Edinburgh, Aberdeen, Dundee, Inverness, and London.

People (cross section).

Fiona Black (fashion writer)
1-year course on fashion writing at London College of Fashion. Back
to *Kilmarnock Standard* for 4 years, because she wanted general
newspaper experience. To *Daily Record* as fashion writer 1979.

Endell Laird (editor-in-chief)
From school to RAF. Then *Dundee Courier*, *Scottish Daily Express*,
Daily Record and *Evening Times* (Glasgow). To *Daily Record* as
deputy editor 1973. To *Sunday Mail* as editor 1981. Editor-in-chief
1988.

Malcolm Speed (news editor)
At 16 to Campbeltown local paper. Then another local; then *Scottish
Daily Mail* ('well trained by a hard taskmaster-news editor'). To *Daily
Record* 1973. News Editor since 1984.

Content by Categories: *4 days, Tuesday 17–Friday 20 May 1988*
Counting only the news pages. Not included are sports pages,
property, competitions, weather forecasts and leaders. Pictures are
included at half the values of texts.)

Category* (sq. cm.)	4-day total and no. of items	1-day av.
A & S	450 (5)	110 (1)
Ag.	—	—
Crash	589 (7)	147 (2)
Crime	4157 (37)	1039 (9)
Crime C	661 (5)	165 (1)
Crime W	—	—
Env.	31 (1)	—
Health	237 (5)	59 (1)
Health A	525 (5)	131 (1)
Human	6697 (29)**	1674 (7)
Int.	464 (11)	116 (3)
Money	25 (1)***	—
Pets	26 (2)	—
Pol.	2198 (21)	549 (5)
Pol. A	2719 (39)	680 (10)
Pol. W	375 (3)	94 (1)
Pol. Ed.	2789 (4)**	697 (1)
Terror	737 (6)	184 (2)
Sport	246 (2)	62 (1)
Stars	6823 (28)	1706 (7)
S & S	998 (6)	246 (2)
War	1661 (2)**	415 (1)
Weather	200 (1)	—

Notes:
* For explanation of categories, see pp. xi–xii.
** *Human* includes the 'Take Four Girls' feature and the Tammy Wynette
feature; *Pol. Ed* includes the Catholic schools controversy; and *War* includes
Scots relief workers in Afghanistan.
*** More recently, the *Daily Record* has introduced a daily 'money' service
listing the 150 most popular shares in Scotland.
    As noted above, *Sport* includes only those news items which appear on news
pages. The 4-day total for the *Sports Record* pages comes to 21 968 sq cm – or a
daily average of 5492 sq cm. That is, of course, by a long way the largest
element in the paper. The *Stars* and the *Human* categories are the next largest,
with daily averages of 1706 and 1674 sq cm.

23 Scotland on Screen: Two Strong Competitors

Both the early evening programmes go chiefly for hard news. Unlike the English regions, they are rarely short of solid events. Wales and Northern Ireland have a similarly strong flow. Both *Scotland Today* (Sc. Tv.) and *Reporting Scotland* (BBC) vary their style towards the end of their half–hours – the former often with an agreeably light touch, and the latter with particular attention to the Arts.

As already noted, Sc. Tv. serves only Central Scotland, most of Argyll, and parts of the inner Hebrides. BBC Scotland covers the whole country. In resources, *Scotland Today* is less well off than some others in ITV: 3 camera crews in Glasgow and 2 in Edinburgh – total 5, compared with TSW's 7 plus 5 single-man units, or Central's 13 crews plus access to 6 1-man freelances.

Scotland Today, Tuesday 17 May

The ITV programme is ready to give extensive time to a big event. In the week of 16–20 May, for example, it gave 8 minutes (out of 26) to a row that reached the House of Commons over behaviour at Scottish–English internationals, and on another day 7 minutes to the rise in violent crime. But on the Tuesday, the day I had chosen for a visit, the prospects at first looked thin.

Eric Wilkie, that day's producer, was less than impressed at his 10 am conference: a Church of Scotland report on a better deal for housing tenants, the launching in Glasgow of Europe's first 'Venture Capital Club' to finance high-risk business projects, a 'loan-sharks' case coming to its climax in Paisley, and others such. Also – a touch of fun – the legendary American singers, the Inkspots, performing at the Garden Festival. All these could be covered but none looked like a strong lead, unless the 'loan-sharks' story could be revealed with all its background.

But the political correspondent, Fiona Ross, thought that the affair of the Townhead Catholic school (as in Chapter 22) was worth further inquiry. She did not guarantee to find anything, but Eric welcomed the idea. The issue, after all, was of great interest to Scottish audiences though individual Protestants and Catholics were wary of discussing it lest they cause offence. Fiona Ross thought it might be possible to find out what the Catholic hierarchy was really thinking, behind its refusal to give clear answers, and also what reaction there was from the Church of Scotland. After the morning conference she set about making telephone calls, the first of which lasted over 20 minutes. She then told producer Eric that there was indeed a story – a possible move by the Catholic church to end segregation and to create 'Christian schools' in conjunction with the Church of Scotland. It was an attempt to be realistic, in the face of Government pressure to merge schools and to bring in parental boards, but it was far from being agreed. In the end, 7 hours later and after further calls, it became the primary item on that night's *Scotland Today*.

Meanwhile Eric was having to allocate crews. At 10.30 am one was already on its way to the Garden Festival for the Inkspots singers, a colourful setting for what could be a cheerful ending to the programme. Another crew was to go to film the Columbian (South American) football team warming up for an international match that night, and it would then go on to Paisley to cover the 'loan-sharks' trial. The third was allocated to the Venture Capital launch, 'on the heavy side', but it might produce something worth using. In Edinburgh only 1 crew was available that day, with at least 3 events to cover. In addition, Eric wanted if possible to get a crew to Duns, many miles away in the Borders, where a racehorse which had won 49 races was preparing to try for a 50th win tomorrow at Perth. The easiest solution was to send a crew by helicopter in the afternoon, but all the Glasgow helicopters turned out to be fully booked. So the Edinburgh crew had to be sent by road to Duns, and 1 of the Glasgow crews was despatched to Edinburgh at midday, with cancelling of its afternoon assignments.

That cancellation had a knock-on effect on the final running order, because 3 planned items had to depend on library film or stills and were consequently shortened to about half a minute each. That in turn weakened the middle part of the programme, or so I thought, because it resulted in 9 short items separated by only 1 longer story – and of those 9 at least 2 could easily have been dropped.

Let us look at that running order and at how each item came about. After the opening titles (0.12) and the headlines (0.14), these followed:

1. *Catholic church may move to end school segregation*: 3.15
Fiona Ross's work, taking her most of the day. She said afterwards that her main difficulty was that she had to depend on one
source – but one of whose reliability she was completely certain.
No talks had yet been opened with the Church of Scotland, and
the Archdiocese might well deny the story next day. (They did
not, preferring to stay silent.) Possibly the idea was being floated
to test reactions, but it was a constructive proposal. Since no crew
was available, she had put together in the afternoon a text which
she recorded in a studio, showing as little of herself as possible
and using library pictures of the 3 schools, the Townhead
motorways, and 3 more schools in other districts where integration had taken place (with children seen playing together).
2. *A 12-year-old boy cleared of killing a 62-year-old man*: 1.18.
This had not been on the morning list. It was unusual both
because a charge of culpable homicide against a child is very rare,
but the judge dismissed the case because of evidence of provoca-
tion.
3. *The Venture Capital Club's award of £120 000 for development of
an inventor's pipe-bending machine*: 2.25
Good pictures of the prototype machine bending cold metal
pipes. Alan Saundby, the industrial reporter, said he had expected
'a PR hype' but it had turned out well. It was 'an advanced
product' of a kind that was needed and pictorially effective.
4. *The Church of Scotland's proposals for radical changes in housing
policy*: 2.16
It suffered a little from the late arrival in Edinburgh of the
Glasgow crew (at least when compared with the more measured
BBC Scotland treatment), but they were proposals based on
impartial study and worth reporting. Incidentally, they illustrated
the Church of Scotland's readiness to tackle difficult political
issues.
5.–8. *Four half-minute items*
Leith MP Ron Brown to speak to his constituency party that
evening, after a month's suspension by the party; inquiry into a
meningitis death where a doctor failed to see the signs; another
inquiry into food poisoning in a hospital; and a man fined for
spanking his daughter wins his appeal. (Any of the last 3 could
have been dropped.)
9. *The 'loan-sharks' trial at Paisley*, adjourned for 3 days because of
dispute over a search warrant: 1.40

A dramatic ending to the case had been expected, but the adjournment prevented that. Again, moneylending had become a troubled issue in Scottish cities.

10.–14. *5 more half-minute items*
The anthrax island at Gruinard given a clean bill of health; the Peterhead riot trial continued; a court case over a Stirling District election result; a Glasgow East-End shopping development; and pub owners in conference reject identity cards for young drinkers. (The East-End shopping development was to be covered by that night's co-presenter, Shereen Nanjiani, with the crew coming on from the Garden Festival; but it never arrived, because of being diverted to Edinburgh, thus depriving Shereen and the programme of good pictures of the old Parkhead Forge site – so she had to write a 35-second report instead, to read herself among the short items.)

15. *The Colombian footballers warming up*: 3.54
Pictorially lively, and a bright commentary.

16. *The 'Flying Ace' racehorse*, with trainer and woman rider at Duns, preparatory to possible 50th win next day. (It won.)

Then closing headlines and weather: total 1.40.

17. *The Inkspots*: 2.24
(It had been scheduled as 1.30, but Producer Eric dropped an item to let it run, and it could well have gone on even longer.) Mike Milford, the reporter, had to persuade the singers to put on a special performance because the film crew was delayed. But that let him cut in their most famous song (especially to older fans) – 'Whispering Grass' – and to arrange presentation of a specially grown begonia plant, for them to take back to America. All bright and funny – a neat end to the programme.

Eric Wilkie earlier in the day had spoken of the programme being 'as soft as putty'. By transmission time he was better pleased. Fiona Ross had 'hardened up' the leading story, and the acquittal of the 12-year-old boy in the High Court was an exceptional event. There had been the usual last minute rushes, with 3 items still being edited 15 minutes before transmission, and his final changes had been made only 10 minutes before the start. But it had come out well enough.

As to style and presentation, these were direct and professional. The studio background is a neutral light grey, and the presenters are kept always in medium close-up. That day they were Shereen Nanjiani and Malcolm Wilson – both with convincing authority (in spite of Shereen's youth), and Wilson well known for his key role in *Scottish Questions* at election and other times. Since Gus Macdonald's return to Scotland in 1985, after many years with Granada in the South, the news and current affairs output of Sc. Tv. has been perceptibly extended and strengthened. For the reporting of Scottish politics and the affairs of Central Scotland, it provides a competent service.

People

Michael Mulford, reporter
D. C. Thomson, Dundee, from 1964. General reporter, then crime correspondent, *Courier* and *Evening Telegraph*. First Scottish journalist to be seconded to a police force (Dundee City) for a crime campaign, 1966. To the *Scotsman*, Edinburgh, 1973; Parliamentary Correspondent, Westminster, 1974–9. Then to Sc. Tv., as presenter of *Report* documentary series. Now with *Scotland Today*, for general news and features.

Shereen Nanjiani, reporter-presenter
Glasgow University, philosophy graduate 1983. To Sc. Tv. where she learned journalism on the job.

Fiona Ross, political reporter
Trained as teacher of speech and drama at Royal Scottish Academy of Music and Drama, Glasgow. Taught for 5 years in secondary and further education. To R. Clyde as researcher, 1974; trained as radio journalist, taking over political programme in 1978. To Sc. Tv. as political reporter, 1983.

Alan Saundby, industrial reporter
From Yorkshire, but University of Wales, Swansea – politics and economics graduate 1970. To Canada and US for 8 years; then R. Hallam, then news desk Granada Tv., then news editor Two Counties Radio (Bournemouth); then, having married a Scot, founding editor Moray Firth Radio 1980. To Sc. Tv. 1983.

Eric Wilkie, producer
From National Service to *Perthshire Advertiser* for 3 years. Then 2½ years as Dundee reporter for Outram (*Glasgow Herald, Bulletin, Evening Times*). Then reporter, *Glasgow Herald*, in Glasgow for 5 years. To Sc. Tv. 1957 – reporter-interviewer, then news editor for 12 years, then Editor *Report* series. Producer *Scotland Today* from 1985.

Reporting Scotland, Thursday 19 May

No less competent and professional than its ITV rival, the BBC's early evening programme has the same high standards. It covers a larger territory, since it broadcasts not only to Central Scotland but to the North-East, the Highlands and the Islands – served by Grampian Television for ITV – and to the Scottish Borders. To cover this larger area it has a slightly smaller staff, with altogether 39 journalists compared with the 45 of *Scotland Today*; it has, however, the advantage of staff reporters not only in Glasgow and Edinburgh but in Dundee, Aberdeen and Inverness, and a full-time parliamentary correspondent at Westminster. And it has studio facilities in all those places.

Reporting Scotland tends to be aimed at a slightly higher market than *Scotland Today*, with emphasis on covering the Arts. There was a time a few years ago when it seemed to be suffering from an over-stodgy interpretation of the BBC's public service brief. That has gone, and today its programmes are a pleasure to watch, with a fine blending of serious politics and rather lighter items.

In the latter part of the week of 16–20 May, there was no shortage of news. The advance list for *Reporting Scotland* on the morning of Thursday 19 May had 19 items – of which, in the end, only 6 reached the programme while 3 of the strongest stories were unforeseen. For one of those surprise events, as we shall see, BBC Scotland gained a great advantage over other television companies and over the newspapers by having its Inverness reporter and his camera crew on the spot long before anyone else.

At his 9.30 am news conference producer Brian Currie saw the top part of his programme looking 'very lumpy', so he was looking for lighter relief for the tail end. But soon after the meeting 3 new stories were signalled, all strong. BBC Scotland's parliamentary correspondent at Westminster, Leslie Anderson, confirmed that later in the day the Scottish Office would publish its plans for a 'claw back' of local authority grants. He also said that a report critical of the Scottish Development Agency's decisions on funding the Glasgow Garden Festival and other projects could be expected today from the Auditor General – a blow when the festival had just gone off to a spectacular start. The third, though, was the most surprising story. The Inverness reporter, Andy Webb, had just phoned from Fort William. He had left Inverness early, with his crew, to cover a British Rail showing of their new electronic signalling system on the West Highland line. Over breakfast at Fort William, after the 60 mile drive, he had seen in the *Oban Times* a report about a woman who claimed that a helicopter had landed on her car's roof, frightening her while she was travelling at 70 miles an hour on the Oban–Edinburgh road. Should he abandon British Rail and go to Seil Island where the woman lived, some 50 miles further south? The answer was 'Yes'.

Having settled that, producer Brian went to discuss the 'claw back' with the political correspondent working in Scotland, Brian Taylor. What did the 'claw back' mean, and how could they make it intelligible? Could they interview Malcolm Rifkind or one of the other Scottish Office ministers? From which local authorities would they want a reaction – Edinburgh certainly, because of its overspending, and probably the Strathclyde and Lothian Regions. And what would be the effect on the rates? Rifkind wanted them down, but the regions and districts said it was not possible. Brian Currie was clear in his own mind that, difficult as it might be to explain in simple terms, they must treat it thoroughly, covering every aspect.

Then he dealt with the Auditor General's criticism of the SDA. Just what the audit report said was not yet known, but there was a crew with a reporter already at the Garden Festival. They were shooting a cheerful item about celebration of Australia Day, for the lunchtime news and possibly for later use. By radio telephone they were warned to stand by for something heavier. At 10.50 the BBC's General News Service printer from London provides the first summary of the Audit report, critical of the SDA's early estimates of the Garden Festival costs which are said to have been half the costs now expected. A call is made to the SDA press office in Glasgow, with the reply that a statement will be made later. The summary is also relayed by radio telephone to the reporter at the festival, with a request to try for a comment there too. The chief assistant at the festival says, however, that the figures given by the Audit report are ones he has never seen before. The crew therefore return to base, leaving the reporter to record a voice interview in the afternoon which will be superimposed over general views of the festival site.

By midday producer Brian, though prepared to change his mind if necessary, is almost certain that he will lead with the 'claw back' of money from local authorities, and its implication. Yes, it is heavy, but it's also important. The helicopter story will run second: Andy Webb has located the woman at Seil Island – well before any other reporters – and will be filming soon. A courier is on his way from Glasgow (it will take at least 2 hours to get there and 2 to come back). Webb says the woman is 'very believable'. The third item will probably be about Clydeside shipyard workers lobbying Parliament. They were filmed leaving Glasgow at 6 am, with banners flying; they will be filmed again this afternoon at Westminster, with interviews and comments from MPs. Beyond these there is 'an awful lot'. Stories that would otherwise have had 2 or 3 minutes will have to be 'quick wipes' of 20 to 30 seconds, and others will have to be deferred or ditched.

At 2.30 pm Andy Webb is on the radio telephone from Seil Island. The recording about the helicopter has 'worked out very well'. There were skid marks on the roof of the car and the ledge above the car door had been chipped. Mrs Taylor, the driver, described it as 'a terrific noise' and she had thought her car was going to blow up – until she saw the skids and then saw the helicopter climb away over the hills. Webb said that today there was a search-and-rescue car parked at the foot of her road with 'a very worried looking man in it'. The despatch rider had just left Seil Island for Glasgow and should be there by 5 pm. Reporters from Glasgow offices were only just arriving. (3 or 4 days later, after police inquiries, the Defence Ministry admitted that an RN helicopter had been involved: an exercise had been taking place at the time.)

From 3 pm producer Brian began to monitor the editing of reports. The editing suites in the BBC's Glasgow buildings are inconveniently about 200 yards from the newsroom, along a labyrinth of corridors. But the programme producer and others can watch the editing through screens in the newsroom – watching any 2 of the 3 edit suites in Glasgow, or one in Glasgow and one in Edinburgh. Thus the monitoring and advice on changes are possible without leaving the main newsdesk. Soon after 3 pm the SDA costing of the Garden Festival and a number of other stories were being edited, but the 3 or 4 major items would not be available until well after 4 pm. On the 'claw back', a two-way interview between Glasgow and Westminster was expected at about 5.15 pm.

At 3 pm also, Brian Currie's running order was ready – with, as usual, gaps so that late stories could be slotted in at the beginning, middle or end if necessary. In practice, of the 17 items on the 3 pm list, 5 were dropped before or during transmission (starting at 6.35 pm), to make room for extending each of the 4 major items. The 'claw-back', the helicopter, the shipyard workers and the suspension from Parliament of the MP Ron Brown (not known until after 4 pm) were all judged to be worth more time. Currie regretted having to drop other stories on which reporters and researcher had worked, but there was no alternative. He also regretted postponing one of an Arts series from the Glasgow 'Mayfest', but he replaced that, as a lighthearted end to the programme, with a 1-minute item about a burglarous cat in Aberdeen. The preparation of the 'claw back' explanation was finished only minutes before going on air.

Thus the programme as transmitted ran like this: Titles and headlines, taking 1 minute. Then –

1. *The 'claw back'*: 3.52
   It began clearly enough with a statement that councils were likely to lose £140 million in Government grants during the coming year, because of penalties for previous overspending imposed by the Secretary of State. Graphics showed Strathclyde losing £82 million, Lothian 44 million, Edinburgh District £2.5 million, and Aberdeen £1.3 million. A somewhat confusing explanation followed, too compact for the words to be absorbed. That was followed by a statement issued for the Minister, Ian Lang – he was to have been interviewed from the BBC's Westminster studio soon after 5 pm, but got there only at 5.35 by which time the Telecom line to Glasgow had been lost. Whereas the regional councils had just been quoted as saying that the 'claw back' would increase the Community Charge (or Poll Tax) by about £100 a head, Mr Lang said it would reduce the charge. Viewers were left to work that out for themselves, but it was followed by an interview with the Lothian Region's Labour leader saying that it would mean 2500 redundancies among council workers and a 'huge' increase in Community Charges.

2.–3. Tacked on to this were *two items about overspending by Stirling District* and a *dispute at Dumbarton*: together 2.00
   The Stirling item had lively pictures (perhaps a visual relief after the 'claw back') of triumphant Labour councillors opening champagne bottles, even though they might be about to be fined £3000 each.

4. *The helicopter*: 2.58
   (Brian Currie, justifying its placing, said 'When shall we next get a story about a helicopter touching down on the roof of a car?')

5. The *shipyard workers lobbying at Westminster* and initial of lack of Government support for their industry; 2.18

6.–8. *3 'wipe' items*
   The Seamen's Union being fined in Edinburgh, 0.25; unemployment in Scotland below 300 000 for the first time in 6 years, 0.33,

and an animal rights group claiming to have contaminated meat in a Coatbridge supermarket, 0.24. (The third was a last-minute unlisted entry.)

 9. *The Audit report on the SDA and the garden festival*: 1.14
    A brief voice report, over general views of the Festival, of the criticisms of SDA cost estimates; and a statement from the SDA saying that since their chief executive would be appearing before the Public Accounts Committee next week they could say no more.

10. *Ron Brown, MP, suspended from Parliament for seizing the Speaker's mace and failing to apologise adequately*: 2.36
    With a very vigorous response from the MP, interviewed outside the Commons.

11. *The Scottish football team on its way to Wembley*: 1.07
    For a Scottish audience, presumably a 'must'. But cut short during transmission because of the contaminated meat late entry. (3 'wipe' items had already been ditched.)

12. *The hundredth anniversary of 'Highers'* (the Scottish equivalent of 'A' levels): 3.52
    A delightful reconstruction of the earliest such examinations, with Edinburgh schoolgirls in Victorian dress, then neatly cutting to shots of an exam scene today, including a close-up shot of a boy's shoes, under his desk, rubbing alternate legs, presumably as he thought of answers.

13. The burgling cat in Aberdeen: 0.55

Followed by end headlines and the weather. Total 25.00.

Among comments after the programme was over were these. Producer Brian Currie was 'content' overall. Much had happened during the day, so that he had had a wide choice. The only worries had been over the lateness of the 'claw back' material and the arrival of the helicopter tapes only 50 minutes before transmission. The helicopter editing had been done by a researcher-reporter, Fiona Henderson, who had only arrived from BBC R. Foyle (in Northern Ireland) a week or two before. It had come out well.

Leslie Anderson, the parliamentary man at Westminster, said it had been 'a busy day' but he liked that: the early indication about the 'claw back' and the Audit report, then the shipyard men in the afternoon, and finally the interview with Ron Brown and getting the shots of his marching away from Westminster unbowed. Viv Lumsden, one of the two co-presenters that day, brushed aside any worry about the sudden death of 3 'wipe' items – of which the presenters had not been warned. 'The first indication you get', she said, 'is a horrible silence'. (Actually it was a silence of not more than 1 second.) The football story had been chopped short, and as she looked up at the teleprompt to begin the 'wipes' the text of the exams centenary came up instead. So she simply read it, having never seen it before. Dealing with that is instinctive, she said 'for people at home don't know it's not *your* fault'.

As to style, *Reporting Scotland* has 6 regular presenters on whom to call. All 6 are cool, clear in speech, and pleasing to see and hear. All are experienced reporters, though only 2 have had many political assignments. The men dress mostly in plain suits and the women in a variety of clothes, depending on the season. The impression is friendly, orderly and perhaps rather formal.

If there are criticisms of a reliable news magazine, mine would be two. One is that there is an almost too conscious caution, common in the BBC. In Scotland as in other parts of the BBC, the mantle of responsibility hangs heavily. BBC senior staff believe that they are a bigger target for Government and other hostile snipers than are the ITV companies, and they play safe accordingly. It will not soon be forgotten that it took Granada Tv. to uncover corruption in Scottish local government, while BBC Scotland and Sc. Tv. stood back from reporting what was happening under their noses. Some of that caution remains in BBC Scotland.

The second is a lesser criticism. The presenters, individually, are good. *Reporting Scotland* could, however, establish a stronger identity with its audiences if there were fewer changes. The usual combination of a woman and a man works well, particularly since the woman often takes the lead. But there is no evident logic in the way the presenters are switched round – and the most incisive of Scotland's recent political interviewers, Kirsty Wark, has been lost much of the time to London, with only end-of-the-week appearances in the North.

People

Leslie Anderson, parliamentary correspondent
Copy boy, *Scottish Daily Mirror*, Edinburgh 1957. Reporter, *Lennox Herald*, Dumbarton. Then reporter, *Scottish Daily Mail*; then *Scottish Daily Express*, deputy industry reporter. To BBC Scotland 1978 as reporter; industrial correspondent 1979. To Parliament 1984.

Louise Batchelor, Arts reporter and programme presenter
Reading University, English. Home Counties Newspapers, 1974–7 (mostly at Milton Keynes). *Oxford Mail* 18 months. Then to Radio Scotland 1978. To tv. as reporter, 1980. *Newsnight*, London 1982–3. Then back to BBC Scotland. Two children.

Brian Currie, producer
From school to *Wishaw Press*; then attachment to *Glasgow Herald* as reporter (same group as Wishaw paper). Back to Wishaw, then to *Evening Citizen* (Glasgow) as sub-editor. Brief spell at Reuters, London. In 1974 to Radio news (BBC), London; then to combined radio/tv. newsroom, BBC Scotland. Programme director, then assistant producer; latterly producer, *Reporting Scotland* and election programmes.

Fiona Henderson, researcher-reporter
Stirling University, English graduate 1984. 1 year in East Africa. Falmouth journalist course, 1985–6. BBC R. Foyle (Londonderry) 18 months. To BBC Scotland 1988.

Conclusion

If all the early evening news programmes in the UK were as reliable as the two described here, there would be little to complain about. The priority given to political, social and economic affairs is shown in the content analysis. Both programmes have their own parliamentary correspondents at Westminster and make good use of them – a valuable facility which the English regions lack (both BBC and ITV, though most of the ITV companies could well afford to provide this for themselves). Both are in close touch with the Scottish Office, the major local authorities, and the health services in Scotland. Both cater for the Scottish interest in football, rugby, and even ski-ing; and both keep an eye (the BBC especially) on Scotland's considerable achievements in the Arts. No charge of bias can justly be made against either, apart from the inevitable socio-centralism. They serve their audiences well.

Content by categories: *television, totals for 4 days, 24–27 May 1988*
(Excluding headlines and weather forecasts.)

Category*	Scotland Today (*Sc. TV.*)		Reporting Scotland (*BBC*)	
	No. of items	*Total duration (min./sec.)*	*No. of items*	*Total duration (min./sec.)*
A & S	1	2.00	5	5.21
Crash	4	1.38	–	–
Crime	10	20.56	8	15.42
Crime C	1	0.28	–	–
Env.	1	2.54	3	1.29
Health A	3	1.45	3	6.39
Human	5	8.30	4	1.36
Money	2	2.10	3	1.03
Pets	1	1.56	–	–
Pol. A	33	65.38	21	46.37
Pol. W	1	2.30	1	1.44
Pol. Ed.	1	2.18	1	2.40
Sport	3	9.45	3	6.12
Stars	1	0.30	1	1.31
Weather (news)	2	1.06	–	–

Note:
* For explanation of categories, see pp. xi–xii.

24 BBC R. Scotland and James Gordon's R. Clyde

R. Scotland calls itself 'The national network' – justifiably, because it covers events in the whole of Scotland and can be heard throughout the country. R. Clyde is limited to west Central Scotland, but there it can be heard by nearly 2 million of the nation's $5\frac{1}{2}$ million people. In news gathering, R. Scotland is well staffed not only in the central belt but with reporters in Dundee, Aberdeen and Inverness, giving it a total of 43 journalists. When necessary, it can also call on the small stations in Solway, the Borders, Stornoway, Orkney and Shetland.

In its news service, R. Scotland is modelled on R. 4, with thorough cover and concentration on the political, economic and social affairs of Scotland and with R. 4's own UK and international material to draw on. In its general programming, R. Scotland blends highbrow and popular interests – with, for example, most of its music being on the popular side but also with excellent concerts provided by its BBC Scottish Symphony Orchestra. Among its many other series are *In the Country*, mainly naturalist; the weekday *Head-on* debates and the weekday Kirsty Wark single-topic phone programmes; Jimmy Mack from all over Scotland and *The Gathering*, mostly Jimmy Macgregor's but with others contributing to its talk and music. All these have elements of news within them.

At R. Clyde the newsroom is smaller, with only 18 journalists, but by ILR standards that is big. Clyde's 2 top people are former journalists – James Gordon, its creator and managing director, and Alex Dickson, its programme controller. They believe in the importance of their news service; that will not change with deregulation. Also there are news elements in others of R. Clyde's programmes, such as Sheila Duffy's individual interviews. Like other ILR stations, R. Clyde's output is predominantly music – pop and rock for the young (15–25) on FM and a broader range on MW – but R. Clyde also carries more speech than most, with up to 30 per cent of what the

IBA used to call 'meaningful speech' on medium waves. It runs all
night, repeating some of the daytime and early evening features and
bringing in new ones. And, it is worth remembering, it was the huge
success of R. Clyde that finally jolted the BBC into creating R.
Scotland in 1978 as a wholly Scottish full-time service, instead of
relying on limited 'opt-outs' from R. 4.

Audience figures can be confusing, but however you look at them
both R. Clyde and R. Scotland come out well. Within its compact
west central territory, R. Clyde has a weekly reach of 52 per cent – just
short of 1 million people. That puts it among the top 6 of the 45 ILR
companies. Serving the entire country, R. Scotland has a weekly reach
of 24 or 25 per cent – which means that, over the whole area from
Shetland to the Borders, about 1 320 000 people listen to R. Scotland
at some time in the week. Given R. Scotland's policy of a high speech
ratio, these are good figures.

Numerically, within west central Scotland, ILR's JICRAR gives
R.Clyde a weekly reach of 987 000 and R. Scotland 467 000. But in
daily rather than weekly terms, the BBC's research puts R. Scotland
level with R. Clyde, partly because of its steady audience for *Good
Morning Scotland*. Both studies agree that R. 4 in Scotland reaches
about half the weekly audience of R. Scotland. JICRAR puts R. 1 as
the closest competitor both of R. Clyde and of the 5 other ILR
stations. BBC research, looking at Scotland as a whole, gives ILR's 6
stations a total reach of only 37 per cent, or just over 2 million people;
though individually, within their limited transmission areas, 4 of the 6
(including the biggest, R. Clyde) have over 50 per cent.

When deregulation comes, R. Clyde may well extend itself by
starting secondary 'opt-out' stations in Greenock and Stirling. At
present both are on the edges of R. Clyde's area, and both would need
new transmitters. Even before deregulation, R. Clyde is negotiating to
merge with North Sound in Aberdeen. With a pre-tax profit of
£608 205 in 1987–8, R. Clyde is in a strong position. For the smaller
companies such as Moray Firth, in Inverness, deregulation will mean
that they must carry the full costs of transmission – which is at present
subsidised through the IBA. They could then become subject to takeover bids from bigger companies which, unless carefully handled,
could weaken their local identity.

R. Clyde news

Since the summer of 1988, R. Clyde has run a split service, with FM transmission of a programme aimed at the young (15–25) and AM carrying the previous Clyde format. The main news remains on AM (or MW), with bulletins on the hour every hour – up to 10 or sometimes 15 minutes at peak times of 8 am, 1 pm and 5.30, but only 2 to 6 minutes at other times. There are headlines on the half-hour. On FM, in keeping with the style there, the bulletins are no more than a fast 90 seconds on the half-hour, with no news on the hour.

The difference is evident in the traffic reports from Clyde's helicopter: 'I'm over Kingston bridge now, all the traffic is moving along, as far as I can see both sides are clear – Good Morning', which takes 5 seconds on FM, whereas on AM up to 30 or 40 seconds can be used. And in interviews, for example if 200 men are paid off, MW will talk to a worker who has been there for 20 years while Clyde FM will talk to a young apprentice for only a sentence or two.

Among the news elements on Clyde are brief reports daily from Parliament at 7 pm and 10.30 pm, a law report for 15 minutes on Monday evenings, Sheila Duffy's interviews on Tuesday, both reviews for 20 minutes on Tuesdays and Wednesdays (Alex Dicksons'), health hints on Tuesdays, an industrial programme on Thursdays, and 40 minutes on politics on Fridays. The format can vary, of course, but these are regulars. One of the early presenters of the Friday *Clyde Comment* (the political programme) was Donald Dewar, more recently Shadow Secretary of State for Scotland.

Taking the morning news of Thursday 2 June 1988, at 7 am the bulletin had 7 items. At 8 am it had the same 7 – with 2 extended and 1 shortened – plus 2 new items, making a 10-minute programme instead of 5 minutes. At 9 am there were 8 items, 1 being new. The lead in all three programmes was the British Government finally losing the *Spycatcher* case in Australia, after a long and costly High Court hearing. It was given 0.52 at 7 am, with a revised and extended version running to 1.15 at 8 am, and a shorter and further revised item at 9 am. (The BBC's *Good Morning Scotland* ran it third at 8 am, for reasons given later, at 1.17.)

Andy Dougan, the duty news editor that morning, said of his decision: 'It was far and away the lead story'. It was 'completely new' because of the time factor with Australia. It had been edited on arrival from IRN in the early morning, but he had re-edited it for the 8 am bulletin to include an interview with the British Deputy High Commissioner in Canberra, who said that the British Government still believed that the retired spy, Peter Wright, had had a duty of confidentiality. But he accepted that in Australia the case was closed.

Dougan rewrote the introduction for each bulletin 'to make it sound slightly different'.

Second in the running order was President Reagan arriving in London that morning on his way back from his last Moscow summit, and Mrs Reagan taking her last chance to meet the Queen. There was 'nothing new' in that, Dougan said – though the BBC had chosen to lead with it. As a follow-up R. Clyde had travel agents in Scotland reporting a greatly increased interest in holidays in the Soviet Union – but at £600 for a two-week holiday.

The other items in the 7, 8 and 9 am news were all solid stories, sharply presented, and none in the categories of *Crime*, *Sex* or *Stars*. One item, about legal action against the Seamen's Union, came from North Sound in Aberdeen – through an arrangement among the 3 Scottish ILR stations to share news. Another, in a lighter vein, at the end of the 8 am bulletin, came from Moray Firth Radio – a Scottish National Party man being expelled by a British Legion Club in Ross-shire for refusing to stand during the national anthem.

In all, R. Clyde provides a reliable news service run by experienced professionals and free of slang, gossip or superficiality.

BBC *Good Morning Scotland*

The great advantage that the BBC's morning news has over Clyde and the other ILR stations in Scotland is that it can draw on the BBC's UK and international news services. A further advantage that Scotland, Northern Ireland and Wales have over the BBC's local radio in England is in the greater staff and resources that they enjoy. As a result, R. Scotland provides competitive and well presented views, comparable to R. 4's in London.

Taking again the morning of Thursday 2 June, *Good Morning Scotland* began at 6.30 and 7 am by leading with the *Spycatcher* decision in Australia, for the same reasons as R. Clyde. It was a dramatic end to a long court case, with Peter Wright receiving £450 000 in costs from the British Government and £500 000 in royalties for his book. But at 8 am *Good Morning Scotland* dropped that to third place, because of 2 new stories. At about 7.40 am it received through London a live broadcast of President Reagan's farewell words on leaving Moscow for London, and of Mr Gorbachev's reply. That was rapidly edited for use as the lead at 8 am. What they said was no more than a summing up of what they had said the previous day – perhaps a reason for still not putting it first – but with the promise of further reduction in nuclear forces it was a historic and quite moving occasion.

Also between 7 and 8 *Good Morning Scotland* received a graphic report from a BBC reporter at a coal mine in West Germany, where 29 bodies had been recovered during the night after an explosion. 30 men were still missing, but hope of finding any alive was receding. That took second place, putting *Spycatcher* down to third.

There was another surprise to come, after the Australian report – a first class 'exclusive', though it was not claimed as such. It said that in London that morning the management of the Norwegian shipbuilders Kvaermer – known to be negotiating to take over the Govan yard, the biggest still working on the Clyde – was to meet the Govan management and trade unions to discuss 'a slim down operation' at the yard. In strictly Clydeside terms, it was the biggest story of the day. It was in none of the papers, and at midday R. Clyde had still been unable to get any confirmation from British Shipbuilders. As a frustrated R. Clyde news editor said, 'If it's Kenny MacIntyre it's right'. It was the work of the BBC reporter Kenny MacIntyre, and it was correct.

Producing *Good Morning Scotland, Good Evening Scotland* and the 1 pm programme is a combined operation of the newsroom and current affairs. They work with apparent harmony, one preparing the bulletins and the other the 15 to 25 items required for each of *Good Morning Scotland* and *Good Evening Scotland*. All three programmes are entirely speech; most of the features must be news-related, and a number are usually live interviews of three or four minutes. In contrast with the sparse staffing of English local radio in early morning, *Good Morning Scotland* has 6 people present by 5.30 am every weekday morning. One is usually the editor, news, or one of his deputies, and another the programme producer. 2 of the 3 regular presenters will be there – Joanna Hickson, Neville Garden and Mike Russell – all experienced broadcasters, well able to improvise if there is a hitch, and capable of interviewing anyone from a dustman to the Prime Minister.

On a rough calculation, putting together the half-hourly figures, between 450 000 and 500 000 people in Scotland listen to *Good Morning Scotland* each weekday morning – most for no more than half an hour, but a few for much or all of the programme. The two departments, in addition to the daily output, also co-operate on three weekly programmes: *Corridors of Power*, a political review; *Newsweek Scotland*, for 60 minutes on Saturday mornings; and *Weekly Report*, a fast-moving discussion on Friday and Saturday evenings.

Finally, let me come back to Kenny MacIntyre as an example of a journalist with initiative. He would not claim to be any better than others in BBC Scotland, but he has an exceptional record. He comes from Tobermory in the Isle of Mull, and after leaving school he set up his own building company. The Tobermory distillery closed about 1977, owing him a lot of money, so his company went into liquidation. He then set up as a freelance reporter, working mostly for BBC R. Highland and R. Scotland in Mull and Argyll, but from 1981 to 1983 was full time with R. Highland in Inverness. He then moved to the BBC's Edinburgh newsroom – on a contract, not staff – and to Glasgow in 1987.

The Govan shipyard 'exclusive' mentioned above was, to him, routine. Two more notable ones had occurred earlier in the year. One was the Auditor General's critical report on the Scottish Development Agency's investment in projects where, it said, there was no need for public money. That led to the SDA's chief executive having to appear before the Public Accounts Committee, and it got much publicity because the Glasgow Garden Festival was involved. How did MacIntyre get his information?

> I was in the SDA five or six weeks earlier and someone mentioned that they'd just had their last session with the Audit Office. They couldn't tell me what it was about, so I started nosing round. Then from the Scottish Office I managed to get a little information, and I worked on that. In the end, we [*Good Morning Scotland*] were able to do it a day before [publication], with much of the detail.

The other, in two stages, was the Ford decision to set up a plant in Dundee – a major investment, with 500–600 new jobs – and then the decision to withdraw when a single-union agreement could not be reached.

Conclusion

R. Scotland owes its existence partly to R. Clyde and partly to concern in the BBC in London lest the pressure in the mid-1970s for a Scottish Assembly might lead to Scottish broadcasting coming under the Assembly's control. R. Clyde had set the way with all-Scottish programming; and its news service, within a generally popular format, has been possibly the best among all ILR companies. BBC R. Scotland, founded by the BBC's governors from 1978, has in turn developed a high quality of journalism – of which *Good Morning Scotland* is an example. It now stands level with the best of British broadcast news, on R. 4.

25 East and West: the *Scotsman* and the *Glasgow Herald*

The *Scotsman* and the *Glasgow Herald* are old rivals who enjoy their rivalry. The *Herald* tells us every day that it is 207 or more years old: *The Scotsman* is a little younger. One dominates the West of Scotland, the other the East. Both are 'heavy' newspapers, with good cover of national and international events and with substantial business news. Both have had unhappy periods: the *Herald* in the mid-1960s and early 1970s, with changes of owner and editors who moved away from its broadly liberal tradition; and *The Scotsman* more recently with management policies which demoralised its journalists and caused a competent editor to resign.

Today (1988–9) both look healthy and are a pleasure to read. The *Herald* is clearly the better off, with more advertising and generous editorial space. *The Scotsman* has had a new editor since January 1988. He has restored self-confidence and given the paper fresh vigour, though its resources are less than its rival's.

He is Magnus Linklater – born in Orkney and educated at Eton, news editor and features editor of the *Sunday Times* 1975–83, managing editor of the *Observer* 1983–6, and editor of Maxwell's short-lived *London Daily News* 1986–7. The *Glasgow Herald*'s editor since 1981 is Arnold Kemp, an Edinburgh man at one time with the *Guardian* in London, but deputy editor of *The Scotsman* 1972–81. Both are 'writing' editors, in the sense of writing frequently for their own papers – Linklater the more visibly active in his newsroom day by day; Kemp with a quieter style but close control in Glasgow.

Edinburgh, Thursday 26 May 1988

Linklater holds editorial conferences at 11.30 am and 4.45 pm. For the morning meeting there is an 'early schedule' which lists about 30 items, without judging priorities. For the 4.45 meeting the list is in order of importance, with separate sections for the front page and other pages. The editor's questioning is brisk. Thus at 4.45 – after warning from Peterhead that the trial of prisoners for riot and assault could reach a verdict this afternoon, a day earlier than expected – he orders most of the right-centre page (the main features page) to be cleared for a background piece. What about the SAS, he asks. Is any more known of their role? Not yet, but the Aberdeen reporter is working on it. Linklater wants at least a 200-word 'sidebar' on the SAS: say who went in to end the riot, for it was neither the police nor prison officers.

At the end he sets down his view on priorities for page 1. First, the Peterhead trial of the verdict has come. Second, Leith MP Ron Brown facing censure by his constituency party at a meeting tonight – a short holding story for the first edition, and a full report later. Third, South Africa: 2 white policemen sentenced to hang for torture and murder of a black, the first such conviction in some years. Fourth, the court order in London that newspapers there must give the police their unpublished photos of a riot outside Murdoch's newspapers plant in Wapping. Another possible: a siege in Glasgow where bank robbers are holding hostages.

In practice Linklater's projection of the front pages holds good for all editions, except that the South African story goes to page 7 to make room for the Glasgow siege which ends about 6 pm, without casualties, after 14 hours of police action. Also space on page 1 has to be made later for another item: it was on the general list, but its implications were not seen until it came up on the BBC's *Reporting Scotland* at 6.35 pm, where it was the second item. It was a call by the Principal of Strathclyde University for a form of privatisation of higher education. It had not been mentioned at the 4.45 pm conference.

As seen by news editor Jim Seaton, it was an average though busy day. In mid-morning he knew that there would be at least 6 or 7 stories to cover in the afternoon, and he did not have 6 reporters to cover them. He therefore had to draw on the specialists or semi-specialists, as often happens. Rob Brown (whose work on the Catholic Schools controversy we have already encountered in Chapter 23) was on standby for the big Peterhead feature, expected to be for Saturday. Meanwhile in the morning he had written a preparatory piece on an EEC conference due next day in Glasgow on minority languages (33 of them, including Gaelic). Also reporters had to be committed to the General Assembly of the Church of Scotland and the Free Church Assembly – the latter upstaging the former by praising Mrs Thatcher, after her cool reception by the Church of Scotland on the previous Saturday.

The first warning that the Peterhead trial was near its end came at 2.45 pm and the jury's verdict at 5.35. By then Rob Brown had most of his feature ready – 'the most violent explosion at Scotland's powder keg prison' he called it – with a lengthy account of 5 days of riot and wrecking, with serious injury and death threats to two prison officers. Brown had been to Peterhead the previous week, to collect his information. His account ended at 5 am on the sixth morning, when the floodlights illuminating the roof were suddenly extinguished, and masked men with stun grenades burst through the barricades. As Brown concluded, 'an even harder set of hard men were "taking the hall"'.

That was the cue for the SAS 'sidebar', of some 400 words, setting out the evidence on the black-jacketed, gasmasked men. It had been put together partly through Scottish aircraft enthusiasts who collected information about unusual flight movements from air traffic control logs. An Augusta A109 helicopter of the kind used by the SAS arrived at Edinburgh airport from Wiltshire on the Friday afternoon, refuelled, and went on to Aberdeen, where it remained until 5.49, when it left. That aircraft, however, was known to have landed at a private airport in Peterhead on an exercise after a previous riot at the prison and it had stayed in the area for some days. The pilot paid for his fuel in cash. Circumstantial evidence, but convincing. In its way, a scoop for *The Scotsman*.

On the Graham Hills story – the Principal of Strathclyde University on partial privatising of higher education – *The Scotsman* had not been represented at the conference where he was speaking. Its Glasgow office had, however, collected a copy of his text. In the late afternoon a young reporter, a recent arrival from the Cardiff postgraduate journalism course, had to seek reactions from student bodies and University teachers. She wrote the front page story and it was credited with her name. 'A good test for her', news editor Jim Seaton said. (Rob Brown is also a Glasgow graduate who completed the Cardiff course in 1985.)

Linklater, in the newsroom at 6.55 pm, has just written one leader and revised another. He has to go out to speak at an art gallery function with Orkney connections, but the will be back by 9 pm. He still has no doubt about leading with Peterhead and he believes (correctly, as it turns out) that the *Herald* will lead with it too. He wants the Wapping court ruling on the front page – it is important, and one of the leaders is about it – but he thinks the *Herald* will put it inside (also correct). About Graham Hills he is not sure, having just heard about it; but when he returns at 9 pm he endorses the decision to put it on page 1.

Of the Graham Hills story, Seaton says it is 'quite amazing' and deserves a front page place. Chief sub-editor Bobby Campbell agrees, with the Glasgow edition especially in mind. Later they hear from the Glasgow that Hills himself says he doesn't know what the fuss is about – he's said it before. Apparently it's been in the *Herald* before, but never on television or in *The Scotsman*. The newsroom stands by its decision. On the court ruling on Wapping photographs Campbell thinks that also to be important: 'it's the cumulative effect – *Spycatcher*, Cavendish, the murdered soldiers in Ulster and the requirement of pictures there; it's the creeping encroachment of State hands on the media'. So, yes, it should go on page 1.

Linklater is back at 9, as promised. The Leith Labour Party meeting has ended earlier than expected, and there is a good picture of the MP Ron Brown. With Campbell, therefore, the page 1 plan is revised. The Peterhead story is stripped across the top of the page (and continued on page 2), with the Ron Brown picture below beside bold headings 'Storm in a teacup, says Brown'. The Glasgow seige is on the right, Graham Hills below, and Wapping stripped across the bottom. That layout stays for the whole night.

The Glasgow edition – and the emphasis on trying to get a good Western story on the front page every day – was one of Linklater's innovations at *The Scotsman*. Getting a 4.45 pm news list that indicates priorities for each page is another. He has sought better planning of pages and layouts, and more considered use of pictures. 'You must', he says, 'have the pictures in front of you when planning a page'. He has aimed also at attracting young readers with extra Arts pages, a cinema page on Mondays and a 'younger profile' for the paper. Finally, with the management, he is trying to restore good relations with the staff after the bruisings of the previous year.

'Exclusives'

In 1985, in the pilot study for my previous book *News, Newspapers and Television*, I looked closely at 'exclusives' in a week in Scotland.

Analysing exclusives is not easy, because some are claimed when in
practice other papers or broadcasters have the same or a similar story,
while others are not claimed because the paper or broadcaster does
not know whether others may have it too. That study, after careful
cross-examination, concluded that of 16 genuine exclusives in that
week 4 each were in *The Scotsman* and the *Glasgow Herald*, 3 in the
Daily Record, 3 on BBC Sc. tv., and 2 on Sc. Tv. Radio was not
included. While events prevented such a thorough analysis in 1988–9,
I suspect that the figures would be similar – probably with an increase
in the total number.

While at *The Scotsman*, I sought from its Industrial Editor, Keith
Aitken, an account of how he alone had received 3 exclusives in the
previous week – one the page 1 lead, on the return to Scotland as
British Coal's area director of Albert Wheeler, a controversial figure
during the 1984–5 coal dispute. He had now been given charge not
only of the Scottish coalfields but of many of the English and Welsh
mining areas. Another concerned negotiations between the Coal
Board and the SSEB (South of Scotland Electricity Board) and was
said by John Seaton to have had the SSEB 'jumping up and down in
impotent rage'. Aitken's answer was simply that he had built up good
contacts over many months, and was careful to maintain their
confidence.

Rob Brown, when questioned about his exclusive on the Catholic
hierarchy's proposals to the Scottish Office on restricting the number
of non-Catholics in their schools (Chapter 22), said he had felt that
the controversy was reaching 'an interesting stage'. So he decided to
seek an interview with Fr Lynch, the Catholic representative on
Strathclyde education committee. But instead of talking on the
telephone, he went on the Saturday to see Fr Lynch at home in
Ardrossan. His aim was to fill in the background; but out of it he
learned of the Catholic lobbying of the Scottish Office to secure a
ceiling of non-Catholic numbers. He got it because he had taken the
trouble to go to Ardrossan and talk it over 'face to face'.

Moving now to the 'exclusives' in the *Glasgow Herald*, an example
is its economics editor, Alf Young. Much of his work is analytical and
inquisitive. Take two of his news stories in the week of my study,
neither claimed as an 'exclusive', but both with information not to be
found anywhere else. One, already mentioned in Chapter 2, concerned
the funding of Scottish universities. It was based on a research report
by the Fraser of Allender Institute in Glasgow. The report was to be
released at a 10.30 am press conference, but BBC R. Scotland at 8 am

broadcast a brief item on the loss of public funds by three universities.

Young went to the press conference and studied the document. He concluded that 'it was not a simple message of university cuts leading to an impact of job losses and loss of economic activity' – the line taken next day by other newspapers. It was a more complex story, for two of the three universities covered by the Fraser report had succeeded in offsetting their severe loss of Government funding by raising money from industry – not always for the teaching that they thought most important, but an extraordinary achievement nevertheless. That became a front page story in next day's *Herald*, together with an extended article on one of the centre pages. 'I like complicated stories', Young said. 'I look forward to teasing something out, something I haven't anticipated'.

His other notable story of that week – an exclusive in the strict sense, since nothing appeared elsewhere until after the *Herald* carried it – was on the forthcoming annual report of the Highlands and Islands Development Board (HIDB). It spoke of 'an air of guarded optimism in the Highlands', in spite of a rundown in offshore oil contracts, and it had an interview with the HIDB's chairman. Young got that interview because he maintains contact with the HIDB and is respected for his grasp of economic issues, and because the chairman wanted to project a view of the Highlands that differed from 'Central Belt perceptions'. He therefore responded to an approach from Young. Among the points reported were that the Dutch owners of the offshore yard in Lewis, in the Outer Hebrides, now said that they had 'the highest labour productivity they have had anywhere in the world'. That is far removed from the conventional vision of the islanders as easy-going, slow workers.

As with examples in the Midlands and South-West, I cite Young's work as creative journalism. Other examples can be found at the *Glasgow Herald*, *The Scotsman* and elsewhere. Young himself regarded the items quoted here – included because they happened while I was at the *Herald* – as less important than his writing on matters such as inward investment in Scotland and, conversely, on the rundown of Scottish shipbuilding. His own background is unusual: a good physics degree at Glasgow University, 2 years of teaching in school, then a Master's degree in education; next, 6 years of teaching others to teach ('I felt a bit of a fraud'). From 1976 to 1978 he worked for the Labour Party in its Scottish headquarters – in contact with the trade unions, the Scottish Office, and Cabinet Ministers during the 'devolution' period. Then to R. Clyde at the age of 35 ('I learned a great deal but the end product was hardly satisfying'); and onwards to print journalism at the *Sunday Standard*, *The Scotsman* ('I ran with the Guinness affair for a year, on the inside track on one or two stories'), and to the *Herald* in the autumn of 1986. Summing up, 'totally untrained, extremely lucky, and enjoying it'.

Memorable also is the work of the *Herald*'s Monday columnist, Murray Ritchie. He provides a half page of critical information on a single topic each week. One such dealt with the use of public money (SDA, Historic Buildings Council, Glasgow District, and Strathclyde Region) to convert into high-class flats the old Trinity College in Glasgow's West End – a fine building in a prime site. With completion of the conversion, preference was given in buying of the flats to people or interests connected with the project. It was a valid disclosure of maladministration. Another such article dealt with the disciplinary procedures of the Law Society of Scotland, indicating that there was one rule for small firms and another for the big. That led to threats of legal action. Later, the president of the Law Society said in its journal that they would have sued the *Herald* but they could not afford the lawyer. The cost of litigation in such cases, he said, was too high. A further example was an article revealing the misery and overcrowding in the Lennox Castle Hospital for mentally handicapped people, near Glasgow. Ritchie's report led to a change of policy in relation to Lennox Castle – 'a case of journalism changing the course of events', as he said, 'and very satisfying.'

Glasgow, Thursday 31 May 1988

The *Glasgow Herald* has three editorial conferences, each lasting about 20 minutes, at 12 noon, 5 pm and 7.30. Arnold Kemp, as editor, chairs all three. The first is a general review of prospects, with particular attention to the features. It is part of Kemp's policy that features should 'respond to the news', so many are written on the day. Today's conference is anyway dominated by the Reagan–Gorbachev summit in Moscow. The *Herald*'s political editor is there, and with any luck he will be writing both for the front page and for the centre-page features.

At 5 pm the News Editor presents an updated list, in order of priorities as he sees them, with some 20 staff items and 6 or 7 from PA. The Night Editor, John Duncan, adds his comments and assessments. Kemp leaves most of the talking to others but indicates his view. The

Moscow Summit is still top of the list, with an extra item on Nancy Reagan visiting the Hermitage in Leningrad. Copy from the *Herald*'s man is expected from 7 pm: it is being sent via the United States, because that seems to be the quickest way. The disarmament talks are apparently not going too well. Second on the list is the forming of a new 'Scottish Conservative Candidates' Association' – not at first sight very exciting, but important because the previous association was wound up by the party's Scottish headquarters because its members were so critical of Government policy. The *Herald*'s Scottish Political Correspondent has found out about it – and its pledge to be 'a loyal body' – and the paper may have it to itself (and does).

An item lower down the list interests John Duncan, who sees it as likely for page 1. Lawyers for the Scots Guards have been in talks all day with BBC lawyers, because the controversial Falklands play *Tumbledown* is due to have its first screening tonight. The News Editor mentions 3 other late entries – a tip off from the ICI's big explosives plant at Ardeer that there has been an emergency, with staff having to take cover in bunkers for 20 minutes; a call from a police officer, apparently an inspector, who is considering whether to meet a reporter for non-attributable information; and an extraordinary letter to the Prime Minister from a Glasgow woman working in a school for blind children. All three are being followed up.

Before the 7.30 pm conference John Duncan has sketched out a front page plan. He has two good pictures from the Summit – one of Nancy Reagan at the Hermitage and one of the President below Lenin's bust in Moscow. Because the *Herald* is in process of testing its new printing plant which will give it high-quality colour pictures later in the year, Duncan sees this as a chance to try a new style of layout with two deep pictures side by side on page 1. (Echoes, to me, of pictures determining news priorities in television – but the summit was almost certain to be the lead anyway.) The copy from Moscow has been in since 6.35 pm, comfortably early; it is 'fine', Duncan says at the start of the 7.30 meeting.

At the conference Kemp agrees to the Night Editor's proposal, and afterwards Duncan tells me why he made his decisions. Moscow, he says, matters most because of the nuclear disarmament talks. The talks seem deadlocked, but they are still talking and both sides seem committed to reaching an agreement. He also likes the pictures that he has chosen – and getting it right when colour comes is important to him, too. On *Tumbledown* he is no less sure. 'It's another BBC drama, with severe fire from certain quarters. It's interesting to see how their new management react. They've cut 12 seconds, a matter of hours before transmission'. He also expected reaction from midnight onwards, which could bring more to the story. (*The Scotsman* also led with Moscow and had *Tumbledown* as the second story.)

For its third item the *Herald* had the new Conservative candidates' association, 'the good boys', as Duncan put it. He found some of the material in the report 'quite fascinating' – especially an interview with Lord Goold, the party chairman in Scotland, who wanted 'discussion without going into public disagreement'. Duncan was also hopeful that no other newspaper would have the story. None did. And for his fourth front page item he took the letter to Mrs Thatcher from the woman in Glasgow who, although working at the school for the deaf, could not afford to buy her daughter new shoes. That was because of the changed social security regulations. 'She's obviously a woman who's never resorted to the press before. She's putting a plaintive plea to Mrs Thatcher'. It was a very articulate letter, Duncan said.

On how the *Herald* got the first story of the Conservative candidates' association, Scottish political correspondent William Clark said it was 'built on a contact basis'. At the weekend he had heard of the new 'loyal' association. He knew the man who was to chair the association, so arranged an interview. From that he went on to other interviews. Thus the report was put together.

One other piece of routine but constructive journalism: the follow up to the police officer's anonymous call that afternoon. The information was handed over to the crime reporter, James Freeman. The officer had telephoned, it seemed, because of anger over criticism in the *Herald* of police behaviour. He had said that the force was dangerously under-manned, with sometimes only 3 on duty where there ought to be 18 or 20. Freeman said that, whether or not the officer telephoned again to arrange a private meeting, he would make inquiries over the next few days. From the information given on some of its news pages he must be at least a sergeant or an inspector. Freeman said that the call could be a plant by the police federation, but it could be justified. Whether the man rang back or not, he would talk to the federation and try to get numbers from a series of areas, not just one. It would take some days but it was worth pursuing.

The *Herald*, however, is not without faults. It retains one or two columnists who should have been put out to grass long ago. And with the coming of its high-grade colour, it has yet (mid-winter 1988) to find a satisfactory layout on some of its news pages. Some lack the clear simplicity of design more often to be found in *The Scotsman*. These are flaws, but they do little damage to the quality of its news.

A final point: women at the *Herald*. There are few either there or at *The Scotsman*, but the Glasgow paper has a distinguished women's editor in Anne Simpson, winner of many awards. Her pages tackle anything from food and fashion to women's rights, here and abroad, but with a special interest in Glasgow's growth as a centre of design – a renaissance, she says, with 'funky confidence'. The *Herald* is also one of the few places where two women with young children operate 'job sharing', each doing 2 days a week in the office and some work from home. Both were on the staff before having their children, one being the social affairs correspondent, and they now work in tandem for features.

Conclusion

The sales figures themselves tell the story – *The Scotsman* nearly level with the two highest regional morning newspapers in England, both in areas of higher population, and the *Glasgow Herald* with a daily average higher still. Both are 'quality' papers in the best sense. As can be seen from the content analysis which follows, their priorities are headed by the political, social and economic news, with the total for both newspapers well above either sport or the business pages. Politically, both tend towards a middle road – the *Herald* at times a little to the left of *The Scotsman* – but both have a good record of impartial reporting. Complaints, of course, are frequent enough from Conservatives and Labour, and from the Scottish Nationalists who feel that they are neglected (or did until the Goven by-election of November 1988). But in reality there is little ground for objection. Overall, the *Glasgow Herald* has the advantage of better editorial funding and years of prosperous stability. Of both, nevertheless, it can fairly be said that they serve Scotland well.

People

Keith Aitken
Edinburgh University, politics and sociology. ('Politics more use than sociology: it teaches you to weigh arguments and present a case'.) TRN trainee, Edinburgh and Newcastle 1979–81. *The Scotsman*

Parliamentary Correspondent, London 1981–5. Labour Correspondent, London, 1985–8. Industrial Editor, Edinburgh, since 1988.

Rob Brown
Glasgow University, politics. Cardiff postgraduate journalism course 1984–5. Freelance 1 year. *The Scotsman* since 1987.

James Freeman
From school (Stonehaven) to D. C. Thomson, Dundee, for 11 years. Then to *Glasgow Herald*, 6 years as general reporter, then Crime reporter.

Arnold Kemp
Edinburgh University, modern languages. Then to *The Scotsman*, 1959. The *Guardian*, London, 1962–5. Back to *The Scotsman*, production editor 1965–70; London editor 1970–2; deputy editor 1972–81. Editor, *Glasgow Herald*, from 1981.

Anne Simpson
From school to *Yorkshire Post*, 1968. Meant to go to University later but didn't. Worked in news and features. To *Glasgow Herald* to start Woman's page, 1976.

Alf Young
See text pp. 226–7.

Content by categories: *4 days, 17–20 May 1988 with also a daily average*

(Features are not included; these are figures for news only.)

Category*	Glasgow Herald				The *Scotsman*			
		Total		Daily av. (sq. cm.)		Total		Daily av. (sq. cm.)
A & S	19	6116	5	1529	47	6834	12	1708
Ag.	–	2732	–	683	–	3795	–	949
Crash	6	379	1	95	7	269	2	67
Crime	33	4254	8	1063	34	4193	8	1048
Crime C	9	1743	2	436	7	882	2	220
Env.	7	870	2	220	10	1210	2	302
Health	3	350	1	90	6	653	1	163
Health A	6	812	1	203	12	1309	3	327
Human	11	972	3	243	11	927	3	232
Int.	25	4188	6	1047	58	8667	14	2167
Money	4	283	1	71	2	196	1	49
Business pages	–	12940	–	3235	–	18832	–	4708
Pets	2	272	1	68	–	–	–	–
Pol.	46	6069	11	1517	65	9015	16	2254
Pol. A	67	10152	17	2538	70	10663	17	2666
Pol. Ed.	13	2780	3	695	10	1010	2	202
Pol. W	4	396	1	99	1	54	–	–
Terror	4	819	1	205	6	1532	2	383
Sport	–	16688	–	4172	–	17152	–	4288
S & S	–	–	–	–	1	135	–	–
Stars	9	1000	2	250	7	1173	2	293
War	4	501	1	125	5	498	1	124

Note: For explanation of categories, see p. xiv.

The *A & S* category for both papers is unusually high in that week because of the Glasgow Mayfest. Within the features pages, not counted here, there are often news elements.

26 You, the Jury

The case for the prosecution is that journalists too readily accept what Government Ministers and others in authority tell them, that they are spoonfed by the rich and powerful, that they are influenced by the conservatism of their superiors, that they trivialise and fabricate the news, and that personally they are a boozy lot who collaborate with their rivals in the pub instead of using their own judgements. In short, that they supply bad news. The case for the defence is that, while some of the popular national newspapers based in London may indeed be guilty on some of those charges, the great majority of regional or local newspapers are not, and never have been guilty (apart perhaps from an addiction among journalists to have a pint or two in the pub, but even this is now less common than it used to be). And as to broadcasting, whatever the position in the early days of radio and television, in the past 50 years radio news has proved its reliability while television news, after a shaky start, has done so in the past 30 years.

But it is for you, as the public jury to decide. This book is about the news provided by regional daily newspapers and by the broadcasters in the regions. The evidence in the book is based on a series of random visits – random in the sense that I could afford only a limited time at each of the 24 news-producing units that I visited, and that neither they nor I could foresee what events would occur on those days. It is for you to reach your own conclusions, if you have had the time and interest to read this far – and I offer delighted thanks if you have. In reaching your judgements, it may be profitable also to think of what newspapers you read, and how often you read them, and of which news broadcasts you watch or listen to. Are you receiving the kind of service that you want? Do you regard it as reliable? Does it, above all, give you the information you need as a responsible citizen who votes in national, regional or local elections? And, for that matter, in managing and enjoying your daily life?

Of course sport, the arts and the human stories are important too. Most men – and some women – want good sports reporting; many women and a fair number of men want to read the women's pages,

234

and many want to hear about theatre, cinema, television and the arts. Human stories, by their nature, also attract interest; they are, in the old saying, what people talk about at home or in the pub. Stories about unusual happenings to individuals or families are part of the day's news. But for newspapers and broadcasting news the most vital duty is in the reporting of political events, the social environment, industry and the economy. So these are the primary elements that, as defence council, I ask you to consider.

Let us therefore look back at whether journalists are too ready to accept what people in authority say. The short answer is to look at how (Chapter 17, pp. 158–60) TSW's Chris Rogers dealt with the Defence Procurement Minister on the rundown of the Royal Naval Dockyard at Plymouth, or for that matter at how (Chapter 3, pp. 21–2; and Chapter 5, pp. 44, 47–8) BBC *Look North*'s Judith Stamper questioned Mr Arthur Scargill about his refusal to talk to the Coal Board. Or look at the reporting of the Land-Rover strike at Solihull by BBC R. WM, BBC *Midlands Today*, and the *Coventry Evening Telegraph* – with both sides in the dispute covered, plus interviews with men on the picket lines. Much the same applies to the reporting by Central News West.

Look also at the creative aspects of much journalism – the *Birmingham Post*'s uncovering of the sale of Birmingham girls into marriage in Yemen (Chapter 15, pp. 146–8), the *Yorkshire Post*'s exposure of the proposed planting of 66 acres on Cam Fell in North Yorkshire, the TSW reporting of kidney transplants at the Exeter hospital, the work at the *Glasgow Herald* of Alf Young and Murray Ritchie, and the work of Kenny MacIntyre at BBC R. Scotland. Look further at the sequence of reports on the Catholic schools controversy in Central Scotland – with *The Scotsman* reporter discovering and disclosing that the Catholic Church had been putting to the Scottish Office its case for restricting the number of non-Catholics in its schools, then the *Daily Record* building on that to explain why the non-Catholic families in Glasgow's Townhead were so anxious to have access to St Mungo's school, and then another day later Sc. Tv.'s Fiona Ross reporting that the Catholic Church was considering a move to end segregation and establish 'Christian schools'. (The *Glasgow Herald*, too, had been involved through being the first to report the concern of the Townhead parents over closure of the non-denominational school there.) And there are a number of other examples of initiative in the preceding chapters.

Perhaps the most significant, both in human terms and in creative journalism, is the reporting on the Birmingham hospitals (Chapter 2, pp. 9–10 and Chapter 13, pp. 125–8) by Peter Hoskins and Clare Harrison of the BBC's *Midlands Today*. Without their persistance, it might have been many months before the crisis in the hospitals became a public issue. Hoskins was probably correct in saying that once the surgeons at the children's hospital realised the value of publicity, they began to 'manipulate' the media. He and Clare Harrison must nevertheless be seen as having done great public service through their work.

The charge of being spoonfed by the authorities does not stand up. It may be true that some – though not all – of the stories mentioned above would eventually have come to public knowledge. The girls sold into marriage in Yemen almost certainly would not, and the hospital crisis could have become much worse before being brought into the open. Nor does the charge of triviality stand up – certainly not in any of the newspapers or broadcasting units that I visited, though of journalism in some of the weekly newspapers it may be true.

As to the influence of proprietors or of the senior management in broadcasting, the case is not so cut-and-dried. The *Yorkshire Post* is not so strongly Conservative as it was 30 years ago, and outside election periods its reporting seems broadly neutral. The editor of the *Huddersfield Examiner* is its co-proprietor, and the paper's long Liberal tradition is upheld by impartial reporting. The *Coventry Evening Telegraph* is now owned by the American Ralph Ingersoll, who has no known view of British politics apart from respect for Mrs Thatcher, and the editor is apparently left free to make his own judgements. Much the same is true of the *Western Morning News*, even though it is owned by the very Conservative Lord Rothermere. The editors of the two 'heavy' Scottish newspapers appear to be left to make their own judgements without any advice from above – Arnold Kemp being now well established at the *Glasgow Herald*, while *The Scotsman*'s management must have been thankful to secure Magnus Linklater to pull it out of its troubles. At the *Daily Record* the editor is reluctant to talk about his proprietor, Mr Robert Maxwell, whom he sees at least once a month; but since the paper, like its readers, is traditionally left of centre, he has no difficulties.

The one valid criticism is that people in authority find it easier than others to secure attention in the newspapers and in broadcast news. That is not only because they are generally more articulate than trade union officials or working people, but also because, being policy-makers, they have more to say. With a Labour government just as much as with a Conservative one, Ministers could count on being heard when they wished – though sometimes with critical questioning which made them uncomfortable. Much the same applies to leading industrialists: they are more likely to get a hearing when they want it than are trade union leaders or shopfloor workers. Again, though, it is not always that way – as shown in BBC R. WM's treatment of the Land Rover company's private poll of workers, using at least once an ex-directory telephone number (Chapter 11, pp. 90–3, 95–6).

Two other areas where the case for the defence is not cut-and-dried: the ethnic dimension, especially in the Midlands and in West Yorkshire; and the malaise in the middle and upper ranks of the BBC. The Midlands and West Yorkshire both have large ethnic communities. BBC Radio in both areas has tried to provide for them and to involve them in productions, as in R. WM's *East and West* evening series (Chapter 2, pp. 10–11; and Chapter 11, pp. 94–5, 97). These, again, are constructive programmes. Both the *Yorkshire Post* and the *Birmingham Post* have tried to concern themselves with ethnic groups, particularly the young, but neither has yet recruited an ethnic journalist. The *Guardian* bursaries for training ethnic journalists at the City university may possibly change that, if television does not swallow them all.

The malaise in the BBC – because of the belief that the Governors will not support critical or inquisitive journalism – has done much damage. 'Play safe' has too often become the rule, not least in news and current affairs. The Governors' decision in 1966 to stop transmission of the *Real Lives: at the Edge of the Union* programme undermined editorial confidence. The programme was about an extremist on the Nationalist side in Northern Ireland and an extremist on the Loyalist side. It was a worthy programme, in my view, having seen an uncut version. That had been preceded and was followed by other hurtful decisions. In all four of the regions in my study, I encountered in the ITV newsrooms people who had left the BBC not so much because of the higher pay offered by YTV or Central or others, but because of sadness and disillusion with what was happening to the BBC. But, at the same time, it seemed to me that confidence was beginning to be recovered in the newsrooms of Leeds, Birmingham, Plymouth and Glasgow. There was still a sense of caution and a concern with not taking too many risks, for no support could be expected from higher levels, but there were signs of a determination to restore responsible standards of journalism.

In spite of those troubles, and smaller staff and less money, the

BBC's early evening news programmes in Yorkshire and the Midlands seemed to me marginally better than those of YTV and Central. They could not send reporters or crews to so many events, but on the major items they did well. In the South-West, again with competent programmes from both TSW and BBC, I would have put TSW marginally ahead – though the South-West happens to be one of the areas where the audience figures are better for the BBC than for its ITV rival. In Central Scotland the quality of the two programmes seemed to me about level, each with its own strengths. Inevitably these are subjective judgements; and readers will reach their own conclusions in their own areas.

THE BIG AND THE SMALL

The largest daily sales outside London – an average of just under 300 000 – are for the *Manchester Evening News*. Most of its customers are in Manchester, Salford and Stockport, though the delivery vans go as far south as Crewe and north to Blackpool. It carries from 48 to 80 tabloid pages, depending on the volume of advertising, which is heaviest on Thursdays and Fridays. Its earliest editions are on sale by midday – and in principle repeat nothing that has been in the morning papers, except where there are fresh aspects of the news – and the last edition goes to press at 4.15 or 4.30 pm, or later if necessary (Budget day, for example). It normally has 2 or 3 pages of national and international news, but most of its space is for Greater Manchester events.

Michael Unger, its editor, says that the main difference between an evening and a morning newspaper is 'time'. The *Manchester Evening News* has to 'treat news on the run', putting stories in as they happen. That makes it harder to edit, especially when it is not immediately clear how or why something has happened. Readers sometimes complain that a particular report is wrong in detail whereas the *Telegraph* next morning got it right – but then the morning papers will have had 10 or 12 hours' longer in which to check. Not that it receives many complaints, for it does all it can to be accurate.

Its approach to news is catholic, since it has to provide for all ages and all interests. It has a weekly centre-page feature by a young writer who is highly popular with young readers but less than intelligible to me – beginning, for example, thus:

Listen, I'm not a philistine and I have a collection of smoked glass ducks to prove it. I can appreciate art as much as the next man. Actually, probably more because the man sitting next to me at this moment, hastily scanning a Stockport County programme, doesn't look as though he has gazed upon an exhibition of cubism in many a year. Unless, of course, one can find artistic worth in the rather anarchic way we play football in Stockport.

But then on another day it has a political commentary from the *Manchester Evening News*'s man at Westminster, on a third day an up-market piece on fashion, and on a fourth something on the politics of sport in South Africa. On a quick check of content by categories, the top group on the news pages comes out as the political, social and economic content, but with *Crime* and *Crash* not far behind. Unger is concerned about the paper carrying 'almost too much' in the political category rather than too little, but corrects that by saying 'what we put in is very good and very selective'.

With a total of 114 journalists, working 9-day fortnights, it is well staffed. The *Express and Star* at Wolverhampton (sales 245 000) has 160 journalists on a 5-day week – probably the biggest staff outside London, apart from the *Daily Record* in Glasgow. Of the 114 at the *Manchester Evening News*, only 9 are women.

Among its major achievements of 1988, the *Manchester Evening News* counts its reporting of the Burnage High School inquiry into the murder of a 13-year-old Asian boy by a white boy in the school playground. It was a long inquiry, dealing not only with the events that led to the murder in a school with a headmaster committed to anti-racism but also with the conduct of the police. Manchester City Council did not want the report to be published: the *Manchester Evening News* published it almost in full, in an 8-page special report. Had it not done so, it is unlikely that any action would have followed. Similarly, it was the *Manchester Evening News* and Unger individually who uncovered vital facts in the Stalker case, when the RUC was preventing inquiry into allegations of 'shoot to kill' – again, a significant public service by the newspaper.

When asked about his competitors, Unger cites Piccadilly Radio (ILR) and Granada tv. (especially its 3.25 pm news). The latter is a source of complaints to the *Manchester Evening News*, if Granada carries something that the newspaper does not have. The former (Piccadilly) is ruthless in lifting stories from the *Manchester Evening News*, as soon as they are published. In the fringe areas, papers such as the *Bolton Evening News* are also competitors. But editing the paper, Unger says, is 'wonderful'. 'You never know what you're going to do when you come to work in the morning, and the adrenalin pumps. You find yourself involved in the front page lead ... There's Burnage, there's Stalker, there's no end to it'.

At the other end of the scale from the *Manchester Evening News*, there are the smallest of radio stations – BBC R. Orkney and R. Shetland, which started in 1977 each with only 2 all-purpose people (reporter, presenter, producer) and a secretary. Now they have 3 or 4 broadcasters each. They were established because these were the most remote of British communities, each with a strong character of its own and needing basic daily news including shipping, fishing and local weather. At first they were on air only for about 2 hours a day, 'opting out' from the R. 4 of R. Scotland service in the morning, midday or early evening. They were followed soon after by R. nan Eilean in Stornoway, and much later by R. Tweed and R. Solway. They were also the model for R. Foyle at Londonderry – a remarkable station in that it won the confidence equally of Catholics and Protestants in that area – and in Wales for R. Gwent and R. Clwyd. The Irish and Welsh stations, however, had larger staffs.

Another small but successful operation is ILR's Moray Firth Radio in Inverness. It has a total staff of 28, including those who sell advertising time and make many of the ads., and within that staff 5 are full-time journalists in Inverness, and a sixth part-time (based in Elgin to the east). It broadcasts news on the hour from 7 am to 6 pm, with up to 8 minutes at 8 am, 7 at 1 pm, and a 'news hour' of news, information and music from 5 to 6 pm. In spite of its small staff, its bulletins are at least as adequate as in most English ILR stations. It serves a thick strip of the north-east coast of Scotland, from Wick in the north to beyond Elgin in the east – almost 200 miles, but probably with no more than 150 000 people, if that. Its weekly reach is between 56 and 59 per cent. It makes a modest profit, which in such an area is in itself a minor miracle. With deregulation and the coming of national commercial radio – if it ever reaches the far north – Moray Firth might seem to be at risk, but since 80 per cent of its revenue is from local advertising it may well survive. It also has the local advantage of being audibly Scottish. The threat to it lies in the costs of transmission to an extensive area, at present subsidised by the IBA. But by 1993 an answer to that may have been found.

At the other side of the River Ness, a mile away, is BBC R. Highland which is also, with Stornoway, the joint headquarters of

Gaelic radio – Radio nan Gaidlead. From a small operation in the 1970s, this has grown into a substantial service – not least with news and current affairs in Gaelic, and a weekly international hook-up. Gaelic is up to 5 hours a day – still far short of the output of R. Cymru in Wales, but growing. Gaelic television comes from Glasgow, though again on nothing like the scale of S4C in Wales. But the Gaelic current affairs programme, broadcast weekly, claims 'an enviable number of exclusive stories'.

PEOPLE – THE BRIEF BIOGRAPHIES

For young people thinking of becoming journalists, the footnotes on 'People' may show the variety of routes that their predecessors have taken. Many have gone straight from school to a local newspaper, weekly or daily: in the past, that was the common way. More recently, from the 1950s onwards, a growing number have gone from school either to a pre-entry course or to a university. For non-graduates, two of the best known courses are at the London School of Printing and at Napier College of Edinburgh, but there are many more. The quality of teaching is very variable.

For post-graduates the 1-year courses at the City University in London, University College Cardiff, Lancashire Polytechnic at Preston, Falmouth (radio only), Portsmouth and other technical colleges all provide a useful start. The best of these courses will guide students to likely jobs, with attachments during the year. Local and regional newspapers or radio are the main targets. Direct entry into television is difficult, unless you can win one of the prized places with one of the BBC's schemes or with ITN.

Some newspapers used to run their own training, the *Liverpool Post* and the *Guardian* among them, but the NUJ – mistakenly in my view – made that nearly impossible. The only surviving course of that kind, so far as I know, is that of Thomson Regional Newspapers (TRN), based in Newcastle, but taking trainees from all of TRN's newspapers. Quite possibly, other such opportunities will open in the near future.

For a determined person, nevertheless, it is still possible to make the transfer into journalism at the age of 35, as Alf Young's biography (Chapter 25) shows.

1993: THE YEAR OF CHANGE

The Government has committed itself to maintaining the regional structure of broadcasting both for independent television's Channel 3 (C3) and within the BBC. That was an important and welcome point in the Home Office White Paper, *Broadcasting in the 90s*, published in November 1988. Much will change in 1993, or sooner, but the regional services will stay on at least 2 television channels. In radio the BBC is being allowed to complete its chain of local stations, speech-based, while the ILR (commercial) stations will no longer be required to carry news. Many, such as R. Clyde, will certainly continue to do so; others may choose to drop news, which is expensive, but that choice is likely only where their local service is already inadequate.

For both the BBC and the new C3 companies, however, there will be problems in funding the news. For all its activities, the BBC's primary source of money is the television licence fee. From 1992 the Government intends to reduce the licence fee progressively, year by year. The Peacock Committee, set up by the Government in 1985 to consider broadcasting finance, in all its calculations assumed that there would be no rundown of the licence fee before 1996, if then. Further, Peacock's first recommendation – coming before all others – was that the Government should legislate for the inclusion of sockets in all new television sets, to provide for subscription services. The French Government had done so in 1975, to help the introduction of subscription television 10 years later (the average life of a tv. set being about 10 years). Without a built-in socket, a decoder attached to a set is likely to lower the quality of the picture.

With the British Government's decision not to make sockets compulsory, and with the decision to reduce the licence fee progressively from 1992, Mrs Thatcher's Cabinet has begun to undermine the financial foundations of the BBC. To say as the White Paper does (para. 1–3) that the BBC 'will continue as the cornerstone of public service broadcasting' is either eyewash or self-delusion. If the Government wants to preserve that cornerstone is must retain the licence fee, determined annually by the Retail Price Index, at least until 1996. Failing that, it is likely that the BBC from 1992 or 1993 will find that it can no longer fund all its existing local radio stations; and it may have to enforce yet another series of economies on its regional television services in England, Wales, Scotland and Northern Ireland. Unless there is a change of Government policy, the BBC is being condemned to a slow death.

For the commercial television companies who win C3 franchises from January 1993, there are other dilemmas. To begin with, the new Independent Television Commission (ITC) which will replace the IBA has to decide what areas it will offer for tendering. Will it, for example, leave both the Thames Valley west of Reading and the Gloucestershire area as part of the Midlands? It might make more sense to link the Thames Valley with London and Gloucestershire with Bristol. And what of Scotland? Will it continue to be divided in three or will it be linked as one unit? In any event, companies bidding for a franchise will be allowed, as things stand, to bid for 2 regions. So we may finish with only 6 or 8 regional companies instead of 15. If that then leads to a company providing separate early evening and other news for 2 or 3 separate areas – as Central already does and YTV seems likely soon to do – will the quality of the programme remain? Although that separation makes a lot of sense, and Central has an acute problem of identity whenever it treats its three areas as one, experience suggests that such splitting leads to a loss of quality.

An even greater problem for the new C3 franchise holders will be the money they can afford to spend on news. They will be required by law to provide a regional service, and in theory the ITC will be watching their performance, ready to pounce with its yellow and red cards (the latter summarily withdrawing the franchise). But having put so much of their money into making the highest bid and paying the Treasury, it is doubtful whether the winners will spend much on retaining the existing standards of regional news. The one real safeguard – and the cause for modest optimism – is that audience figures for the early evening news programmes are generally good, so advertisers will be ready to book time beside the news.

For Radio, the Government promises not only deregulation but more broadcasting – three new national channels, more local radio, and new 'community' stations, all commercially or privately funded. The IBA can immediately authorise new ILR stations, and the new Radio Authority will take over before long. The only requirement is that new stations should combine 'local identity and cultural diversity'. Whether that will permit the pirate stations – particularly the ethnic ones – to become legal is not clear. Also, of course, there are questions about frequencies and the power of transmission.

In principle, what the Government is trying to do in providing for wider choice and more freedom of operation must be right. But there will be dire consequences from the cutback on BBC funding and the competitive tendering for C3 franchises. In radio the reorganisation of frequencies and the opening of new channels may lead to even more jamming than exists already, especially at night. As ever, the ultimate safeguard will be in public reaction. So, once again, it is for you the jury to help to influence the standards of British broadcasting.

A LAST SALUTE

In picking Yorkshire, the Midlands, the South-West and Central Scotland I may have been lucky. Every one of the 24 offices or studios that I visited was of interest. In radio, the least impressive was Mercia Sound, but it is also among the most profitable. In newspapers, the *Birmingham Post* was having the hardest struggle, being desperately understaffed and underfunded. In television, I have watched early evening news programmes in the South-East of England and elsewhere that were far below the standards of those reported in this book. And, if time and space had permitted, I would have liked to write more about Wales and about the North of Scotland, where remoteness and strong character seem to make for good journalism. As it is, I hope that the case for the defence – and the encouragement – of journalists and journalism has been made. I did not set out with a preconceived conclusion. It grew out of 8 months of agreeable observation.

Appendix A: Newspaper Sales and Owners

For those not familiar with the structure of British newspapers and British broadcasting, here is a brief summary. The national newspapers, based in London, are grouped by the Audit Bureau of Circulations as 'Popular' and 'Quality'.

The 'populars', with their average daily sales for January to June 1988 and their ownership are these:

The *Sun*	4 147 000	Rupert Murdoch	(News International)
Daily Mirror	3 082 000	Robert Maxwell	(Mirror Group Newspapers)
Daily Mail	1 793 000	Lord Rothermere	(Associated Newspapers)
Daily Express	1 679 000	Lord Stevens	(United Newspapers)
The *Star*	1 014 000	Rupert Murdoch	(News International)
Today	408 000	Rupert Murdoch	(News International)

And the 'qualities':

Daily Telegraph	1 139 000	Conrad Black	(Argus Corporation)
The *Guardian*	470 000	Scott Trust	
The *Times*	451 000	Rupert Murdoch	(News International)
The *Independent*	375 000	No primary proprietor	
Financial Times	286 000	S. Pearson plc	

Rupert Murdoch is an Australian who has taken US citizenship in order to own television stations in America; Conrad Black is Canadian, and Lord Rothermere lives in France. The *Independent* has many shareholders, none of whom can own more than 10 per cent; its prime mover is its editor, Andreas Wittam Smith. The *Guardian* is owned by the Scott Trust, a unique body which ploughs back profits into the operating company, Guardian and Manchester Evening News plc.

Among the nationals, Lord Rothermere's group has the largest interest in regional newspapers. S. Pearson, through its subsidiary The Westminster Press, also has a number of papers. So do United Newspapers. Rupert Murdoch has no regional interests. Maxwell's *Mirror* group owns the *Daily Record* in Glasgow, with sales per head of population in its distribution area far above the *Sun*'s (768 000 daily in January–June 1988, and rising to 770 000 in the autumn of 1988 – proportionately the biggest in Britain). Maxwell also has a minority interest in a number of ILR stations and a controlling interest in R. Tay.

United Newspapers have 6 regional daily newspapers but no substantial holdings in radio.

The main regional groups, together with sales figures and ILR holdings, are these:

1. *Northcliffe* (part of Associated Newspapers), 11 dailies – *Gloucester Citizen*, 40 000; Exeter *Express and Echo*, 36 000; *Grimsby Evening Telegraph*, 75 000; *Hull Daily Mail*, 108 000; *Leicester Mercury*, 149 000; *Lincolnshire Echo*, 34 000; *Western Morning News* (Plymouth), 56 000; *Western Evening Herald*, 59 000; Stoke-on-Trent *Evening Sentinel*, 107 000; *South Wales Evening Post* (Swansea), 69 000; Torquay *Herald Express*, 31 000.

   Also Associated Newspapers minority holdings in Piccadilly Radio (Manchester), GWR (Bristol and Swindon), Plymouth Sound, Thames Valley (Reading, 2CR (Bournemouth), and LBC (news, London based). And 17 weeklies.

2. *Thomson Regional Newspapers* (part of International Thomson, based in Canada), 12 dailies – *Press and Journal* (Aberdeen), 109 000; *Evening Express* (Aberdeen), 77 000; *Belfast Telegraph*, 148 000; *Lancashire Evening Telegraph* (Blackburn), 56 000; *South Wales Echo* (Cardiff), 96 000; *Western Mail* (Cardiff), 78 001; Cleveland *Evening Gazette*, 75 000; The *Scotsman* (Edinburgh), 90 000; *Evening News* (Edinburgh), 114 000; *Evening Chronicle* (Newcastle), 148 000; The *Journal* (Newcastle), 60 000; *Evening Post* (Reading), 32 000. Also 12 weeklies.

3. *Westminster Press* (part of S. Pearson), 9 dailies – *Bath and West Evening Chronicle*, 24 000; Bradford *Telegraph and Argus*, 82 000; Brighton *Evening Argus*, 95 000; *Northern Echo* (Darlington), 89 000; *Evening Despatch* (Darlington; n.a.; *Oxford Mail*, 41 000; *Evening Echo* (Southend), 62 000; *Evening Advertiser* (Swindon), 37 000; *Yorkshire Evening Press* (York), 55 000.

   S. Pearson own 20 per cent of Yorkshire Television and are shareholders in BSB, but no radio interests. Also 12 weeklies.

4. *United Newspapers* own 4 dailies, apart from *Daily Express* and *Star*. West *Lancashire Evening Gazette* (Blackpool), 52 000; *Yorkshire Post* (Leeds), 93 000; *Yorkshire Evening Post* (Leeds), 143 000; *Star* (Sheffield), 140 000. United Newspapers have magazine interests but no radio or television.

5. *Eastern Counties Newspapers*, with 4 dailies. *East Anglia Daily Times* (Ipswich), 51 000; *Evening Star* (Ipswich), 36 000; *Eastern Daily Press* (Norwich), 91 000; *Eastern Evening News* (Norwich), 51 000. Also weeklies.

6. *EMAP* (East Midlands Allied Press), with 4 dailies. *Northamptonshire Evening Telegraph* (Kettering), 41 000; *Leamington and District Morning News* (previously 'Heart of England Newspapers', sold to EMAP 1987), n.a.; *Peterborough Evening Telegraph*, 34 000; *Scarborough Evening News*, 19 000. Also owns about 10 per cent of Radio Cornwall (Ipswich). And 28 weeklies.

7. *Reed*, owns 4 dailies and 1 daily free newspaper (Birmingham). *Evening News* (Bolton), 53 000; *Evening Gazette* (Colchester), 31 000; *Evening News* (Hereford), n.a.; *Evening News* (Worcester), 29 000. (The Hereford and Worcester papers were formerly 'Berrows'.) Reed also have IPC Magazines and other publishing, and a holding in Marcher Sound (ILR, Wrexham).

8. *Lonrho*, with 3 papers in Scotland and the *Observer* in London. *Glasgow Herald*, 124 000; *Evening Times* (Glasgow), 181 000; *Paisley Daily Express*, 12 000. *Also 15 per cent of Border Television. And 16 weeklies in Scotland.*

9. *Ingersoll*, based in Princeton, New Jersey, USA, with 3 dailies in England. *The Post* (Birmingham), 27 000; *Evening Mail* (Birmingham), 233 000; *Coventry Evening Telegraph*, 91 000. Also weeklies.

10. Others with multiple interests. *D. C. Thomson*, with 2 dailies. *Dundee Courier*, 124 000; *Dundee Evening Telegraph*, 47 000. And *Sunday Post*, 1 400 000 (UK). Also a number of magazines, and a holding in Central Television. *Midlands Newspapers Association. Express and Star* (Wolverhampton), 245 000; (second biggest daily outside London); *Shropshire Star* (Telford), 98 000. And weeklies. *Iliffe, Burton Mail*, 22 000; *Cambridge Evening News*, 47 000. Also 25 per cent of *Coventry Evening Telegraph*; and weeklies. *Portsmouth and Sunderland Newspapers. The News* (Portsmouth), *93 000; Sunderland Echo*, 67 000. And weeklies. *Trinity International. Liverpool Post*, 72 000; *Liverpool Echo*, 204 000. *Guardian and Manchester Evening News, Manchester News*, 289 000 (highest daily sale outside London). The *Guardian* (national, London based, 470 000). Also substantial holdings in Anglia Television and Piccadilly Radio (Manchester); and 12 weeklies or bi-weeklies, in Surrey and NW England. Owned by Scott Trust, as noted above.

11. *Independents*. Not to be neglected – indeed often to be respected – are the independent companies each with a single daily newspaper. Among them are these: *The North-Western News and Mail* at Barrow, created by a management buy-out from Westminster Press (sales 22 000). In Belfast there are 2, unrelated, the *News-letter*, with average daily sales of 42 000, and the *Irish News* with 44 000. The *Greenock Telegraph*, belonging to Orr Pollock and Co., sells 21 000 a day. The *Evening Courier* at Halifax, at 37 000, belongs to Halifax Courier Holdings Ltd. The *Huddersfield Examiner* has a long Liberal history and is the primary product of Huddersfield Newspapers Ltd, with sales around 44 000 a day.

In Nottingham T. Bailey Forman run the *Evening Post*, along with profitable breweries, and are famed for their fight with the National Union of Journalists some years ago. The Kent Messenger Group, based in Maidstone and Chatham, have the *Kent Evening Post* and 8 weeklies. The *Oldham Evening Chronicle* is the sole daily produced by H. J. Hirst, Kidd and Rennie. South Shields has the *Shields Gazette* (27 000). Southern Newspapers, in Southampton, have the *Southern Evening Echo* (85 000). Finally, North Wales Newspapers in Wrexham have the *Evening Leader* (28 000), serving both sides of the northern Welsh Border.

Nearly all of these companies combine publication of their daily paper with a series of weeklies, and nearly all protect themselves by distributing also 'free' papers consisting mainly of advertising. The dailies and weeklies are of variable standards – some dependent on crime, courts, accidents and other such news, while others provide a more extensive cover of highlights from the national and international news and more detail of local government, politics, industry in their areas and readable features.

Appendix B: Television Audiences

The figures are for the week of 15–21 October, 1988. They are intended as a guide to the number of people watching, day by day, the early evening news programmes in the regions. Please remember, though, that there can be considerable variations week by week. The figures come from BARB/AGB – the Broadcasters' Audience Research Board Ltd, a joint company of the BBC and ITV Association, and their research contractor AGB. They are BARB copyright, and I am grateful to BARB for permission to use them.

To provide the most simple comparison of ITV and BBC early evening news audiences, the first table for each area has 4 columns only – (1) and (4) TVR, which is the number of homes or individuals watching the particular channel expressed as a percentage of all homes or individuals within the transmission area. Columns (1) and (4) are for the ITV homes and individuals; columns (7) and (8) are for BBC homes and individuals.

Below that is an extended chart with 8 columns, including the preceding programme and sometimes the one following. The additional columns are (2) the number of houses (in thousands) watching ITV, (3) percentage of sets then switched on to ITV rather than BBC or C4, (5) numbers of individuals viewing (in thousands), and (6) percentage of individuals then watching ITV rather than BBC channels or C4. For the BBC, columns 7 and 8 are repeated for convenience of comparison.

TABLE A1: *Yorkshire* (Chapters 3–6)

Date	(1) *YTV* (homes) (%)	(4) *YTV* (indivs) (%)		(7) *BBC* (homes) (%)	(8) *BBC* (indivs) (%)
Mon. 17					
Calendar	27	17	*Look North*	20	14
Tues. 18	30	19		20	13
Wed. 19	29	19		16	10
Thurs. 20	28	19		16	10
Fri. 21	27	18		21	14

249

TABLE A2: *Yorkshire (extended)*

	YTV (1) (homes)	(2) (000)	(3) (%)	(4) (indivs)	(5) (000)	(6) (%)		BBC (7) (homes)	(8) (indivs)
Mon. 17									
5.45 news	24	534	43	15	839	40	*Neighbours*	23	15
Calendar	27	592	46	17	925	44	6pm news	20	14
Fashion							*Look North*		
Tues. 18									
5.45 news	27	600	45	17	950	43	*Neighbours*	19	12
Calendar	30	659	49	19	1012	48	6pm news	20	13
Prove it							*Look North*		
Wed. 19									
5.45 news	29	636	47	18	1001	45	*Neighbours*	19	12
Calendar	29	653	47	19	1051	46	6 pm news	16	10
Emmerdale Farm							*Look North*		
Thurs. 20									
5.45 news	27	605	47	17	927	44	*Neighbours*	20	14
Calendar	28	627	48	19	1016	48	6pm news	16	10
Emmerdale Farm							*Look North*		
Fri. 21									
5.45 news	20	445	35	13	715	35	*Neighbours*	21	14
Calendar	27	591	46	18	963	45	6pm news	21	14
Living it up							*Look North*		

As with all such surveys, the figures are a general guide rather than an exact measurement.

In case anyone is confused: the difference between Column (1) and Column (3) is that (1) is the percentage of all homes which are *actually switched on* at that time, whereas (3) is the percentage of switched-on homes which are *at that time watching YTV*.

From Monday to Thursday, ITN's 5.45 network news held about level with *Neighbours* on BBC1; but on Friday *Neighbours* was well ahead, with a substantial switch to YTV's *Calendar* as soon as *Neighbours* ended. ITV's *Emmerdale Farm* coming after *Calendar* on the Wednesday and Thursday pulled down the audience for *Look North*; but next day the BBC's *Look North* held its audience in competition with *Living it up*.

TABLE A3: *Midlands (East and West)* (Chapters 10–13)

	(1) *(homes)*	(4) *(indivs)*		(7) *(homes)*	(8) *(indivs)*
Mon. 17					
Central News	26	18	*Midlands Today*	22	16
Tues. 18	24	16		20	12
Wed. 19	27	18		16	11
Thur. 20	27	19		16	11
Fri. 21	24	15		22	15

In the Midlands, throughout the week, the '*Neighbours* effect' is evident. There was substantial switching from the BBC to Central News at 6 pm each day. Nevertheless BBC's *Midlands Today* appears to have had audiences of up to 1 250 000 and Central News up to 1 600 000.

The '*Neighbours* factor' is less evident in the South-West. Indeed, the BBC kept ahead of TSW until *Coronation Street* at 7.30 on the Monday, *Jack the Ripper* at 9 pm on the Tuesday, and *This is your Life* at 7 pm on the Wednesday. In spite of limited resources, *Spotlight* achieved good audiences – generally level with *Today* or ahead of it. But both, as noted earlier, are strong programmes.

On average, *Scotland Today* and *Reporting Scotland* run neck to neck in Central Scotland. The '*Neighbours* effect' is small, but *Take the*

252

TABLE A4: *Midlands (extended)*

	CN (1) (homes)	(2) (000)	(3) (%)	(4) (indivs)	(5) (000)	(6) (%)		BBC (7) (homes)	(8) (indivs)
Mon. 17									
5.45 news	22	743	41	14	1215	41	*Neighbours*	21	16
Central News	26	905	46	18	1549	46	6pm news	22	16
							Midlands Today		
Tues. 18									
5.45 news	21	733	40	14	1234	40	*Neighbours*	20	13
Central News	24	839	43	16	1402	44	6pm news	20	12
							Midlands Today		
Wed. 19									
5.45 news	23	784	44	15	1263	43	*Neighbours*	16	12
Central News	27	927	50	18	1518	49	6pm news	16	11
							Midlands Today		
Thurs. 20									
5.45 news	22	736	44	15	1310	46	*Neighbours*	17	12
Central News	27	913	51	19	1616	52	6pm news	16	11
							Midlands Today		
Fri. 21									
5.45 news	19	664	39	12	1007	38	*Neighbours*	21	13
Central News	24	814	43	15	1330	43	6pm news	22	15
							Midlands Today		

TABLE A5: *South-West (Devon and Cornwall)* (Chapters 17–18)

	(1) (homes)	(4) (indivs)		(7) (homes)	(8) (indivs)
Mon. 17 Today	25	16	Spotlight	36	23
Tues. 18 Today	27	16	Spotlight	34	24
Wed. 19 Today	26	16	Spotlight	26	16
Thurs. 20 Today	27	15	Spotlight	27	15
Fri. 21 Today	26	16	Spotlight	37	23

High Road pulls audiences in its direction. The figures for both Sc. tv. and BBC Scotland are good.

As to the North of Scotland, Grampian is generally about 35 per cent ahead of BBC Scotland in the early evening, except on Fridays. For Border tv., there are no comparative figures for the early evening as seen north of Carlisle.

To illustrate the changing pattern of audiences in spring and summer, I am indebted to Central Television for this list of people watching the early evening news programmes in February, March and April 1988. These are the average daily numbers of individual viewers (in thousands), as in column (5) of the preceding tables.

254

TABLE A6: *South-West* (extended)

TSW	(1) (homes)	(2) (000)	(3) (%)	(4) (indivs)	(5) (000)	(6) (%)		BBC (7) (homes)	(8) (indivs)
Mon. 17									
5.45 news	23	148	40	13	201	34	Neighbours	27	21
Today	25	161	39	16	241	37	6pm news	33	22
News View	20	127	33	13	198	33	Spotlight	36	23
Tues. 18									
5.45 news	25	159	42	14	216	37	Neighbours	26	19
Today	27	168	42	16	243	40	6pm news	29	19
Prove it	22	140	34	15	238	34	Spotlight	34	24
Wed. 19									
5.45 news	25	157	42	14	210	35	Neighbours	28	21
Today	26	168	42	16	249	40	6pm news	26	16
Emmerdale Farm	27	173	45	19	298	47	Spotlight	26	16
Thurs. 20									
5.45 news	25	159	46	14	217	40	Neighbours	26	19
Today	27	168	45	15	236	43	6pm news	27	15
Emmerdale Farm	25	159	42	16	251	43	Spotlight	30	19
Fri. 21									
5.45 news	21	133	36	12	187	33	Neighbours	29	19
Today	26	166	41	16	247	41	6pm news	30	19
Friday people	15	92	23	10	160	26	Spotlight	37	23

TABLE A7: *Central Scotland* (Chapters 21–23)

Date	(1) (homes)	(4) (indivs)		(7) (homes)	(8) (indivs)
Mon. 17 *Scotland Today*	28	19	*Reporting Scotland*	27	20
Tues. 18 *Scotland Today*	24	16	*Reporting Scotland*	26	16
Wed. 19 *Scotland Today*	28	19	*Reporting Scotland*	27	18
Thurs. 20 *Scotland Today*	29	19	*Reporting Scotland*	24	18
Fri. 21 *Scotland Today*	29	19	*Reporting Scotland*	19	12

TABLE A8: *Central Scotland* (extended)

Sc. Tv.	(1) (homes)	(2) (000)	(3) (%)	(4) (indivs)	(5) (000)	(6) (%)		BBC (7) (homes)	(8) (indivs)
Mon. 17									
5.45 news	24	309	36	17	543	38	*Neighbours*	32	21
Scotland Today	28	357	41	19	621	41	*6pm news*	33	23
Bless this house	26	371	43	17	554	38	*Reporting Scotland*	27	20
Tues. 18									
5.45 news	29	364	40	20	625	40	*Neighbours*	29	20
Scotland Today	24	304	36	16	510	34	*6pm news*	24	15
Strike it lucky	32	413	44	24	764	47	*Reporting Scotland*	26	16
Wed. 19									
5.45 news	29	367	43	19	624	42	*Neighbours*	30	21
Scotland Today	28	356	40	19	620	41	*6pm news*	28	19
Emmerdale Farm	32	405	45	22	706	46	*Reporting Scotland*	27	18
Thurs. 20									
5.45 news	28	362	45	17	547	38	*Neighbours*	27	22
Scotland Today	29	367	45	19	420	43	*6pm news*	24	17
Emmerdale Farm	33	324	39	17	542	37	*Reporting Scotland*	24	18
Fri. 21									
5.45 news	22	279	34	14	458	33	*Neighbours*	25	18
Scotland Today	29	366	43	19	608	42	*6pm news*	27	18
Take the High Road	34	437	52	23	737	51	*Reporting Scotland*	19	12

TABLE A9: *Seasonal variation*

To illustrate the changing pattern of audiences in spring and summer, I am indebted to Central Television for this list of people watching the early evening news programmes in February, March and April 1988. These are the average daily numbers of individual viewers (in thousands), as in column (5) of the preceding tables.

Week	Midlands	London	North-West	Yorkshire
5	1846	1661	1225	1143
6	1724	1534	1119	1153
7	1561	1568	1175	1206
8	1625	1632	1000	1144
9	1757	1565	1075	1172
10	1697	1525	1075	1181
11	1604	1548	1101	1131
12	1573	1552	1012	1039
13	1539	1477	991	1043
14	1373	1316	855	1055
15	1377	1281	830	922
16	1372	1312	902	973

Index

258